The KILLING OF THE PEACE

The KILLING *of the* PEACE

BY ALAN CRANSTON

New York

THE VIKING PRESS

1945

THIS EDITION IS PRODUCED IN FULL COMPLIANCE WITH ALL APPLICABLE WAR PRODUCTION BOARD CONSERVATION ORDERS

FIRST PUBLISHED BY THE VIKING PRESS IN AUGUST 1945

PUBLISHED ON THE SAME DAY IN THE DOMINION OF CANADA
BY THE MACMILLAN COMPANY OF CANADA LIMITED

PRINTED IN THE UNITED STATES OF AMERICA
BY AMERICAN BOOK—STRATFORD PRESS, INC., NEW YORK

TO CHARLES—

WHO DIED IN WORLD WAR II

"A small group of willful men kept us from assuming our world obligations in 1919–20, and the same thing can happen again.

"I am just as sure as I can be that this World War is the result of the 1919–20 isolationist attitude, and I am equally sure that another and a worse war will follow this one, unless the United Nations and their allies, and all the other sovereign nations, decide to work together for peace as they are working together for victory."

—PRESIDENT HARRY S. TRUMAN

(Speaking as Senator before the United States Senate, November 2, 1943.)

PREFACE

WE HAVE come to assume that after World War I we went isolationist simply because we were tired, tired of war and tired of the world.

We have come to believe that the United States Senate, led by skilful Henry Cabot Lodge, was supported by a good part of the people of this land when it kept us out of the League of Nations and apart from the world.

The fact is, isolationist sentiment was a product of the fight to prevent American participation in world affairs. It was not the cause of it.

All surveys of opinion in 1918 and 1919, and even in 1920, showed that the American people wanted to join a world organization to preserve the peace. Most of the press supported the idea, and most of the pulpit; so did business and labor, and war veterans and gold star mothers. And so did most of the United States Senate—76 out of 96 Senators voted for the League of Nations!

But a little group of powerful men wanted to keep us out. They well knew the sentiment of the nation. Their leader said in 1919:

"I think a majority of the people of the country desire a League. . . ."

They understood they would lose in an open fight. But they conceived a subtle strategy that would fool and defeat the people.

The strategy was successful. The little group of dissenters kept us out. They isolated America.

And so the United States abandoned her Allies, refused to join the League of Nations, forgot about the war criminals, and signed a separate peace with Germany. The United States, after winning World War I in 1917 and 1918, thus lost it in 1919 and 1920.

I do not believe that the League of Nations was a perfect instrument to preserve the peace. I do believe that when we refused to join the League of Nations and retreated into isolation, we sabotaged an instrument that—well used and wisely perfected—could have prevented the drift toward World War II that commenced when we withdrew from the world. I do believe that when we abandoned our Allies and signed a separate peace with Germany, we told Adolf Hitler and Germans like him that the rest of the world could be surely divided and perhaps conquered.

This book is the story of how it all happened; the story of how a handful of men caused us to withdraw from the world; the story of how we lost World War I.

It is told in the hope that the telling will make it more difficult for any little cabal to do the same thing again.

It is told in the hope that the telling will help us win lasting victory in World War II.

THANKS

Most of all to Professor Denna Frank Fleming of Vanderbilt University for his invaluable criticism of the entire manuscript, and for his monumental *The United States and the League of Nations, 1918–1920,* indispensable background for the writing of this book.

To Erma Celventra Fischer, for her intelligent research—reporting in retrospect, really—and for her many sound suggestions.

To my wife, Geneva, for her fine reporting, too, and for her advice on the manuscript and for her help on all the odds and ends that go along with doing a book, and for her constant encouragement—and patience.

To Ulric Bell, of Americans United for World Organization, to Denys P. Myers, of the old League to Enforce Peace, to the Library of Congress, the New York Public Library, the *New York Times,* and to all those whose writings and records have helped preserve the story of the first fight in the United States for world organization.

To the publishers listed below for their generous permission to quote from the books named. The page numbers in brackets following the book titles indicate the portions of *The Killing of the Peace* in which I have drawn on these books as a source for quotations:

The Bobbs-Merrill Company, Indianapolis. *As I Knew Them,* by James E. Watson. [pp. 48-49, 142-43, 149-51]

Doubleday, Doran & Co., New York. *Unfinished Business,* by Stephen Bonsal. [pp. 105-106, 205-206, 219] *Woodrow Wilson As I Knew Him,* by Joseph Tumulty. [p. 190]

Harcourt, Brace & Co., New York. *Fighting Years,* by Oswald Garrison Villard. [pp. 183-84]

Harper & Brothers, New York. *Henry White, Thirty Years of American Diplomacy,* by Allan Nevins. [pp. 41, 69, 83-85, 87, 94-95, 99-100, 107, 179-80, 253]

Houghton Mifflin Company, Boston. *Beveridge and the Progressive Era,* by Claude G. Bowers. [pp. 27, 42-43] *The Intimate Papers of Colonel House,* Vol. IV, arranged by Charles Seymour. [pp. 33-36] *Mein Kampf,* by Adolf Hitler. [pp. 38, 252-53]

The Macmillan Company, New York. *Public Opinion,* by Walter Lippmann. [pp. 276-77]

Charles Scribner's Sons, New York. *The Aftermath,* by Winston Churchill. [pp. 38-39] *The Senate and the League of Nations,* by Henry

Cabot Lodge. [pp. 74, 101-102, 207-209, 236] *Henry Clay Frick, the Man,* by George Harvey. [pp. 111-13]

Yale University Press, New Haven. *Survey of American Foreign Relations, 1928,* by Charles P. Howland. [pp. 280-81]

University of North Carolina Press, Chapel Hill. *The League to Enforce Peace,* by Ruhl J. Bartlett. [p. 139]

Also to the Estate of Willis Fletcher Johnson, for quotations from *George Harvey, A Passionate Patriot* (Houghton Mifflin). [pp. 62, 263, 265-66]

1916

May 27, 1916. President Wilson and Senator Lodge

Two men sat down to dinner at the same table this night in the Willard Hotel in Washington, D. C.

One was Woodrow Wilson, President of the United States.

The other was Henry Cabot Lodge, Senator from Massachusetts.

They came to address a convention of the League to Enforce Peace, a new and powerful movement for the creation of a world organization to keep the peace.

It was known that one of the speakers would strongly endorse the proposal. He had publicly proclaimed his conviction that only international force could preserve peace.

After dinner, he spoke first, declaring that the limit of voluntary arbitration of disputes between nations had been reached.

"If we have reached the limit of voluntary arbitration, what is the next step?" he asked. And he answered, "I think the next step is that which this league proposes, and that is to put force behind international peace, an international league or agreement, or tribunal, for peace. We may not solve it in that way, but if we cannot, it can be solved in no other....

"I know, and no one, I think, can know better . . . no one can, I think, feel more deeply than I do the difficulties which confront us. . . . But the difficulties cannot be overcome unless we try to overcome them. I believe much can be done....

"I know the difficulties that arise when we speak of anything which seems to involve an alliance. But I do not believe that when Washington warned us against 'entangling alliances' he meant for one moment that we should not join with the other civilized nations of the world if a method could be found to diminish war and encourage peace."

He closed with these ringing words: "This league certainly has the highest of all aims for the benefit of humanity, and because the pathway is sown with difficulties is no reason that we should turn from it. It is the vision of a perhaps impossible perfection that has led humanity across the centuries. If our aspirations are for that which is great and beautiful and good and beneficent to humanity, even when we do not achieve our end, even if the results are little, we can at least remember Arnold's lines:

> 'Charge once more, then, and be dumb!
> Let the victors, when they come,
> When the forts of folly fall,
> Find your body by the wall!' "

There was warm applause as Senator Lodge sat down.

And there followed a hush as former President William Howard Taft got to his feet to introduce Woodrow Wilson, who had driven him from the White House four years before. The whole meeting had been arranged in the hope of gaining President Wilson's support for the idea of world organization, but no one was certain that he shared Lodge's convictions. Not even White House intimates knew what he intended to say, for he had kept the notes for his address in his desk drawer in a folder no one was permitted to touch.

Taft, who was head of the League to Enforce Peace, made it clear in his introduction that no one had a right to infer that Wilson's presence committed him to the program of the movement. "We think by his presence, however," he smiled, "that he shows sympathy with our general purposes."

There was a sense of great expectancy as the President started to speak.

"We are participants, whether we would or not, in the life of the world," he said, and the people felt a glow. "The interests of all nations are our own also. We are partners with the rest. What affects mankind is inevitably our affair."

The President spoke slowly, and with great emphasis he said:

"I am sure that I speak the mind and wish of the people of America when I say that the United States is willing to become a partner in any feasible association of nations. . . ."

He explained that he had not come to discuss a program. "I came only to avow a creed and give expression to the confidence I feel that the world is even now upon the eve of a great consummation, when some common force will be brought into existence which shall safeguard right as the first and most fundamental interest of all peoples and all governments, when coercion shall be summoned not to the service of political ambition or selfish hostility, but to the service of a common order, a common justice and a common peace.

"God grant that the dawn of that day of frank dealing and of settled peace, concord and co-operation may be near at hand."

The people stood and thrilled to the thought that they were applauding the first proposal ever made by the responsible head of a great nation to lead it into a commonwealth of nations.

Woodrow Wilson, Democrat, had chosen the time and the place for the declaration with great care. The League to Enforce Peace had been founded largely by leaders of the opposition party. When he spoke out under its auspices, in full agreement with former President Taft and Senator Lodge, Republicans, seemingly all hint of partisanship in the proposition had been thrust aside.

October 30, 1916. A Tale Told on a Train

In the presidential campaign of 1916, Woodrow Wilson and his Republican opponent, Charles Evans Hughes, both came out strongly in favor of world organization. The campaign slogan of the Democrats—"He kept us out of war!"—meanwhile placed the Republicans in a hopeless dilemma and kept them there. Every effort to reply seemed to imply that if Hughes was elected he would take us to war.

On the eve of the election, Senator Henry Cabot Lodge made a desperate effort to wreck Wilson's strategy by proving it was based on fraud. He threw the nation into an uproar by telling a tale told to him by a man who had heard it from another man on a train between San Francisco and Ogden.

Lodge charged that when President Wilson sent a stiff warning to Germany after the sinking of the *Lusitania,* he tried to add a secret postscript explaining to the Germans that the blunt note was not to be taken seriously—that it was simply meant to satisfy the outraged people of the United States. Cabinet members found out about the postscript before the note was sent, said Lodge, and in a stormy meeting they forced Wilson to kill it by threatening to resign and expose the duplicity.

The Cabinet members flatly denied the startling story that Wilson had sought to deceive the American people by pretending to tell the Germans one thing while actually telling them another. The fact was that Secretary of State William Jennings Bryan had proposed a modification of the note to Germany. Other members of the Cabinet, together with Bryan's assistants in the State Department, had opposed the modification, and Wilson had agreed with them.

A stump speaker campaigning for Wilson asked him for comment. Wilson replied by telegram:

"LET ME SAY THAT THE STATEMENT MADE BY SENATOR LODGE IS UNTRUE. . . ."

November 1, 1916. "Stagecoach Tittle-Tattle"

It was obvious to the nation that Lodge did not have his facts straight, and he was assailed from all sides. The *New York Times* said it wondered how the renowned Cabots and Lodges of early New England would regard their descendant, and exclaimed:

"Can you imagine George Cabot . . . spreading stagecoach tittle-tattle at second or third hand as political or Gospel truth?"

The Gentleman from Massachusetts was in an indefensible position. He issued a statement saying: "The President of the United States has denied that there was any postscript to the *Lusitania* note and we are all bound, of course, to accept the President's denial just as he makes it."

No member of the Senate, and perhaps no other American of the day, would have felt more deeply the embarrassment of his position than did Henry Cabot Lodge.

A stern aristocrat, he was accustomed to vast respect. His reserve sometimes led his colleagues in the United States Senate to refer to him in the cloak rooms as the "Ambassador from Massachusetts." Some, resentful of his austerity and particularly of his habit of quoting precise, nasal French to a largely mono-lingual Senate, liked to quip, "Lodge's mind is like the soil of New England—naturally barren but highly cultivated." He was one of the best dressed of Senators, too, and his thin figure was always erect, always proud. His white hair and his white beard and his white mustache were always clipped, always combed.

Never before had Henry Cabot Lodge been subjected to the ridicule of the nation. Never before had it seemed conceivable that any President of the United States would ever call Henry Cabot Lodge a liar.

November 10, 1916. Three Men and Woodrow Wilson

Not until three days after the election of 1916 was it finally determined that Woodrow Wilson would stay in the White House for a second term.

Wilson finally won when he captured California's twelve electoral votes—despite the pre-election predictions that California was a "strong and safe Republican state" certain to support Charles Evans Hughes.

Republicans all over the land at once accused Senator-elect Hiram Johnson of electing Wilson. He had bolted the Republican Party in 1912 to run for Vice President with Theodore Roosevelt on the Progressive Party ticket. He was still feuding with the regular Republicans in 1916, and did not even speak to Hughes when he swung through California during his campaign, even though they were in the same Long Beach hotel for several hours. Johnson ran for the Senate as a Republican as well as a Progressive, however, and carried the state by the huge margin of 296,815 votes—while Hughes lost the state by 3773 votes.

Republican politicians felt that there had been some sort of a deal, that Hughes had been traded off for Johnson. The *Los Angeles Times* charged Johnson with treachery, labeled him "The Benedict Arnold of California."

Some Republicans blamed Theodore Roosevelt, too, for helping elect Wilson, even though he had supported Hughes. They felt that Western Progressives had split the vote as in 1912, when their bolt elected Wilson over Taft and TR. A Republican wrote a sarcastic letter to the *New York Times:* "Kindly inform me if our deserting leader [Mr. Roosevelt] is the author of a book entitled *The Winning of the West*?"

And there were some Republicans who felt that Henry Cabot Lodge had done his bit for Woodrow Wilson by his wild, last-minute charge about the *Lusitania* note.

1917

January 13, 1917. The Anniversary of St. John

The affair of the tale told on the train rankled in two minds—Wilson's and Lodge's. Wilson, like Lodge, was not a man to forgive and forget personal affronts. Like Lodge, he knew how to hate.

Lodge found this out—and for him it was an important discovery—when the good Rector Roland Cotton Smith of the Church of St. John in Washington innocently invited both the President of the United States and the Senator from Massachusetts to speak at a celebration marking the hundredth anniversary of his church. Both accepted the invitations.

But when Wilson discovered that Lodge was to speak, he notified Rector Smith that he would be unable to attend—unless Lodge was taken off the program.

Horrified, Rector Smith hurried to his old friend Lodge for advice. What Lodge said to Smith and what Smith said to Wilson is not exactly known.

But Lodge addressed the celebration, and Wilson stayed away.

January 22, 1917. "Now It Appears to Be Possible"

The idea of world organization won wide and growing support in the United States in 1916 and early 1917.

The United States Chamber of Commerce reported that 96 per cent of more than 700 business groups polled favored creation of some sort of a society of nations. A survey of 99 leading newspapers showed that 91 favored world organization, while only 8 opposed it.

After the Washington meeting, the League to Enforce Peace developed into a strong, nation-wide organization, and soon had branches in all states except Minnesota, Nebraska, and Nevada. It sought in countless ways to show the American people that their happiness and welfare depended upon a stable, peaceful world, and that there would never be a stable, peaceful world unless Americans joined with other peoples to build it. Meetings were held, pamphlets were distributed, letters were sent to civic, church, educational, business, labor, fraternal, and other leaders.

Many governors and mayors proclaimed League Sundays and League Weeks. Former President Taft was among many powerful people who toured the country under League to Enforce Peace auspices. Another who spoke at their meetings was Edward A. Filene, the noted Boston business leader. Filene predicted that unless a concert of nations was constructed after peace came in Europe, the world would soon see the greatest depression in history, followed by the worst war in history.

About the only prominent American who took a position against world organization was the aging pacifist, William Jennings Bryan.

Abroad, too, there was growing support for the idea. The British, French, and German governments all sent friendly messages to a League to Enforce Peace dinner held in New York late in 1916.

Now President Wilson, after a careful estimate of the trend of American and world thought, came before the Senate of the United States to talk over the proposition. He said:

"I have sought this opportunity to address you because I thought I owed it to you, as the council associated with me in the final determination of our international obligations, to disclose to you without reserve the thought and purpose that have been taking form in my mind in regard to the duty of our Government in the days to come when it will be necessary to lay afresh and upon a new plan the foundations of peace among the nations."

He stated that no covenant of peace that did not include the New World would suffice to prevent future war once the battle raging in the Old World was done. He declared that when the time came for a settlement the United States would be willing to add its authority and power to the authority and power of other nations to guarantee world peace and world justice.

"It is right that before it comes this Government should frankly formulate the conditions upon which it would feel justified in asking our people to approve its formal and solemn adherence to a League for Peace," he said. "I am here to attempt to state these conditions."

He proposed that the "League for Peace" should not be based on a peace dictated by one group of nations to another, but a peace of equality and of common participation in common benefits. He proposed that the peace should bring government by the consent of the governed, should provide free access to the seas for great nations and freedom of the seas for all nations, and should limit the size of armies and navies so they would be powers for order and not instruments of aggression and of selfish violence.

"I am proposing, as it were, that the nations should with one accord adopt the doctrine of President Monroe as the doctrine of the world; that no nation should seek to extend its policy over any other nation or people, but that every people should be left free to determine its own policy, its own way of development, unhindered, unthreatened, unafraid, the little along with the great and powerful. . . .

"There must be, not a balance of power, but a community of power, not organized rivalries, but an organized common peace. If the peace presently made is to endure, it must be a peace made secure by the organized major forces of mankind."

President Wilson's heart was warmed by the great applause that accompanied him as he made his way from the Senate chamber, and he remarked, "I have said what everybody has been longing for, but has thought impossible. Now it appears to be possible."

January 23, 1917.
"Of All in Congress Who Listened . . ."

Mark Sullivan, a young Washington correspondent, heard Wilson address the Senate, and reported to his newspaper, ". . . of all in

Congress who listened to Wilson's words this day, and of all throughout the country who read it, probably it occurred to very few to question the project Wilson here proposed."

One man who sat in the Senate and listened intently to Wilson's words, and who then read the printed text of the address over and over again, was Henry Cabot Lodge.

Despite Wilson's statement that he addressed the Senate as the council "associated" with him in the "final determination" of the international obligations of the United States, Lodge had reason to believe that Wilson's view of the powers of the Senate in world affairs was very different from his own. For in a book written in 1908, before he became President, Wilson had said:

"One of the greatest of the President's powers I have not yet spoken of at all—his control, which is very absolute, of the foreign relations of a nation. The initiative in foreign affairs which the President possesses without any restriction whatever is virtually the power to control them absolutely. The President cannot conclude a treaty with a foreign power without the consent of the Senate, but he may guide every step of diplomacy, and to guide diplomacy is to determine what treaties must be made if the faith and prestige of the government are to be maintained. He need disclose no step of negotiation until it is complete, and when in any critical matter it is completed the government is virtually committed. Whatever its disinclination, the Senate may feel itself committed also."

To Senator Lodge, this was plain heresy. At the turn of the century, when engaged in one of his many treaty fights with a President, he had expressed his own doctrine:

"It is . . . a . . . serious matter when misapprehension of this kind [as to the functions and powers of the Senate] is found among those who are charged with the conduct of government. . . .

"Practice and precedent, the action of the Senate and of the President, and the decision of the Supreme Court, show that the power of the Senate in the making of treaties has always been held . . . to be equal and co-ordinate with that of the President, except at the initiation of a negotiation which can of necessity only be undertaken by the President alone. The Senate has the right to recommend entering upon a negotiation, or the reverse . . . the right to amend, and this right it has always exercised largely and freely."

Lodge had acted in accordance with this doctrine many times.

When President Cleveland, Democrat, sent a treaty to the Senate in 1897 proposing to establish a method of arbitration of disputes between the United States and England, Lodge helped bury it in the Foreign Relations Committee.

When President McKinley, Republican, endorsed the same treaty after his inauguration, Lodge so ruined it by amendments that the Senate refused to ratify the wreck.

Even when President Theodore Roosevelt, Lodge's dearest friend, sent some arbitration treaties to the Senate, Lodge fought them. He persuaded the Senate to amend them so that all settlements of disputes by arbitration would have to be approved by the Senate—thoroughly upsetting the proposed arbitration machinery. TR withdrew the treaties from the Senate, and wrote an angry letter to Lodge declaring he would not give "the impression of trickiness and insincerity by solemnly promulgating a sham."

When President Taft, still another Republican, proposed arbitration treaties with several nations, Lodge took up the fight again, declaring that arbitration of disputes between nations was too great a step forward in international relations. "Great and lasting advances are those which have been slowly made," he warned. Led by Lodge, the Senate so gutted the treaties by amendments that Taft refused to sign them. Later, when he was out of the White House, Taft remarked, "I put them on the shelf and let the dust accumulate in the hope that the Senators might change their minds, or that the people might change the Senate; instead of which they changed me."

And now President Wilson, Democrat, had come before the Senate and was proposing not arbitration with one nation, not arbitration with a handful of nations, but arbitration with all the nations of the world through the creation of a League for Peace!

Senator Lodge had advocated the very same thing in his address before the League to Enforce Peace. However, now that the proposal was beginning to take shape—now that it had been discussed before the Senate by the President—he felt he should bring his own position up to date.

The Gentleman from Massachusetts sat down at his desk to prepare a speech for delivery in the Senate.

February 1, 1917. Lodge Addresses the Senate

Senator Lodge took the floor of the Senate early in the afternoon to read a long, carefully prepared address. It was the product of long days and late nights of intensive work.

He drew to quite a degree upon his address of 1916 to the League to Enforce Peace. Several passages were virtually identical. Again he declared that the limit of voluntary arbitration had been reached.

"If, then, voluntary arbitration and voluntary agreements, by convention or otherwise, without any sanction, have reached their limits, what is the next step?" he asked. And again he answered, "There is only one possible advance, and that is to put a sanction behind the decision of an international tribunal or behind an agreement of the nations; in other words, to create a power to enforce the decree of the international courts or the provisions of the international agreements. There is no other solution."

Lodge had gone on from there, in 1916, to point out that no one knew better than he the difficulties that would rise in the way of this solution, but that the only thing to do was to try to overcome them. Now, in 1917, he set out to prove they could *not* be overcome.

"I confess that when I first began to consider it some two years ago, it presented great attraction to me," he said, "but the more I have thought about it, the more serious the difficulties in the way of its accomplishment seem to be. . . .

"The first difficulty comes when the League is confronted by the refusal of a nation involved in a dispute with another nation to abide by the decision of the League."

The result would be war, not peace, he warned:

"You would be compelled, if a decree of the League were resisted, to go to war without any action on the part of Congress and wholly on the command of other nations."

Senator Lodge's little excursion into internationalism was at an end. Once more he was the nationalist, the isolationist, the opponent of Presidents who talked of establishing peaceful methods of solving international arguments.

He proceeded to point out other difficulties. Since the United States would have but one vote in the proposed League, he said, we might be compelled to submit to decisions made by the smaller and weaker nations. We might find the League interfering in our domestic affairs, perhaps ordering us to admit Asiatic labor.

"These are not fanciful cases drawn from the regions of the imagination," he said. "They are actual living questions of the utmost vitality and peril today. In them is involved that deepest of human instincts which seeks not only to prevent an impossible competition in labor but to maintain the purity of the race."

Lodge assailed the conditions Wilson had declared must be met if we were to enter a league to preserve peace. It didn't matter, he said, whether the peace was dictated or not; it mattered only that the peace be just and righteous. However, he wanted to know who was to decide whether a government really rested on the consent of the governed? If we decided that the government of Armenia by Turkey didn't rest on the consent of Armenians, were we to go to the rescue of the Armenians, or were we to exclude the Turks from the league? And what if anyone were sufficiently malevolent to ask if we secured the Louisiana Territory by vote of Louisianians?

When Wilson spoke about limiting the size of armies and navies, why didn't he mention the merchant marine? And when he spoke about freedom of the seas, why didn't he mention the matter of planting mines on the high seas?

Why did Wilson confine his proposal of free access to the seas to great peoples, and forget about lesser folk? Were we to give Germany a corridor to the Persian Gulf because she is a great nation, while denying Switzerland access to the seas because she is a small nation?

Did the proposal that the Monroe Doctrine become the doctrine of the world mean that the United States should regard European colonization anywhere in the world as an unfriendly act? If it didn't mean that, Lodge wanted to know this:

"Or does the President's proposition mean that the Monroe Doctrine is to be extended to all the world and thereby be abandoned under the law laid down by John Fiske in regard to myths—that when we find a story of something which has happened everywhere we may be quite sure that it never happened anywhere—so that if we have a Monroe Doctrine everywhere we may be perfectly certain that it will not exist anywhere?"

Lodge in 1916 had quoted Washington's "entangling alliances" phrase in support of the league idea. Lodge now quoted the same phrase *against* the league idea:

"There is no lurking place for a league for peace 'supported by the organized major force of mankind' in the sentences of George Washington. . . ."

The Gentleman from Massachusetts did not evoke the brave lines of Arnold for this occasion. He turned instead to Browning, prefacing the choice with a sarcastic reference to Wilson's lofty purposes:

"Of course, we all agree most heartily with the proposition that peace—just and righteous peace—is infinitely better than war; that virtue is better than vice; that, in Browning's words:

'It's wiser being good than bad;
It's safer being meek than fierce;
It's fitter being sane than mad.'"

February 2, 1917. "I Abhor Wilson"

Senator Lodge's feelings about the man in the White House, no matter how bitter they might become, would never exceed those of a former occupant of the White House, Theodore Roosevelt.

TR's ill will for Wilson dated back to 1912, when Wilson defeated him for the presidency. TR was outraged when practically the first thing Wilson did after he was sworn into office was to apologize to Colombia and offer the little nation $25,000,000 for TR's famous seizure of Panama. Soon after the World War began in Europe, TR was all for American intervention, and he contemptuously charged that Wilson's efforts to keep us out were supported only by the "professional pacifists, the flubdubs and the molly-coddles."

Scorn and hate for Wilson intermingled and grew into the consuming passion of TR's later years. "I abhor Wilson," he wrote to his son Kermit. "I am simply unable to understand how the American people can tolerate Wilson," he told Lodge. Once, inviting a friend to visit him at Sagamore Hill at Oyster Bay, he wrote, "Come down for a night or a week; we'll hold a commination service over Wilson, and curse him out of the book of Ernulphus and with the Greater and Lesser anathema."

"No opinion that Roosevelt held, no action which he took, can be considered apart from that hatred," wrote Henry Pringle, TR's biographer.

For a long time, TR had strongly favored the idea of a world organization to preserve the peace. When he went to Norway in 1910 to accept the Nobel Peace Prize, he declared, "It would be a master stroke if those great Powers honestly bent on world peace would form a League for Peace, not only to keep the peace among themselves, but to prevent, by force if necessary, its being broken by others . . . the ruler or statesman who should bring about such a combination would have earned his place in history for all time and his title to the gratitude of all mankind."

TR devoted much of his book *America and the World War,* published in 1915, to his proposal for a world league. "Under the proposed plan there would be a strong likelihood of bettering world conditions," he wrote. "If it is a Utopia, it is a Utopia of a very practical kind."

TR and Lodge were lifelong friends. TR once said of the Senator from Massachusetts, ". . . he was my closest friend, personally, politically, and every other way." The two men consulted each other on virtually every important political move either made. Neither the scattering of TR-Lodge letters made public up to now, nor their biographies, reveal consultation on this particular phase of their war on Wilson. It is significant, however, that their abandonment of internationalism, and their opening attacks on Wilson's idea for a League for Peace, were made at the same time, and were in some ways identical.

Lacking the floor of the Senate as a forum, TR spoke in the pages of the February 1917 issue of *Metropolitan Magazine*. Implying that Wilson favored world organization in order to win some "temporary acclaim or advantage" to "the detriment of mankind," the former President pointed out all the conceivable difficulties involved in establishing a League for Peace. Like Lodge, he charged that the United States might have to submit to decisions made by the smaller and weaker nations. Like Lodge, he said we might find the League interfering in our domestic affairs.

All the same fanciful cases posed by Lodge were posed by TR—from the threat that the League might order us to admit Asiatic labor to the danger that the Monroe Doctrine might be abolished.

"These apostles of feeble folly . . . offer yet one more quack nostrum for international wrong. . . ." said TR of all who advocated world organization in 1917. He dismissed his former advocacy of world organization with the assertion that his statements of 1910 and 1915 had been "in the realm of mere speculation."

Lodge explained his 1916 advocacy of world organization in a letter to former Senator Albert Beveridge of Indiana: "It was not a question that was up then."

April 2, 1917. "It Is a Fearful Thing . . ."

"I have called the Congress into extraordinary session," a haggard and gray Wilson told a tense and sober Congress, "because there are serious, very serious, choices of policy to be made, and made immediately, which it was neither right nor constitutionally permissible that I should assume the responsibility of making."

The President of the United States summed up in cold, concise terms the story of wanton destruction and aggression by Germany, and he declared:

"The challenge is to all mankind."

His request for a declaration of war was greeted by wild applause, stamping feet, lusty cheers.

Yet, strangely, the call for war was not the high point of Wilson's address. That part seemed underplayed, toned down, automatic.

Wilson poured all his eloquence and feeling into these final stirring words:

"It is a fearful thing to lead this great peaceful people into war, into the most terrible and disastrous of all wars, civilization itself seeming to be in the balance. But the right is more precious than peace, and we shall fight for the things which we have always carried nearest our hearts—for democracy, for the right of those who submit to authority to have a voice in their own governments, for the rights and liberties of small nations, for a universal dominion of right by such a concert of free peoples as shall bring peace and safety to all nations and make the world itself at last free.

"To such a task we can dedicate our lives and our fortunes, everything that we are and everything that we have, with the pride of those who know that the day has come when America is privileged to spend her blood and her might for the principles that gave her birth and happiness and the peace which she has treasured.

"God helping her, she can do no other."

1918

January 8, 1918. The Fourteen Points

On the East Front, the Germans were dictating peace terms to a beaten Russia.

On the West Front, they were preparing new offensives.

The forces of freedom needed inspiration, needed a declaration of the things they were fighting and dying for. They needed leadership.

President Wilson went before Congress to raise a banner to the sky.

His message was carefully designed as an instrument of propaganda, a guide for America and the Allies, and for all freedom-loving people everywhere. It held out hope for every nation, big or little, friend or foe, and even to people who had no nation of their own but longed for one.

It promised a world fit and safe to live in, where every peace-loving nation would live its own life, free of the fear of force and aggression. It proposed a world where the causes of war would be controlled by international agreement.

The pattern of the peace to come was set down concisely in Fourteen Points, designed for translation and distribution on leaflets and placards all over the world.

Through the Fourteen Points ran the theme of the concert of free peoples, and the grand finale was the League of Nations.

Point 1 would abolish secret diplomacy, and substitute open covenants openly arrived at.

Point 2 would guarantee freedom of the seas except for international enforcement of peace.

Point 3 would reduce economic barriers between all nations joining in the maintenance of the peace.

Point 4 would reduce armaments to the lowest point consistent with domestic safety.

Point 5 would adjust colonial claims in the interest of the inhabitants as well as the colonial powers concerned.

Beginning with Point 6, the appeal turned to particular peoples whose rights had been trampled in the dust. One, a desperate effort to keep a badly needed ally in the war, pledged a free and independent Russia. Others promised to liberate Belgium, to free France, to liberate the nations of Central Europe and the Balkans, to adjust the frontiers of Italy along lines of nationality, to free minorities from Turkish domination but to permit an independent Turkey, and to create an independent Poland with access to the sea and including territories inhabited by Polish populations. Again and again there was the pledge that these things would be guaranteed by international covenants.

Point 14 would make all the others possible. It said:

"A general association of nations must be formed under specific covenants for the purpose of affording mutual guarantees of political independence and territorial integrity to great and small states alike."

July 4, 1918. "The Great Stage of the World"

Since winter, the Germans had swept close to Paris, after inflicting an incredible peace on Russia that deprived her of 34 per cent of her population, 32 per cent of her farmland, 54 per cent of her industry.

Yet American troops were pouring into France, and Marshal Foch was calm and determined. Even Germans were saying, "Our military situation is brilliant—and hopeless."

The fire of the Fourteen Points was spreading all over the world. There was rebellion in Hungary, desertions among the Czechs and Slovaks, trouble for the German General Staff all over the Balkans, and even some strikes inside Germany.

On this Independence Day, President Wilson journeyed to Mount Vernon, still and remote beside the lazy Potomac River. And standing there on the gentle slopes of a green hillside, once again Wilson set forth the war aims of the people fighting for freedom, and again he declared that the fundamental of the peace must be a concert of nations.

"These great objects can be put into a single sentence," he said. "What we seek is the reign of law, based upon the consent of the governed and sustained by the organized opinion of mankind."

Wilson spent a few moments recollecting the story of the American Revolution, and he closed by saying:

"I stand here now to speak—speak proudly and with confident hope—of the spread of this revolt, this liberation, to the great stage of the world itself."

Sometime in August 1918. A Meeting at Beverley Farms

Tall and thin, with solemn eyes obscured by thick horn-rimmed spectacles, a heavy, immobile face, and a slow and awesome way of speech, Colonel George Harvey was a plotter of plots, a man of wild imagination and vast ambition. He always managed to convince even the most casual observer that he was a puller of strings, a power behind great affairs—and he often was.

Colonel Harvey was the "discoverer" of Woodrow Wilson. He had happened to attend the inauguration of Wilson as President of Princeton University in 1902, and he had remarked that day to Abraham Lincoln's son, "That man could win the people. I want to know more about him."

The Colonel got to know Wilson very well indeed—he moved right in. Four years later, he attracted wide attention with the first recorded hint of a destiny that lay ahead:

"It is with a feeling almost of rapture," he said at a New York dinner honoring Wilson, "that I occasionally contemplate even a remote possibility of casting a ballot for the President of Princeton to become President of the United States."

Four more years passed and Wilson was elected Governor of New Jersey, with the astute political guidance of Harvey, who was one of the nation's foremost publicists. "He was Woodrow's first political friend, the one who started it all," said Mrs. Wilson.

Then, in 1911, as the campaign to put Wilson in the White House gathered momentum, the two men split. The opposition to Wilson had dropped sinister hints of Harvey's links with "interests" in Wall Street. Far too bluntly, Wilson told Harvey his support had become a dangerous liability. Hurt and angry, Harvey withdrew his support. Wilson sent him belated thanks for all he had done, begging, "Forgive me, and forget my manners," but the wound never healed. Although in after years the two men often slept in the same hotels, attended the same meetings, sometimes sat at the same banquet tables, they spoke to each other only once again—at a futile White House meeting that failed to bring them together.

Even so, Colonel Harvey backed President Wilson strongly on many issues, and he fervently endorsed his expression of American war aims. In 1917 and 1918 he edited both the sedate *North American Review* and a powerful, less inhibited magazine called the *War Weekly*. Of the Fourteen Points address, Harvey wrote in the *War Weekly,* "Wilson's declaration was a veritable masterpiece. He has never done and we doubt if anybody living could have done better." Of the Mount Vernon address, he editorialized, "As long as generations to come read the history of our share in the great World War just so long will this 1918 Fourth of July address of President Wilson at Washington's tomb be read and admired as a dominant monument in our history."

Now, in August, while Allied offensives were driving the enemy back to the Somme, and convincing the German General Staff that the war was lost, Colonel Harvey was invited to the home of Ex-Senator Albert Beveridge at Beverley Farms, Massachusetts, to meet with Theodore Roosevelt and Beveridge, who were planning to fight Wilson's peace plans. The exact day of the visit is unknown.

Beveridge, who had bolted the Republican Party in 1912 to be Chairman of the Progressive Party convention, had always favored a form of United States imperialism. He detested the idea of a League of Nations, and he hoped to smash it.

TR's passionate hatred for Wilson had grown to new heights since his desire to command a division in France had been denied. He had dreamed of military glory ever since he had charged up San Juan Hill with his Rough Riders, and he was surprised and hurt when his services were not accepted with delight in 1917. "I wish respectfully to point out that I am a retired Commander-in-Chief of the United States Army," he wrote to Secretary of War Newton D. Baker, giving three generals as references. He went to see Wilson at the White House, and reported afterwards, "I complimented him upon his war message and told him it would rank with the world's greatest state papers if it were made good and I told him I wanted a chance to help him make it good."

TR's desires became a public issue, and Wilson finally felt compelled to make a public statement refusing his services. The statement was hardly diplomatic. After acknowledging TR's fine vigor and enthusiasm, it said, "But this is not the time for compliment or for any action not calculated to contribute to the immediate success of the war. The business at hand is undramatic, practical, and of scientific definiteness and precision . . . I am too much interested in the cause we are fighting for to be interested in anything but success . . . whatever the argument of policy or of personal gratification or advantage."

General Pershing stated years later that the Secretary of War made the decision against TR. Marshal Joffre had informed Baker it cost from ten to fifteen thousand lives to train a division commander.

But TR laid all the blame on Wilson. His hate for him became an obsession—the "gospel of vengeance" Henry Pringle called it.

TR had taken to raging up and down the land, thundering denunciations of Wilson's conduct of the war.

Now that the war was coming to a victorious end, he would commence denouncing Wilson's conduct of the peace.

There were two instruments TR wanted to use in his battle against Wilson to supplement his own vast energy.

One was the Republican Party. TR was not always a devout Republican. He had not hesitated to bolt and wreck the party in 1912 to run his Bull Moose campaign as a Progressive. When he visited Wilson at the White House in 1917, he was back in the Republican fold, but his desire to command a division was paramount, and he told a friend, "I am going to tell Wilson that if he will give me this division, I will give him my promise never to oppose him politically in any way whatsoever."

The other instrument was Colonel Harvey, and his *War Weekly*. Harvey had planned to kill his powerful publication when Germany was defeated. Now he altered his plan. There was another war to be fought.

TR and Beveridge pledged 20,000 subscribers to Harvey for two years, according to William E. Dodd, then of the University of Chicago and later United States Ambassador to Germany.

Harvey pledged he would attack Wilson and Wilson's peace plans relentlessly.

Colonel Harvey's abrupt about-face concerning the League of Nations cannot be explained by his ill feeling toward Wilson. Up to August 1918, there was no evidence that it blinded Harvey's approach to any of Wilson's international policies.

The turn-about cannot be explained by partisan motives. For most of his life, Harvey called himself an "Independent Democrat." Soon after Will Hays became Chairman of the Republican National Committee in 1916, Harvey declared, ". . . the sooner he goes home and takes his damned old party with him, the better it will be for all concerned." On April 13, 1918, only four months before he went to Beverley Farms, Harvey outraged the Republicans by urging that 1918 elections be called off and the Democrats left in control of Congress until the war was won.

Friends of Harvey have termed it "contemptible slander" to say that this meeting caused his desertion of the League of Nations. Yet they have failed to offer any other explanation of his sudden switch to the opposition.

September 27, 1918. "The Common Will of Mankind"

Bulgaria had raised the flag of truce, the United States had received a peace feeler from Austria-Hungary, and the Germans were in headlong flight from Greece and were falling back from France.

President Wilson declared that the only hope of the world to secure lasting peace when the fighting was done was through creation of a League of Nations:

"And, as I see it," he said in a Liberty Loan address in New York, "the constitution of that League of Nations and the clear definition of its objects must be a part, in a sense the most essential part, of the peace settlement itself."

Wilson sought to eliminate all hint that the plans for the peace were his, or any man's.

"No statesmen or assembly created them; no statesman or assembly can alter them," he said. "They have arisen out of the very nature and circumstances of the war. The most that statesmen or assemblies can do is to carry them out or be false to them."

He seemed deeply concerned lest the peace program become a partisan plaything.

"As I have said, neither I nor any other man in governmental authority created or gave form to the issues of this war," he emphasized. "I have simply responded to them with such vision as I could command. But I have responded gladly and with a resolution that has grown warmer and more confident as the issues have grown clearer and clearer. It is now plain that they are issues which no man can pervert unless it be willfully. I am bound to fight for them, and happy to fight for them as time and circumstance have revealed them to me as to all the world."

The millions engaged in the fight for freedom drew into closer and closer array as the purposes of the struggle became more distinct, he declared.

"It is the peculiarity of this great war that while statesmen have seemed to cast about for definitions of their purpose and have sometimes seemed to shift their ground and their point of view, the thought of the mass of men, whom statesmen are supposed to instruct and lead, has grown more and more unclouded; more and more certain of what it is that they are fighting for. . . .

"That is why I have said that this is a peoples' war, not a statesmen's. Statesmen must follow the clarified common thought or be broken."

October 13, 1918. "Repudiate the Fourteen Points"

There was a sensational announcement in Washington. Germany was ready for peace—on our terms. President Wilson had received this note on October 6:

> The German Government requests the President of the United States of America to take steps for the restoration of peace, to notify all belligerents of this request, and to invite them to delegate plenipotentiaries for the purpose of taking up negotiations. The German Government accepts as a basis for the peace negotiations, the program laid down by the President of the United States in his message to Congress of January 8, 1918, and in his subsequent pronouncements, particularly in his address of September 27, 1918.
>
> In order to avoid further bloodshed the German Government requests to bring about the immediate conclusion of an armistice on land, on water and in the air.

It sounded like a trick. Wilson and his advisers feared the word "basis" left far too much room for German bargaining at the peace table. The Germans might be seeking a mere breathing spell, an interlude of peace to enable them to regroup their armies.

Wilson replied with a demand for a clear-cut statement of absolute German acceptance of the Fourteen Points.

There had been a delay of several days, while the German General Staff desperately probed for some indication of Allied military weakness, but the demands of the German people for peace grew louder and louder. The German Government dolefully despatched another note to Washington:

> In reply to the question of the President of the United States of America the German Government hereby declares:

> The German Government has accepted the principles laid down by President Wilson in his addresses as the foundations of a permanent peace of justice. Consequently its object in entering into discussions would be only to agree upon practical details of the application of these terms.
>
> The German Government believes that the Governments of the Powers associated with the United States also accept the position taken by President Wilson in his addresses. . . .

The White House now revealed these negotiations, and let it be known that further demands were being made on the enemy.

There was a second sensation later in the day.

Theodore Roosevelt chose this moment to launch his campaign against Wilson and his peace plans. In a torrid statement dictated from his home on Sagamore Hill, he charged that Wilson's negotiations with the Germans were "dangerously close to treacherous diplomacy" and demanded they be stopped.

"I must earnestly hope," he boldly beseeched, "that the Senate of the United States and all other persons competent to speak for the American people will emphatically repudiate the so-called Fourteen Points and the various similar utterances of the President."

October 24, 1918. A Call for Revolt

The morning papers revealed that Wilson had turned over to the Allies the negotiations with the enemy. He had demanded and received certain military and naval commitments from the Germans, and had indicated that no armistice would actually be signed unless the Germans got rid of the Kaiser.

Wilson now advised the Allies that if they agreed to peace on the terms he had reached with Germany, their military chiefs should join with American military leaders to devise armistice terms, provided an armistice was deemed possible from the military point of view. He stipulated that the terms should "fully protect the interests of the peoples involved and ensure to the associated Governments the unrestricted power to safeguard and enforce the details of the peace to which the German Government has agreed."

Hindenburg threw up his hands in horror when he heard of these instructions. He woefully said they amounted to "a demand for unconditional surrender."

Since Theodore Roosevelt's opening blast, and while Wilson had been carrying on his negotiations with the Germans, the former President had been busy meeting with his intimates, and sending notes back and forth, laying down lines of their campaign. One thing they debated at great length was the League of Nations. Beveridge wanted to fight it openly, but TR was afraid to. TR knew the people of the United States favored world organization. "My own judgment," he told Beveridge in a note dated October 17, "is that in dealing with the League of Nations we should not say we totally reject the idea. . . ."

TR also feared that the Republican party might split wide open if he took a stand too different from former President William Howard Taft's support for world organization, and he wrote again to Beveridge on October 21, "I am insisting upon Nationalism as against Internationalism. I am saying with a bland smile whatever Nationalism demands. I will then adopt with that extra consideration any wise and feasible plan for limiting the possible area and likelihood of future wars. Mine is merely a platonic expression, designed to let Taft and his followers get over without too much trouble, and also to prevent any accusation that we are ourselves merely Prussian militarists."

Now TR was ready to open up. He made public a telegram to Senators Henry Cabot Lodge, Hiram Johnson, and Miles Poindexter of Washington, calling upon the Senate to halt Wilson's negotiations with Germany, and declaring:

"I also earnestly hope that on behalf of the American people it will declare against the adoption in their entirety of the Fourteen Points of the President's address of last January as offering a basis for peace satisfactory to the United States."

TR asked the Senate to pass a resolution declaring that American peace aims had never been formulated or accepted by the American people.

The telegram avoided all mention of the League of Nations although, of course, any attack on the entire Fourteen Points was actually an attack on the League of Nations.

It was a call to revolt against the peace program so steadily stated by Wilson, so steadily endorsed by the American people and praised by our Allies, and now accepted by the enemy.

The scattering criticism of the war aims had been so slight that David Lawrence made the flat statement, "Although Mr. Wilson outlined his famous Fourteen Points in January 1918, no dissent was heard in Congress."

All over the world, the Fourteen Points had won endorsement. They had unquestionably speeded the downfall of Germany. Lloyd George and the French Chamber of Deputies had expressed themselves in favor of world organization.

For days now, the press had been full of reports from Allied capitals warmly approving Wilson's peace negotiations with Germany on the basis of the Fourteen Points. The plan for a concert of nations seemed to express the everlasting desires of almost the entire human race for peace and happiness. It had kindled a flame in the hearts of men and women in unknown corners of the earth. Even in an outlying province of far India, a missionary wrote to a friend in the United States:

"Somehow the people have heard extracts of what President Wilson has said and it has gripped their hearts as nothing else has done since the war began."

October 25, 1918. "Elections Are at Hand"

Wilson considered the Roosevelt telegram a challenge not only to his leadership but to the very foundations of world peace.

It was evident that if the Republicans won control of the Senate in the coming elections, TR, who was once more generally accepted as the leader of the party, and Senator Lodge, who would become leader of the Senate and Chairman of the powerful Foreign Relations Committee, would be in a position to threaten his peace plans.

Wilson felt he could not remain idle in the face of this threat.

Many party politicians, who feared they might be defeated without Wilson's support, had been pleading with him to help them out. They pointed out that in Civil War days a Republican named Abraham Lincoln had not hesitated to advise the people not to "swap horses in midstream."

Some Cabinet members urged Wilson simply to call for election, regardless of party, of men who would support full American participation in the peace. The politicians argued that this would anger loyal Democrats, and that election of internationalist Republicans would be no help when the peace treaty came before the Senate if their election enabled Lodge to become chairman of the Foreign Relations Committee.

They also warned Wilson that a Democratic defeat at the polls would weaken him at the coming peace conference where, when it got down to details, he would inevitably face a terrible struggle in keeping the Allies in agreement with the American peace program.

Wilson determined, finally, to appeal to the voters for election of Democrats. He issued a public letter to all Americans:

My Fellow Countrymen:

The Congressional elections are at hand. They occur in the most critical period our country has ever faced or is likely to face in our time. If you have approved of my leadership and wish me to continue to be your unembarrassed spokesman in affairs at home and abroad, I earnestly beg that you will express yourselves unmistakably to that effect by returning a Democratic majority to both the Senate and the House of Representatives. . . .

The leaders of the minority in the present Congress have unquestionably been pro-war, but they have been anti-administration. . . .

This is no time for either divided counsels or for divided leadership. . . .

I need not tell you, my fellow countrymen, that I am asking your support not for my own sake or for the sake of a political party, but for the sake of the nation itself in order that its inward unity of purpose may be evident to all the world. . . .

I submit my difficulties and my hopes to you.

Woodrow Wilson

October 26, 1918. In Senator Lodge's Office

Wilson's plea delighted virtually all Democrats.

It also delighted certain politically astute Republicans. Soon after the message was carried in the morning papers, several of the latter met in Senator Lodge's office.

There was a remarkable coincidence that perhaps escaped Lodge's attention as he conducted the meeting and master-minded the statement that issued from it. Twenty years before, when President McKinley had called for election of a Republican Congress at the close of the Spanish-American War, Lodge had come to his support. Lodge had said then that a victory for McKinley's political opponents would say to the world that the people of the United States repudiated the result of the war and repudiated the man leading the nation back to peace.

It was on October 26, 1898, that Lodge issued a statement saying, "I think it should be the duty of every patriot to stand behind him and to hold up his hands and not to cross him."

Twenty years later to the day, the statement issued from Lodge's office after Wilson's plea said:

"Some time ago, the President said 'politics is adjourned.' Now, in the closing days of the campaign—delayed by the united efforts of all parties for the Liberty Loan—now, when all public meetings have been given up owing to the influenza epidemic, the President sends out a direct party appeal calling upon his countrymen to vote for Democrats because they are Democrats without any reference to whether such Democrats have been or are in favor of war measures and have a war record which deserves support. . . .

"Republicans are loyal enough to fight and die, as they are doing by the thousands; loyal enough to take up great loans and pay enormous taxes; loyal enough to furnish important men at no salary on some of the great war boards in Washington. But they are not loyal enough, in the President's opinion, to be trusted with any share in the Government of the country. . . ."

October 28, 1918. "Rub It In, Teddy!"

Senator Philander Knox of Pennsylvania, who had been Secretary of State in the Taft administration and was reputedly one of the best-dressed of Senators, delivered a speech in the afternoon that showed a pale trace of the TR influence.

The bald, paunchy Senator, nervously fingering his wing collar and shaking straight the crease in his striped trousers, declared that Congress, and Congress alone, had any mandate from the people to declare war and the aims of war.

Knox, who seemed very ill at ease, failed to propose any alternate war aims. The fact was, TR's best friends in the Senate were convinced the American people backed Wilson thoroughly on his negotiations with the Germans and supported his plan for a League of Nations. There was no serious thought among them of trying to pass the resolution TR had demanded in his telegram. They admired his bold challenge of everything Wilson did, but, for the moment, few were stout-hearted enough to go as far as TR in attacking him.

The great TR himself spoke in New York in the evening, and 5000 of his enthusiastic followers fought their way into Carnegie Hall to hear him, while thousands more milled around in the streets outside, completely overwhelming the police.

TR strode to the center of the stage in full dress, and his famous smile beamed from right to left at the wildly applauding audience. After four minutes of cheering, yelling, hand-clapping—and beaming—TR was about to launch his address when someone in the audience yelled:

"Rub it in, Teddy!"

"Put down the barrage!" howled Teddy.

There was more laughing and cheering, and then the crowd let TR get in a few words.

"You have just stood up and heard the 'Star-Spangled Banner' played," he shouted to the topmost gallery, "and I hold that any man who stands up with his heart full because of what the tune symbolizes, that man is entitled to vote in this country and to vote for any party he pleases."

That was the keynote for the two-hour, 20,000-word attack that followed. TR was at savage heat. Wilson the man, Wilson the war leader, Wilson the planner of peace—all were mercilessly torn to small shreds.

Individuals broke in on TR whenever they felt like it, and he would jovially put aside his manuscript and bark back at them. Once a man in the gallery shouted, "Three cheers for a fighting man!"

"I'd have been in the fight if I'd been allowed!" shouted the Colonel.

Once a man bellowed, "Unconditional surrender!" TR's response was rather startling. The *New York Times* reported: "The Roosevelt teeth clicked audibly."

TR brought mad laughter once when he fumbled foolishly with his papers, and muttered loudly, "I've seen it stated that the President counted up the notes to and from Germany last Friday and found that Germany was one note behind. So to be fair, instead of writing one to Germany, he wrote one to the American people."

"Hit him hard, Teddy!" came the happy cry.

Teddy shouted that in the cloak rooms of Congress, this bitter jest was whispered, "Here's to our Tsar, last in war, first toward peace, long may he waver!"

All TR's mighty powers of lung and invective were brought to bear as he thundered:

"He asks only for support of himself. There is not the slightest suggestion that he disapproves of disloyalty to the nation, . . . I do not doubt that he feels some disapproval of such disloyalty; but apparently this feeling on his part is so tepid that it slips from his mind when he contemplates what he regards as the far greater sin of failure in adherence to himself."

Then, baring his teeth and closing his fists:

"President Wilson says that Republicans are not good enough to serve the Republic in Congress at this time. But they are good enough to die for the Republic in the Army and Navy!"

TR declared: "When it comes to the peace negotiations we should emphatically repudiate the famous Fourteen Points announced by the President last January." He offered a long, detailed account of how he, personally, would settle the affairs of Europe, how he would arrange the various countries.

The audience was utterly exhausted at the end, and so was Teddy.

October 30, 1918. "Boot the Democratic Congress . . . !"

The skilful use TR and Lodge made of Wilson's election plea soon had most Republicans in the nation aroused. Even those who wholeheartedly supported his peace plans joined the attacks on Wilson. Taft protested:

"He wishes a Democratic Senate, not because he would seek the assistance of Democratic Senators in the foreign policy concerning which by the fundamental law they are to advise and consent, but because he can mold them to his will without consulting them."

Colonel Harvey, too, behaved like an injured Republican. "Boot the Democratic Congress out of existence!" he blustered.

November 4, 1918. "Fighting Means Struggling for Certain Results"

Colonel House, a small gray Texan, was in Paris representing Wilson in daily meetings with the heads of the British, French, and Italian governments.

They had come together to discuss peace terms, and in the very beginning grizzled old Clemenceau of France turned to fiery Lloyd George of England and inquired with as much innocence as he could bring to his shrewd, cynical face:

"Have you ever been asked by President Wilson whether you accept the Fourteen Points? I have never been asked."

"I have not been asked either," answered the British Prime Minister instantly, and he swung to House: "What is your view? Do you think that if we agree to an armistice we accept the President's peace terms?"

"That is my view," replied House.

"For the moment, unquestionably, we are not bound by President Wilson's terms," interposed Arthur Balfour, the British Foreign Secretary, "but if we assent to an armistice without making our position clear, we shall certainly be so bound."

"Then I want to hear the Fourteen Points," said Clemenceau, as if he had never heard of them.

Colonel House started to read them.

Lloyd George made an ugly face at Point 2, the one guaranteeing freedom of the seas.

"That point we cannot accept under any conditions," he interrupted. "It means that the power of blockade goes. Germany has been broken almost as much by the blockade as by military methods . . . I should like to see the League of Nations established before I let this power go. If the League of Nations is a reality, I am willing to discuss the matter."

He paused, and then added that he would be voted out of office by Parliament in twenty-four hours if he accepted Point 2. "And Parliament would be quite right!"

Orlando blew up when Point 9 was reached. He feared a readjustment of Italian frontiers along "lines of nationality" might limit Italy's territorial ambitions.

When all Fourteen Points had been read, Clemenceau shook his head so violently that his long, overhanging mustache danced. He declared he would not accept the Fourteen Points.

Clemenceau, Lloyd George, and Orlando each supported the complaints of the others to strengthen their own protests; but they soon realized Colonel House was a tough customer. The shrewd Texan feared that if the United States started out by compromising, amendments and reservations would destroy the entire structure of the peace. He had asked Walter Lippmann and another of his assistants to draw up an "interpretation" of the Fourteen Points, and he had virtually memorized it. It gave elementary definitions of each of the points, explained the things they meant and the things they did not mean, and analyzed every reasonable and unreasonable interpretation and distortion anyone might try to make of them. House thus anticipated every protest, and knew the most logical reply. But he was dealing with stubborn men; they deadlocked. House cabled Wilson. Wilson cabled back authorizing him to state that the President of the United States was unwilling to give up the Fourteen Points.

House went to Lloyd George, Clemenceau, and Orlando and told them that if they did not accept the Fourteen Points he would advise the President to go before Congress, state the facts, and ask:

"Should we make peace with Germany, now that she has accepted our terms, or should we go on fighting Germany until she is forced to accept the terms of France, England, and Italy, whatever they might be?"

Clemenceau leaped into the air.

"Would that mean the United States might negotiate a separate peace?"

"It might lead to that," replied House calmly, smiling the smile he used when he wanted to hide his feelings.

Clemenceau, and then Lloyd George, trailed by Orlando, gave way. They signed a memorandum to Wilson. It said:

"The Allied Governments have given careful consideration to the correspondence which has passed between the President of the United States and the German Government. Subject to the qualifications which follow, they declare their willingness to make peace with the Government of Germany on the terms of peace laid down in the President's address to Congress of January 8, 1918, and the principles of settlement enunciated in his subsequent addresses."

There were only two qualifications. One stipulated that the matter of freedom of the seas would be fully discussed at the Peace Conference. The other merely specified that by "reparations" the Allies meant that Germany would pay for all damage done to the civilian population of the Allies and their property.

"I am glad the exceptions were made," wrote Colonel House in his diary, "for it emphasizes the acceptance of the Fourteen Points."

The Colonel went to see Marshal Foch, who had drawn up military terms designed to make it absolutely impossible for Germany to resume war during the Peace Conference.

"Will you tell us, Monsieur le Maréchal," said House, "solely from the military point of view, apart from any other considerations, whether you would prefer the Germans to reject or sign the armistice as outlined here?"

"Fighting means struggling for certain results," replied the Commander-in-Chief of the Allied Armies. "If the Germans now sign an armistice under the general conditions we have just determined, these results are in our possession. This being achieved, no man has the right to cause another drop of blood to be shed."

November 5, 1918. Chairman Henry Cabot Lodge

A cable came to Wilson from Paris, and he decoded it himself. It was the Allied acceptance of the Fourteen Points. Wilson immediately cabled it to the Germans with a note informing them they could obtain terms for a military armistice from Marshal Foch. That done, Wilson awaited another decision. It was Election Day.

The people voted Republican, overwhelmingly.

The Constitution provides that 32 Senators—a third of the Senate—be elected every two years, yet 40 were elected in this one day, for there were 8 vacancies caused by death and resignation. The Republicans won 25 seats, the Democrats 15.

This meant the Republicans had won control of the Senate—by one vote. There would be 48 Republican members, 47 Democrats, and one Progressive.

Neither the leading Republican nor the leading Democratic newspapers interpreted the election as a repudiation of President Wilson's plans for peace.

Internationalism was the issue only in a few of the contests. It was important in Illinois, where Senator James Hamilton Lewis was defeated by a Republican isolationist named Medill McCormick, one-time publisher of the *Chicago Tribune* and brother of Colonel Robert R. McCormick.

Truman Newberry, once TR's Secretary of the Navy, spent more than a hundred thousand dollars in Michigan defeating Henry Ford, who refused to spend a cent. Ford had been very much for the League of Nations, but he had kept a tight lip throughout the campaign, sourly observing now and then that he was only running because Wilson told him to.

Most of the other campaigns had become involved with such issues as prohibition, women's suffrage, the tariff, and complaints about various wartime controls.

The United States had voted Republican with considerable regularity for many years. In 1912 Wilson had garnered less votes than TR and Taft together. In 1916 he had been supported by many Progressives and Republicans who admired his domestic reforms and his efforts to keep us out of war.

Now, in 1918, many concluded that Wilson's appeal for votes—exploited as it was by TR, Lodge, and others—drove enough Republican voters back into the fold to win the election.

The result was that when the new Congress convened in 1919, Senator Lodge would become Chairman of the Senate Foreign Relations Committee.

November 10, 1918.
"I Became Aware of My Own Destiny"

A pastor came into a German hospital to announce the abdication of the Kaiser. He was a dignified old gentleman, and he trembled and tears came to his eyes as he told the wounded soldiers that this war was lost.

One of the soldiers had been shell shocked during a British gas attack at Ypres on October 13—the day Theodore Roosevelt called upon the United States to repudiate the Fourteen Points. He had developed a case of hysterical blindness, but the doctors had promised he would eventually see well enough to take up some occupation. The terrible pain returned to the sockets of the soldier's eyes as the pastor spoke, and he began to weep.

"I could stand it no more. It was impossible for me to stay any longer. While everything began to go black before my eyes, stumbling, I groped my way back to the dormitory, threw myself on my cot and buried my burning head in the covers and pillows . . . I became aware of my own destiny."

The soldier's name was Adolf Hitler; the quotation is from *Mein Kampf*.

November 11, 1918. "Long Live Democracy"

The Germans signed the Armistice at 5:15 in the morning in a railway car on a siding in the Compiègne Forest of France.

The guns were silent on the Western Front at 11:00 a.m.

The world went wild, and Paris went wildest of all, laughing and crying all at once. Even tough old Clemenceau sent an armistice note to sharp Colonel House: "I cannot restrain the desire to open my arms to you and press you to my heart." And House sent a message to Woodrow Wilson: "Autocracy is dead. Long live democracy and its immortal leader. In this great hour my heart goes out to you in pride, admiration and love."

Across the channel in England, Lloyd George dined at No. 10 Downing Street with his friend, Winston Churchill, then Minister of Munitions, and Churchill later recorded his impressions of the night:

"The magnitude and absolute character of the victory induced a subdued and detached state of mind. There was no feeling that the work was done. . . . From outside the songs and cheers of multitudes could be remotely heard like the surf on the shore.

". . . three men . . . seemed to be the masters of the world . . . these men had been drawn together across differences of nationality and interest and across distances of land and sea by the comradeship of struggle against a dangerous foe. Together they had reached the goal. Victory absolute and incomparable was in their hands. What would they do with it? . . .

"These men must come together. . . . They must meet face to

face and settle swiftly after discussion the largest practical questions opened by the total defeat of the enemy. . . . They must seek only the best arrangements possible for the brave nations that had followed them, for a tormented Europe and an awe-struck world."

Across the Atlantic Ocean, the people of the United States danced and sang all day and all night. The *San Francisco Chronicle* gasped, "There never was such a purpose for celebrating before. Please God, there never will be again."

Theodore Roosevelt, suddenly very ill, entered Roosevelt Hospital in New York.

November 18, 1918. "Wilson Has No Authority . . ."

President Wilson announced that he would go to Paris to attend the Peace Conference.

The opponents of his peace plans were appalled. They shared Wilson's belief that his personal power and prestige would insure creation of a League of Nations. Colonel Harvey, according to one of his editors, "remonstrated, protested, pleaded" and the pages of his weekly "teemed and fulminated."

Seeking to undermine Wilson's power and prestige abroad, TR roared from his sickbed, "Our Allies and our enemies and Mr. Wilson himself should all understand that Mr. Wilson has no authority to speak for the American people at this time. His leadership has just been repudiated by them."

"There is no evidence at all . . ." replied the *Review of Reviews*, "that the country intended in this election to disapprove in any manner of President Wilson or of his policies. . . . Never in the history of the United States has any President been as strongly supported in his large policies, regardless of party, as has President Wilson. He may go to Europe feeling that the country is behind him with hearty and sympathetic support."

November 29, 1918. No Senators! No Republicans!

A new storm of criticism came down on Wilson's head when he announced the delegates who would accompany him to Paris.

He appointed Secretary of State Robert Lansing, Colonel House, General Tasker H. Bliss, and Henry White.

There was no Senator on the list!

There was no *real* Republican!

When the Republicans protested, the Democrats asserted Henry White was a Republican. He was a member of the party, an intimate of party leaders, and he did not accept the appointment until he had consulted TR and Lodge. But he had devoted his whole life to diplomacy (TR had once termed him "the most useful man in the entire diplomatic service during my presidency") and he had never been a politician. The party considered him at best a "neutral" Republican.

Many felt that Wilson should have appointed a top Republican, like Taft, or former Secretary of State Elihu Root, both of whom seemed in sympathy with his program. If they helped execute his plans, the party would find it hard to oppose them.

Many felt, too, that Senators of both parties should have been appointed, since the peace treaty would ultimately have to win Senate approval. President McKinley had appointed three Senators to his five-man Peace Commission after the Spanish-American War, but even then the treaty had only passed the Senate by a two vote margin. And afterwards, the Senate had warned McKinley not to appoint any of them to any more peace commissions. They declared the Senate lost its freedom of action when its members became involved in treaty negotiations. They preferred to judge the finished product.

Wilson had considered following McKinley's example, but the presence of Lodge had stumped him. He could appoint no Senators without appointing Lodge. Yet it seemed hardly likely that Lodge would support the League of Nations and the other Fourteen Points. And if Lodge went to Paris and did not have his way, he would return to fight the decisions made there with greater strength than ever—as a Senate leader who had been on the spot, but whose advice had been ignored.

Will Rogers said that Wilson thought it all over and then told the Senators:

"I tell you what, boys, we will split 50-50—I will go and you fellows can stay."

December 4, 1918. A Secret Memorandum

Senator Lodge came to see Henry White as he was packing his bag in his Washington home.

He handed him a secret memorandum, and asked him to show it—in the strictest confidence—to Lloyd George, Clemenceau, and other Allied statesmen.

It informed them that "under no circumstances" should provisions for a League of Nations be included in the peace treaty.

"Any attempt to do this," said the secret memorandum, "would not only long delay the signature of the treaty of peace, which should not be unduly postponed, but it would make the adoption of the treaty, unamended, by the Senate of the United States and other ratifying bodies, extremely doubtful."

It asserted that this represented the views of the Republican Party, and the views of the United States.

Lodge told White he thought the memorandum would strengthen the hands of foreign statesmen against President Wilson.

"This knowledge may in certain contingencies be very important to them in strengthening their positions," he said.

White was thunderstruck. White was also a trained diplomat. He took the memorandum and put it in his briefcase, as if he had been waiting for it. He bade Lodge a cordial farewell, promising to keep him closely informed on developments at Paris.

But he resolved that no one would see the memorandum until the peace treaty was written.

December 14, 1918. "Wilson! Wilson!"

The welcome Paris gave Woodrow Wilson was fantastic. The greatest military conquerors of all time had never known anything like it. Frenzied people packed the boulevards and the housetops to cheer the man of peace. A Frenchwoman penned a summation of the ecstasy:

"Wilson, you have given back the father to his home, the ploughman to his field. . . . You have saved our fiancés; love blooms again. Through you evil is punished. Wilson! Wilson! Glory to you, who, like Jesus, have said: Peace on Earth and Good Will to Men!"

"I knew Paris in the glitter of the Second Empire," said Clemenceau. "I thought I knew my Paris now, but I did not believe she could show such enthusiasm as this. I don't believe there has ever been anything like it in the history of the world."

President Wilson chose this moment of towering strength to announce that creation of a League of Nations was the first and greatest task before the Peace Conference. He declared the League of Nations would be the basis of the treaty and of the peace.

December 15, 1918. "We Shall Win . . ."

Senator Lodge was corresponding with his lieutenants, seeking and offering advice on the plan of attack.

"If you have any suggestion or advice to give me as to the treatment of the situation in making peace, I should be glad to have the benefit of it," he wrote to Colonel Harvey. "I must speak before long and I am naturally anxious to take a sound line on which we can all stand."

A letter written to Beveridge, who thought the group should fight the idea of world organization openly, was remarkable. Lodge declared they should avoid a flat denial of the idea, but should oppose *any method* proposed for actually establishing a League of Nations. He wrote:

"I think it would be a mistake to admit that the League would be a good thing, but I think we should make a mistake if we met the proposition with a flat denial. The purpose of the League—that is, the preservation of world peace—we are all anxious to see, but what we oppose is the method. Now the strength of our position is to show up the impossibility of any of the methods proposed and invite them, when they desire our support, to produce their terms. They cannot do it. My own judgment is that the whole thing will break up in conference. There may be some vague declarations of the beauties of peace, but any practical League that involves control of our legislation, of our armies and navies, or the Monroe Doctrine, or an international police, and that sort of thing, then our issue is made up, and we shall win. We can begin by pointing out these dangers, and that I am sure will be done."

The letter said nothing about any alternate way of preserving world peace.

December 17, 1918. A Council of War

When Theodore Roosevelt read the newspaper accounts of Wilson's wild reception in Paris, he summoned Lodge by telegram.

Lodge hastened to his bedside in Roosevelt Hospital in New York, and as the world planned peace, the two old men held a Council of War.

It was a grim meeting, for TR was terribly ill. He was suffering intense pain; he was blind in one eye, and deaf in one ear. The gay, bully spirit of old was gone. An unsmiling Lodge did not brighten the foreboding atmosphere of the sickroom.

TR and Lodge knew that the bulk of the Senate and the bulk of the American people supported Wilson's plans for a League of Nations. They agreed that the League could not be defeated by an open assault. So they determined to destroy it slowly, bit by bit, piece by piece. They agreed that no matter what precise form the League of Nations took, they would seek to strike out its most vital provisions; and when they failed to strike them out they would cripple them with alterations, until finally even those who originally supported the League of Nations would vote against it.

They would introduce amendment after amendment, and reservation after reservation. Even amendments and reservations that eventually failed to carry would serve a purpose, for they would provoke endless discussion and debate. Eventually, the Senate and the people would become divided and disgusted, and full of doubts and fears.

Then the League of Nations would be defeated.

"There, sitting on the bedside, Senator Lodge and my brother went over every one of the reservations during a session of three hours, changing and deciding upon this one and that and finally every one of them was OK'd by Theodore Roosevelt," said his sister, Corinne Roosevelt Robinson, who was there.

The treaty did not yet exist. The Covenant of the League of Nations had not been written. No official draft of either yet existed. Lodge and TR, however, did their best to foresee the shape the League of Nations would take, and they laid their plans accordingly. They tried to put their fingers on the essential provisions of the treaty, and they determined all possible counter moves, negations, objections, limitations.

It was plain from Wilson's many addresses and messages that the keystone of the League would be an agreement to protect the territorial and political freedom of all members against aggression—and so Lodge and TR agreed to oppose this provision uncompromisingly. It was not easy, of course, to guess at all the provisions that would turn up.

"I do not mean that definite clauses in the League were definitely discussed," explained TR's sister afterward, "but many contingencies of the document, contingencies which later took the form of definite clauses, *were* discussed, and the future attitude toward such contingencies more or less mapped out."

After about three hours, Teddy Roosevelt was exhausted, and Lodge took his leave, promising to return the next day.

December 18, 1918. They Meet Again

The two old men met once more in the sick room, and they polished and refined their plan of battle.

When they parted, Lodge was ready to launch the fight to keep the United States out of the League of Nations.

December 19, 1918. Lodge and the *Chicago Tribune*

Lodge returned to Washington and opened the campaign in the Senate with a short announcement of attacks and discussions to come.

And the *Chicago Tribune* opened the campaign in the press with an editorial applauding the attacks and discussions. The newspaper took care to proclaim the powers and prerogatives of the Senate in regard to treaties, warning:

"The Senate not only has the authority to reject a treaty but it does exercise that authority."

December 20, 1918. The *Chicago Tribune* Again

The *Chicago Tribune* hinted editorially that the still unwritten league would "underwrite all the troubles of the world." The paper again urged that the Senate "indulge" in much discussion.

December 21, 1918. Lodge Outlines the Strategy

Henry Cabot Lodge, in the opening full-dress Senate speech of the campaign planned at TR's bedside, delivered a long lecture to his fellow-Senators on their rights to revise and reject treaties.

He produced for publication in the Congressional Record a painstakingly documented treatise he had written, entitled *The Treaty-Making Powers of the Senate*. It listed all the precedents, all the powers, all the prerogatives Senators might call into play. It was the blueprint, the guide, for the Senate fight against world organization.

"No treaty can become binding upon the United States . . . without the consent of the Senate," said Lodge. "The Constitution also gives the Senate the right to advise as well as to consent, and it is the clear right of the Senate to offer its advice, whether invited or unasked at any stage of the negotiations."

The Gentleman from Massachusetts cited nine cases in United States history when the Senate had been asked for advice or had volunteered advice on foreign policy to Presidents Madison, Jackson, Van Buren, Polk, Buchanan, Lincoln, Grant, and Cleveland. For the benefit of certain Senators who felt they should not discuss the League of Nations until it was submitted to the Senate, he reiterated:

"Let timid souls thus take courage and be cheerful. There is nothing either in law or good manners which stands in the way of advice from the Senate to the Executive."

Perhaps Lodge had dreamed of serving on the Peace Commission despite his opposition to the terms proposed by Wilson and accepted by the Allies and by Germany, for he reminded the Senate that President McKinley had taken Senators to Paris to help negotiate peace with Spain, and he commented, "The fact that these Senators signed the treaty certainly helped its ratification which was strongly contested, and it seemed to me at the time that this was a fortunate circumstance."

It had been clear to Lodge and TR when they talked the whole thing over that they could not afford to put themselves in open opposition to the high purposes for which America had fought the war, and that they could not openly seek to separate us from our Allies. So Lodge praised the close co-operation that had led to the defeat of Germany on the battlefield and declared:

". . . these relations must be continued if we are not to lose at the peace table what we won in the field. To attempt in any way to separate us from our allies now or to prevent unity of action is as harmful as . . . when we were fighting on the plains of Flanders. . . .

". . . we went to war to save civilization. We are as much bound, not merely by interest and every consideration for a safe future, but by honor and self-respect, to see that the terms of peace are carried out. . . . We must do our share to carry out the peace as we have done . . . to win the war, of which the peace is an integral part. . . ."

After making that declaration of principle, Lodge coolly proceeded to deny it in practice. He set out to demolish the Fourteen Points—the terms of peace that had brought the war to an end on November 11.

"The last proposition is the League of Nations," he said, a good deal later in the afternoon, and he put a sarcastic twist into the name. "The words . . . are captivating and attractive. We all are deeply in sympathy with the purposes the words . . . are supposed to imply. But we ought to be extremely careful that in our efforts to reach the millennium of universal and eternal peace we do not create a system which will breed dissensions and wars. It is difficult to discuss it at this time, because no definite plan of any kind has yet been put forward by any responsible person."

With the stage thus set, Lodge swung neatly into the strategy he and TR had devised for the period before the text of the League of Nations was written or known. He started posing hypothetical problems, asking alarming questions, raising great doubts.

"What nations are to be members? . . ." Lodge asked the Senate. "How are these nations to vote? . . . Are the small nations to have an equal vote with the great nations? . . . If this . . . were agreed to, the small nations could determine the action of the League. . . . If nations are to vote in the League on a democratic basis . . . their voting power must be determined by population. . . . This system would give China four times the vote of the United States. . . . If England is to have the right to cast the vote of her possessions, India alone would give her from three to four times as many votes as the United States. . . .

"Are we prepared to allow any association of nations by a majority vote to order the troops and the ships of the United States to go to war. . . . Let us be honest with ourselves. It is easy to talk about a League of Nations and the beauty . . . of peace, but the hard practical demand is, are you ready to put your soldiers and sailors at the disposition of other nations?

"This is the heart of the whole question, but there are others. . . . Are we ready to abandon the Monroe Doctrine and leave it to other nations to say how American questions shall be settled? . . . Are we ready to have other nations tell us by a majority vote what attitude we must assume in regard to immigration or in regard to our tariffs?"

After drawing the Senate's attention to many, many more "dangers and difficulties" involved in any world organization, Lodge suggested that the whole idea be abandoned for the moment. He declared that the important task was to wind up the war with Germany by signing a peace treaty—that was the concern of the world rather than the vague threat of some future war that might never really come. He said in conclusion:

"Is it not our first duty and our highest duty to bring peace to the world at this moment and not encumber it by trying to provide against wars which never may be fought and against difficulties which lie far ahead in a dim and unknown future?"

December 22, 1918.
Senator Jim Watson Accepts an Assignment

It was Sunday morning when Senator Jim Watson's telephone rang. Senator Lodge was calling. He wanted Watson to dine with him that evening at his home at 1765 Massachusetts Avenue. This is the story of their meeting, as Watson told it later.

At dinner Lodge said he wanted Watson to become his special representative in charge of keeping Republican Senators under control in the fight against the League of Nations. Watson was very pleased, and he accepted the assignment. Lodge warned him to keep the whole thing a secret, and to report only to him. Watson agreed.

The Senator from Indiana was new to the Senate, and he had never engaged in a treaty fight.

"Senator, I don't see how we are ever going to defeat this proposition," he said. "It appears to me that 80 per cent of the people are for it. Fully that percentage of the preachers are right now advocating it, churches are very largely favoring it, all the people who have been burdened and oppressed by this awful tragedy of war and who imagine this opens a way to world peace are for it, and I don't see how it is possible to defeat it."

Senator Lodge turned his sharp eyes on Watson. "Ah, my dear James, I do not propose to try to beat it by direct frontal attack, but by the indirect method of reservations."

"What do you mean by that?" puzzled Watson. "Illustrate it to me."

Lodge explained that a "reservation" is a purely American interpretation of a provision of a treaty. While an "amendment" alters a provision of a treaty, a "reservation" simply reserves the right of the United States to observe the provision according to our own interpretation of its meaning. It limits the application of the provision to us. To show Watson what he meant, Lodge told him that there would undoubtedly be a provision concerning mandates in the section of the treaty establishing the League of Nations. He said they would demand a reservation to qualify and limit the provision as far as the United States was concerned. "We can debate that for days," explained Lodge.

He went on to point out other reservations they would demand on other provisions likely to appear in the treaty. He stressed the debate each demand for a reservation would produce, and the doubts and fears and antagonisms they would cause.

After Lodge had talked for two hours, Watson fully agreed that the treaty could be beaten by this method.

Watson saw that in this way the American people, now in favor of world organization, could be prevented from obtaining it.

December 23, 1918.
"Germany Lies Prostrate, Helpless . . ."

A powerful address entitled "No League of Nations to Enforce War" was delivered by Colonel Harvey in New York, and published in his *War Weekly*.

Colonel Harvey went after the idea of world organization with a vengeance. There were no shades, no subtleties in his onslaught. Together, Harvey's attacks and Lodge's attacks would have a devastating effect. Lodge managed to appeal to the people who wanted a *good* League. Harvey's appeal was to those who feared all intercourse with foreign nations.

This night Colonel Harvey bespoke pure and simple isolation. There was no need for a League of Nations, he said. The Armistice was less than six weeks old, but he seemed to have forgotten the entire bloody affair of the war. "Must we, abruptly disregarding the beneficence of the past, fare forth into foreign lands looking for trouble?" he asked.

There was no danger of another war. "The menace no longer exists," he explained. "Germany lies prostrate, helpless—a skulking, whining suppliant at the bar of righteous judgment."

This being so, affairs in the rest of the world were no affairs of ours. We should leave the problem of Germany to others. "What her penalty shall be is no concern of ours," he declared. "It must and should be fixed by those whom she has most grievously wronged. . . . Does anyone imagine that France and England and Belgium and Serbia are incapable of affixing the guilt and exacting the penalty?"

The last words were, "My Country and nothing but my Country!"

December 30, 1918. "The Combination of All of Us"

President Wilson, visiting England before the opening of the Peace Conference, warned against expecting the League of Nations and the peace to be perfect.

Imperfections were bound to be in both, he said in Manchester, for no man, no body of men, could settle everything perfectly.

"Yet," he declared, "if we are to make unsatisfactory settlements, we must see to it that they are rendered more and more satisfactory by the subsequent adjustments which are made possible."

And world organization would make it possible to correct imperfections and injustices by peaceful methods, rather than by war, he said.

The President warned that the United States, now as always, had no desire to become entangled in European power politics. "If the future had nothing for us but a new attempt to keep the world at a right poise by a balance of power," he declared, "the United States would take no interest, because she will join no combination of power which is not the combination of all of us."

1919

January 6, 1919. Death of TR

Theodore Roosevelt died suddenly at 4:00 a.m. of a blood clot in the coronary artery.

President Wilson cabled to Washington ordering that all flags over the White House and other government buildings be flown at half-mast for thirty days.

January 7, 1919. "Must History Repeat Itself?"

Senator Porter McCumber, Republican, said he thought it was time to spike the bad and senseless things he had been hearing in the Senate about the League. The earnest North Dakotan was a man destined to cause Lodge and Watson a lot of trouble.

"Must history repeat itself over and over again?" he demanded. "Must our children's children suffer and die as their fathers have suffered and died to propitiate the God of War?"

One by one, Senator McCumber took up the stock criticisms and disposed of them.

To the charge that American participation in a world organization violated George Washington's "entangling alliances" warning, he replied:

". . . if you justify our alliance with France, Great Britain, and Italy in this war to protect the safety and civilization of the world, then how in Heaven's name can you condemn an alliance to prevent another assault on civilization? How can you in one breath approve the alliance to make war to save the world and in the next breath condemn an alliance to save the world by the prevention of any savage or brutal war which might threaten it?"

To the demand for postponement of the plan for a league, he answered:

"Mr. President, no matter how much we may legislate, how many resolutions we may introduce and pass, three things are certain: The first, already accomplished, is that acting within his constitutional authority the President has appointed delegates to sit with delegates from the other Allied nations to agree upon the terms of peace; second, that these delegates will dictate and agree upon such terms of peace; and third, that they will not rise from their deliberations or attach their signatures to any instrument of peace that shall leave untouched or unsettled the question of the prevention of another such war. If they should do so their action would meet the condemnation of the people of all the countries who have endured the horrors and privations of this war. It will not do in one breath to say that war is wrong and in the next breath that such wrong cannot be checked."

Lodge had charged that the League of Nations would interfere in our domestic affairs. McCumber commented:

"I do not believe there is any possible danger of any intelligent commission ever inserting such an obligation in a treaty of peace. If they should so forget national sentiment, neither France, Great Britain, nor the United States would ever ratify. . . . There is nothing in any League proposal I have heard of which authorizes such an interference with domestic or internal affairs."

Lodge had also charged that the League would threaten the Monroe Doctrine. Said McCumber:

"So far from endangering that doctrine, we would strengthen it . . . The League of Nations which adopts as its guiding principle the independence of every nation of the world . . . certainly cannot be said to endanger our Monroe Doctrine, which guarantees the independence of the nations of the Western world only."

January 12, 1919. The Peace Conference Opens

The Peace Conference opened, and on the very first day, the very first of the Fourteen Points created a crisis. Point 1 read:

"Open covenants of peace, openly arrived at, after which there shall be no private international understandings of any kind but diplomacy shall proceed always frankly and in the public view."

The press had expected to sit in on all the meetings of the Peace Conference, and the world had expected to know all the details. Instead, the doors of the conference room closed in the faces of the reporters—many of them famous men and women who had come to Paris from far places to cover the peace. They muttered and fumed among themselves all morning and all afternoon, and they were white with anger by the end of the day, when a secretary emerged from the conference room to read them a press release consisting of five lines. It revealed that the delegates had met, had considered the conditions necessary to carry out the Armistice, and had then considered procedure.

The indignant correspondents wired bitter accounts to newspapers all over the world.

January 17, 1919. Borah and Johnson for the Defense!

Lodge & Co. had looked forward to obtaining new sources for attack every day in the morning papers when the Peace Conference went to work on the provisions of the peace, but the lack of any news at all about the provisions would serve as well. It would enable them to accuse Wilson of sinister purposes, of meeting furtively behind locked doors to plot dreadful things he was afraid to do in public.

The fact that it would be necessary to defend the first of the Fourteen Points in order to attack the rest of them did not embarrass them. One of their tactics throughout the fight would be to protest in horror whenever it seemed that the Fourteen Points were —or were not—being observed.

Senator Borah seemed badly disillusioned over the secrecy in Paris. It was a betrayal of the Fourteen Points! He read Point 1 to the Senate, and averred in resounding tones:

"And the question now is whether that proposition is to be utterly discarded and disregarded in the proceedings at Versailles!"

Hiram Johnson obtained the floor to complain, "It is humiliating to me to have the President of the United States bottled up in any kind of conference."

Telling the Senate that acceptance of the Fourteen Points was world-wide, he said disapprovingly:

"Yet at the very instant when the Peace Conference assembles . . . the first of these . . . is deliberately violated, and instead of open covenants of peace, openly arrived at, we are given . . . the same old deceptive secret diplomacy and our only news is a communiqué which we know from experience of the past four years is made merely to cover up what has been done. . . .

"So the matter becomes of importance . . . to the whole Nation which has accepted these fourteen covenants concerning peace."

Actually, President Wilson had carefully explained to the Senate that Point 1 did not mean there would be no private meetings. In a memorandum to the Senate on June 12, 1918, he had said:

"When I pronounced for open diplomacy, I meant not that there should be no private discussions of delicate matters, but that no secret agreements should be entered into and that all international relations, when fixed, should be open, above-board, and explicit."

Wilson often compared the conferences to the meetings of the Board of Directors of a corporation or of the Executive Committee of a Trade Union, with private discussions but public decisions. He knew that if the conferees were to be open to argument, and were to be able to change their minds, they must not become publicly committed to a position on every issue that came up. He knew that Washington and Madison and Hamilton had felt the same way at the Constitutional Convention, the most successful meeting of its kind in history. It had been held behind locked doors, a special guard had been assigned to garrulous old Ben Franklin for many days to keep him from blurting out details of the deliberations, and the full account of the debates had been suppressed for fifty years.

Yet the innuendoes about "secret" and "sinister" plottings in Paris, spoken in the Senate and spread far and wide in the *Chicago Tribune* and the Hearst papers, began to put fears and misgivings in many, many minds.

January 25, 1919. A Victory for World Organization

Clemenceau had opened the Peace Conference with a demand that the spoils of war be divided up before anything else was done. He proposed that the League of Nations be taken up last, after everything else was settled.

This sounded suspiciously like the Senators who demanded postponement of the creation of the League, when they really wanted no League at all, and Wilson stated firmly that the League of Nations would be taken up first. He was supported by the representatives of many other nations, for there was a general conviction that otherwise it would never be founded. Wilson knew that the moment peace was made, and the various nations had gotten the territories and reparations they sought, many of them would forget about the League of Nations. And he felt that the peace would be fleeting unless it was based on a world organization.

He finally won his way, and on January 22 the Council of Ten, composed of the leading nations attending the conference, agreed to make the League of Nations the basis of the peace. Now this resolution was approved by the entire Peace Conference:

> The Conference, having considered the proposals for the creation of a League of Nations, resolves that
>
> 1. It is essential to the maintenance of the world settlement, which the Associated Nations are now met to establish, that a League of Nations be created to promote international co-operation, to insure the fulfillment of accepted international obligations and to provide safeguards against war.
>
> 2. This League should be created as an integral part of the general Treaty of Peace, and should be open to every civilized nation which can be relied on to promote its objects.

3. The members of the League should periodically meet in international conference, and should have a permanent organization and secretariat to carry on the business of the League in the intervals between the conferences.

The Conference therefore appoints a Committee representative of the Associated Governments to work out the details of the constitution and functions of the League.

Wilson was appointed chairman of the committee established to draft provisions for the world organization, and he made a short speech about its purposes. Again he stressed that it would provide a peaceful way to do things that had hitherto been done by war.

"Settlements may be temporary, but the actions of the nations in the interests of peace and justice must be permanent," he said. "We can set up permanent processes. We may not be able to set up permanent decisions."

February 8, 1919. A Frankenstein and a Farce

The League of Nations Commission—composed of nineteen men representing fourteen nations—was working as hard as any group of men ever worked, meeting every night beyond midnight after days filled by other problems of the peace.

All the members felt a high sense of participation in a great event. They met without formality, wasted no time on broad orations and narrow details, but set themselves to the tremendous task of drawing a new charter for mankind. "Wilson, in his zeal, worked incessantly," said Lloyd George.

Wilson's greatest role was in persuading the Peace Conference to accept the League of Nations as the basis of the peace. Not a single leading idea that went into the Covenant of the League of Nations originated with him. He became more the editor of the document, piecing into it ideas proposed by others.

The League of Nations was really an expansion of old and new principles, a gathering together of the soundest thoughts on lasting peace since humans first dreamed of banding together to prevent war.

Debate in the Commission mostly concerned the power of the League of Nations. France, still fearful of the nation that had attacked her three times in the memory of living men, wanted it to be a military superstate with absolute military and economic power to suppress Germany or any other nation guilty of disturbing the peace. Clemenceau wanted to have a strong international army commanded by a League General Staff. Wilson knew that the United States Senate would never approve such a strong League. He was trapped between the fears of France and the fears of the Senate. The task before him was to find a workable compromise.

The press, of course, had found ways of learning most of the intimate details of the Peace Conference, and the papers in the United States hinted at the debate going on inside the League of Nations Commission. Colonel Harvey's keen mind sensed the cause of the conflict, and he wrote in his magazine:

"The League of Nations . . . must be either a strenuous body so transcending nationality as to be impossible of American approval, or a futile thing of pious aspirations and impotent achievement."

It was soon reported in Washington that Senate critics of the League of Nations were confronting its supporters with Colonel Harvey's dilemma.

If the League of Nations depended on the compulsory use of armed force against aggressors, they were against it because it was too big and strong.

If the League of Nations depended only on the use of "moral force" against aggressors, they were against it because it was too small and weak.

They predicted that no workable compromise could possibly be found between a Frankenstein and a farce.

February 14, 1919. "A Living Thing Is Born"

"A living thing is born," said Woodrow Wilson as he presented the Covenant of the League of Nations in a public session of the Peace Conference.

"The miasma of distrust, of intrigue, is cleared away. Men are looking eye to eye and saying, 'We are brothers and have a common purpose.' "

The President of the United States slowly read the terms of the Covenant, pausing now and then to look up and explain a provision or amplify some thought. His hearers sensed that here was a new declaration of independence and of international interdependence. The affairs of the world were lifted into a bold, new dimension.

The effort at compromise between the fears and desires of France and the other nations who lived in perpetual dread of their neighbors, and the fears and desires expressed by the leaders of the United States Senate, came in Article 10:

> The Members of the League undertake to respect and preserve as against external aggression the territorial integrity and existing political independence of all Members of the League. In case of any such aggression or in case of any threat or danger of such aggression, the Council shall advise upon the means by which this obligation shall be fulfilled.

Wilson paused to explain, "Armed force is in the background in this programme, but it *is* in the background, and if the moral force of the world will not suffice, the physical force of the world shall. But that is the last resort, because this is intended as a constitution of peace, not as a league of war."

The framers of the League of Nations thought of it as much more than a policeman, and Wilson declared, "It is not in contemplation that this should be merely a League to secure the peace of the world. It is a League that can be used for co-operation in any international matter."

Stars and Stripes, a newspaper edited by enlisted men of the United States Army, published an account of the presentation of the Covenant:

"Standing among the dignitaries of the Foreign Offices, the Sovereigns of States, the members of Cabinets, the diplomatists and the writers who heard President Wilson read the draft of the League . . . were some men in khaki whose 'rank and title' in the registration books reads simply, 'private, USA'—some of the men whose presence in France during the months just passed made possible the League of Nations.

"They saw the printed copies in the hands of the delegates. They knew then that the thing that their comrades had fought and died for through a winter and around the seasons until one November morning was real—it was there on paper for all the world to read. . . .

"It is not yet accepted. It was not even submitted without reservation on the part of some members of the commission that helped draw it up. But it is there, surely a living thing as the President himself called it, with as fair a chance for success among the United States of Civilization as had the constitution of the United States of America when it came before the sceptic and fearful counselors, the doubters, and cynics in the Legislatures of the original States who very likely sneered at the 'idealistic document' as far too impractical to be worthy of their support.

"The privates who heard a draft of the Covenant of the League of Nations believe that their comrades did not die in vain."

February 15, 1919. "In Silence and Amazement"

All over the United States the Covenant was hailed.

"No birth of history, save one, is of greater importance to mankind," said a typical editorial in the *St. Louis Globe Democrat.*

Ex-President Taft praised the solution to the problem of power versus impotency. He said the League of Nations was not a superstate, but a world partnership. He thought all Senators should support it.

"It is not the monster that those who have attacked the plans predicted it would be," declared Senator Gilbert Hitchcock of Nebraska, Democratic leader in the Senate. "Neither is it the helpless sewing circle that one sneering critic predicted it would be."

The critics were shocked. The *New York Sun* reported: "Senators Lodge and Knox read the document in silence and amazement."

They were afraid their colleagues might be stampeded into voicing approval of the Covenant before the best points of attack could be singled out, and they rushed into consultation with Senator Boies Penrose of Pennsylvania and Senator Reed Smoot of Utah. Later a *New York Times* correspondent tried to get Senate comment on the Covenant, but he had to report:

"The attitude of the Senate was almost painfully noncommittal, one of almost complete silence. Senators Lodge, Knox and Borah refused point blank to comment on the League Covenant. Although Republican leaders would not admit it, there was unmistakable evidence of concerted action on their part in opposition to expressions of opinion pending careful study of the project."

Senator Selden Spencer of Missouri was the only Republican willing to talk, and the interview with him was not exactly satisfactory.

"I have not had time to read the constitution carefully," said he, "but what I have read recalls to mind a little story of a preacher who used to live in Missouri. One time we asked him to speak before the YMCA. He laughed a little and said, 'Boys, I cannot make a speech, but in the days when sound was needed more than sense, I was a daisy.' "

February 19, 1919. "Better Get Busy on This!"

The new nations, born out of the ruins of the old empires, were weak and trembling, and the need for a new world based on international co-operation was desperately clear in a Europe seething with revolution and famine and distress.

And while doctors sought to stop the flow of blood pouring from a wound inflicted on Clemenceau by a Paris assassin, the attack on the Covenant of the League of Nations got under way in the United States Senate.

Senator Miles Poindexter of Washington fired the opening shot.

"The question now presented," he soliloquized in the Senate chamber, "is whether or not this high sovereign jurisdiction of the political heirs of Jefferson, Washington and Lincoln is to be in part surrendered and subjected to the control of strangers and aliens."

The tall, good-looking Senator declared the Covenant was a threat to our Constitution, and an imitation of the new Soviet set-up in Russia.

Taft, who was on the West Coast on a speaking tour arranged by the League to Enforce Peace, called a press conference when he heard of Poindexter's attack. He told the reporters acidly:

"These gentlemen who are sitting up with the Constitution using it to defeat the League of Nations are men whom I would not trust overnight."

Ex-Senator Beveridge, more certain than ever that there was only one way to fight the League of Nations, wrote to Colonel Harvey:

"I regard it of *infinite* importance that Lodge and Knox do not make fatal tactical error admitting the Wilson-Taft scheme 'in principle,' and merely criticize this, that and the other details. If they do so, we shall be at a serious disadvantage. If they concede 'the main idea' and just pick flaws, the average busy citizen will say that we are nothing but fault-finders, and that the great plan of this noble world reformer must go through. But if they boldly and clearly assail the *whole thing,* just as we did free silver and anti-imperialism, if they defend the American nation and stand up for our one traditional American policy and strike mercilessly at this and all other schemes to overthrow it, then the average busy American citizen can grasp the issue.

"So I suggest that you see to it that they are given encouragement since, undoubtedly, pressure the other way is being exerted upon them, incessantly. If that pressure weakens them, the result will not be good. Better get busy on this!"

February 21, 1919.
Scapegoat No. 1—A British League of Nations

"This constitution of the League of Nations is the greatest triumph for English diplomacy in three centuries of English diplomatic life," asserted Senator Borah in a long, carefully planned address designed to convince all Americans who disliked England that England would run the League of Nations.

"Yes," he shouted, "when they finally settle down to business, England will have one vote, Canada will have one vote, Australia one vote, and South Africa one vote, whilst the American nation . . . with all her wealth and resources will have one vote. . . ."

The big burly Senator glared across the aisle and shook a thick finger at the Democrats. "I ask you who are in favor of this League, are you willing to give any nation five votes to our one?"

He then went on to prove, according to his logic, that due to her treaties with Italy and Japan and other nations, England would really control many more than five votes. In fact, he said, England would control the entire League of Nations.

He declared that the real purpose of the whole scheme was to guarantee every foot of British soil for all time.

Borah came to a stirring, emotional climax by quoting the late Theodore Roosevelt:

"Any man who says he is an American but something else also isn't an American at all. We have room for but one flag, the American flag!"

Borah sat down at his desk, perspiring and out of breath, and several of his friends came over to shake his big hand and slap his broad back.

"Bill, I'd like to get in the fight against this League of Nations," said Senator Warren G. Harding of Ohio, "but the people of my state are all for it I'm afraid."

The address by Borah was the first of several scapegoat attacks planned as an important part of the campaign against the League of Nations.

The accusation that England would run the League of Nations was intended most of all, of course, to turn Irish-Americans against the League of Nations.

Later, the Senate would ring with the accusation that the Pope would run the League of Nations—in order to turn all anti-Catholics against the League of Nations.

And there would be equally contradictory claims designed to appeal to other prejudices.

February 22, 1919. Scapegoat No. 2—Monarchism; No. 3—Bolshevism

Senator Reed, Democrat of Missouri, carried the appeal to Anglophobes into a second day.

He was sure the British would run the League of Nations, and so they would run us, too. He told the Senate that the terms of the Covenant would prevent us from going to the aid of an Irish rebellion, and would force us to fight anybody who did.

When Senator Reed tired of attacking England, he blandly took a new tack. He said the League of Nations would deliver the United States into the hands of "European monarchs" and "Asiatic despots"—and royalty would rule the world:

"At present, the known signatories are the British Empire, an empire; Italy, a monarchy; Japan, a monarchy or despotism; France, a republic; the United States, a republic. Thus the League will be composed of three monarchies and two republics.

"Who will control it? . . ."

After a time, the master of malice veered off in a new vein. For the benefit of Americans who shuddered at the mere mention of Lenin and Trotsky, Senator Reed asserted that he saw "the menace of world Bolshevism" in the background of the League of Nations.

Although Russia was excluded from the League of Nations, and American and Allied troops were presently fighting the Soviets in Siberia, Reed declared:

"Indeed, that monster is the most earnest advocate of internationalism. Its fangs are plainly visible in the constitution of the League."

And so on.

The morning papers picked up by Taft out West told of Senator Borah's charge that England would run the League of Nations. The afternoon papers told of Senator Reed's charge that England, and also royalty, and also Bolshevism, would run it. The former President of the United States then called another press conference.

"It would be a great tragedy to the history of civilization," he said, "if the Senate can be induced by the protests and narrow views of a small number of Senators who have expressed themselves to defeat this grand covenant of peace. . . ."

Declaring that the people of the United States favored world organization, he described the enthusiasm demonstrated at nine regional conferences held by the League to Enforce Peace.

Some hours later, Taft let off some steam in a personal letter to a friend: "As I write I look out upon the desert of Nevada, and it suggests the waste that war makes. And when I think of the vicious narrowness of Reed, the explosive ignorance of Poindexter, the ponderous Websterian language and lack of stamina of Borah, the vanity of Lodge as an old diplomatic hand on the Foreign Relations Committee, the selfishness, laziness and narrow lawyerlike acuteness of Knox, the emptiness and sly partisanship of Hale, with the utter nothingness of Fall, in the face of this great world's crisis, I confess I don't see where we have any advantage over the women—at least in this juncture.

"I beg of you to believe I am not drunk or wild, but am only roused to the critical situation in world affairs that those who gather around the council board in Paris know, and that these barking critics do not seem to realize.

"It is their American selfishness, their American littleness, blinding them to the real interests of the world, that arouses me."

February 24, 1919. "I Have Fighting Blood in Me . . ."

Woodrow Wilson left Paris immediately after the presentation of the Covenant, for he had to be in Washington long enough to sign any last minute legislation passed by Congress before it adjourned on March 4. As he sailed from Brest he remarked to a friend that he felt like the optimist who fell out of a twelfth story window, and who shouted as he passed the fifth floor:

"I'm all right so far!"

He wired to members of the Senate and House Foreign Relations Committee inviting them to dine with him at the White House, and requesting them to refrain from debating the Covenant until he had a chance to go over it with them.

Wilson determined to land in Boston and to speak there before he proceeded to Washington—with the deliberate purpose of trying to build a fire under Henry Cabot Lodge.

Lodge was infuriated, but he turned the episode to his own advantage by making Wilson's speech in Boston seem to be a gross breach of faith. He scrupulously observed the President's plea for silence, sitting at his desk in stony silence, a hurt look on his face, while Poindexter, Borah, and Reed—who paid no attention to the President's request—carried on the fight. Off the floor of the Senate, Lodge made no secret of his opinion of Wilson's behavior.

"I dare say this is all right under the modern fashion," he snapped, "but to me it is contrary to the principles of conduct on which I happen to be brought up."

When Wilson came ashore in Boston accompanied by his young Assistant Secretary of the Navy, Franklin D. Roosevelt, and followed by Edith Wilson and Eleanor Roosevelt, he was pounced upon by a great many anxious advisers, all of whom began to talk at once in loud voices. It seemed that some of them wanted him to defy the opponents of the League of Nations with a fighting speech. Others, led by Tumulty, Wilson's personal secretary, wanted him to avoid all mention of the League until he met with members of Congress.

Two hundred thousand wildly cheering people were swarming in the streets around Mechanics Hall when Wilson arrived to make his speech. The hall was draped with gay flags and bunting, and over the stage was a huge portrait of George Washington, flanked by portraits of Woodrow Wilson and Theodore Roosevelt. On one wall there was a giant blue flag with a white star—Boston's conception of the flag of the League of Nations. Many people in the audience wore the same emblem in their lapels.

Wilson was introduced by Governor Calvin Coolidge, a warm advocate of the League of Nations.

The advisers who wanted Wilson to use a big stick took up a position to his right under the portrait of TR, and their faces were gloomy as Wilson spoke in general terms of the Paris Conference.

"And in the midst of it all," recounted Wilson, "every interest seeks out first of all when it reaches Paris the representatives of the United States. Why? Because—and I think I am stating the most wonderful fact in history—because there is no nation in Europe that suspects the motives of the United States. Was there ever so wonderful a thing seen before? Was there ever so moving a thing?"

About midway in his address, Wilson began to change his tone, and soon the men standing under the portrait of TR began to beam. The other advisers, grouped on the other side of the stage, began to frown and whisper among themselves, as Wilson exclaimed:

"Any man who resists the present tides that run in the world will find himself thrown upon a shore so high and barren that it will seem as if he had been separated from his human kind forever!"

The President said that some might suggest that America should desert the rest of the world, and nurse her power for her own selfish ends. "I should welcome no sweeter challenge than that," he cried. "I have fighting blood in me, and it is sometimes a delight to let it have scope!"

Great applause interrupted him, for the first time.

He spoke of the utter blackness that would fall on the world, eventually enveloping America, too, if America lowered its lights. He asked if we should one day say, "Here is power to vindicate right," and the next day say, "Let right take care of itself and we will take care of ourselves."

There were cries: "No!" "No!" "No!"

"I have come back to say to you that I have tried in all soberness and honesty to speak your thought!"

The applause leapt to thunder. After revealing his knowledge of the opposition he faced, Wilson changed his tone again, and as if he had been making a mountain out of a molehill, he said, "But I talk as if there were any question."

He paused momentarily, threw out the palms of his hands almost disdainfully, with a smile that bordered on derision. Then he added, with all the earnestness he could command:

"I have no doubt of the verdict of America. . . ."

February 27, 1919. "Wandering with Alice in Wonderland"

"I feel as if I had been wandering with Alice in Wonderland and had tea with the Mad Hatter."

That, said Senator Brandegee, was his impression of the White House meeting with the President of the United States. The Gentleman from Connecticut only offered this judgment after deep consideration. Together with the other critics of the League of Nations, he had flatly refused to say a word to the waiting reporters when the White House meeting broke up after midnight.

Not until late in the morning, after a long conference, were Wilson's opponents ready to talk.

"The President seemed actually befuddled about many most important points," said Lodge.

Senator Knox opined that it was now obvious that the League of Nations was a "betrayal of the people."

Senator Borah had nothing to say—for he had bluntly refused to go to the White House, announcing that nothing the President might say could change his mind about anything.

The colorful statements made by Lodge & Co. dominated the press, of course, overshadowing the pleasantries of such pro-Leaguers as Senator Hitchcock, who had told reporters right after the White House meeting that it had been very constructive, characterized by frankness and good will on all sides.

"Senator Brandegee, an extremely able cross-examiner, took charge of the inquisition," reported the *New York Sun* in a startling account. The newspaper declared that Senators Lodge, Brandegee, Knox, McCumber, and Hitchcock all "agreed" that Wilson had admitted that the United States would lose all control over immigration of Japanese and Chinese, that Ireland would be left completely to the "mercies" of England, and many other amazing things. The *Sun* reported that lame duck Senator Lewis of Illinois was pacing Senate corridors muttering, "He made a great mistake; oh dear, I fear he has made a frightful error."

Senator Hitchcock rose in the Senate in the afternoon to deny that Wilson had said the things attributed to him in the *Sun*. Senator McCumber did likewise from the Republican side of the aisle. Lodge, Brandegee, and Knox, obviously the sources of the *Sun* story, remained silent.

The confusing and conflicting versions of the meeting were never cleared up. The country never knew exactly what had happened inside the White House, but the skilful statements made by Lodge, Brandegee, Knox, and the *New York Sun* gave the general impression that Wilson had been trapped into some bad admissions.

The most reliable testimony concerning the meeting was given by Representative John Jacob Rogers of Massachusetts, ranking Republican in the House Foreign Relations Committee—but it was not given to the public. Rogers, who was opposed to the League of Nations, said in a personal letter to Henry White:

"The White House dinner . . . was a most interesting one and in most respects a memorable one. I thought the President appeared extremely well. He submitted himself to quite rigorous cross-examination for two hours, answering every question, easy or difficult, as fully as possible and with apparent candor. He showed not the slightest vexation, even when Senator Brandegee was pressing him rather closely on certain of the difficulties which to his mind were of importance. I never saw Mr. Wilson appear so human or so attractive as that night. There was no suggestion of a feeling of militant arrogance about him. He apparently tried to give the impression that he was really one of the circle in the East Room, who was answering rather than asking questions only because he had been so recently in Paris, and had been a factor in the preparation of the instrument under discussion."

February 28, 1919. Senator Lodge's Suggestions

Almost every Senator was in his seat, intent and expectant, when Henry Cabot Lodge took the floor to deliver his first speech since the Covenant of the League of Nations had become available.

Only a select few ever knew—and understood—Lodge's purposes and plans. Most, even though they saw him every day, had to rely on hearsay and on their own interpretations of his words and deeds on the Senate floor, for their knowledge of his designs.

The Gentleman from Massachusetts had been working for two weeks on his address, selecting every word and phrase, planning every sentence and paragraph with infinite solicitude.

"We abandon entirely by the proposed constitution the policy laid down by Washington in his Farewell Address and the Monroe Doctrine," he told the Senate.

(Lodge used the word "constitution" for its implications of firmness and finality; Wilson had chosen the word "covenant" for its hallowed connotations.)

The Senator did not take a stand against the League of Nations, even if it did mean overthrowing the precepts of the Founding Fathers.

"Perhaps the time has come when the policies of Washington should be abandoned," he said, "but . . . we ought, at least, as these stately figures pass off the stage of guiding influence, to pay our homage to them and not relegate them to the shades of the past with jeers and laughter. . . ."

Almost as an afterthought, he added, "Standing always firmly by these great policies, we have striven and prospered and have done more to preserve the world's peace than any nation, league or alliance which ever existed."

Lodge moved across the years to Abraham Lincoln, and said, "For Lincoln's government of the people, for the people, and by the people we are asked to substitute in the United States on many vital points government of, for, and by other people."

Yet, the Gentleman from Massachusetts did not advise against accepting the Covenant. "What I ask, and all I ask, is consideration, time and thought."

Lodge proceeded to scrutinize the "constitution" article by article, and he refrained from attacking any of them directly. Some of them he praised. "An admirable proposition!" he exclaimed of one. Some seemed to him a bit vague. "I confess I do not understand what is meant by this." Often he humbly offered an interpretation. "I take it this means. . . ."

When he reached Article 10, he said it was very clear indeed. He said it meant that we would place our army and our navy at the beck and call of the League of Nations. "I am not now arguing whether we should give the guaranty or whether we should not give the guaranty," he hastened to explain, "but I beg my fellow-countrymen to consider well before they give this promise." Lodge planned to concentrate his attack on Article 10, and he did not weaken his position by mentioning the provision that Article 10 would not be invoked without the unanimous vote of all League of Nations members. That provision, of course, meant that the United States would actually use its army and navy only when it chose to do so.

Later, when Lodge came to Article 13—providing for arbitration or judicial settlement of disputes between members of the League of Nations—he demanded, "Are we ready to leave it to other nations to determine whether we shall admit to the United States a flood of Japanese, Chinese, and Hindu labor?" He chose this place to dispose of the provision calling for unanimity. "It is no reply," he declared, ". . . to say that if you follow it through all the windings of the provisions . . . you will find it reaches a point where the League could do nothing about immigration unless it was unanimous. . . ." He declared that "the possibility is there" that the League of Nations might vote unanimously, but he did not point out that the possibility was there only if the United States cast its vote with the other nations. He simply said, "We do not want a narrow alley of escape from the jurisdiction of the League." Then, as if even that "narrow alley" did not really exist, he concluded, "No nation should be compelled to admit anyone within its borders whom it does not choose to admit."

By the time Lodge had gone all the way through the "constitution," he had shown his fellow-Senators countless causes for doubt, skepticism, and fear. He declared it was obvious some amendments were needed, and he offered four suggestions:

Suggestion 1. ". . . let us put three lines into the draft for the League which will preserve the Monroe doctrine. . . ."

Suggestion 2. "Let us also have, if we enter the League, a complete exclusion from the League's jurisdiction of such questions as are involved in immigration. . . ."

Suggestion 3. "There should be some definite provision for peaceful withdrawal from the League if any nation desires to withdraw."

Suggestion 4. "Lastly, let us have a definite statement in the constitution of the League as to whether the League is to have an international force of its own or is to have the power to summon the armed forces of the different members of the League."

Senator Lodge declared that unless the Peace Conference delegates included these simple statements it would be "impossible to avoid the conclusion that they are seeking to do by indirection and the use of nebulous phrases what they are not willing to do directly. . . ."

March 1, 1919. "Do You Believe in Fairies?"

Senator Hardwick, Democrat of Georgia, warned the Senate that he had discovered a secret threat to the United States in the Covenant: Mexico might demand Texas back, and if we refused to give up the Lone Star State, the entire League of Nations would promptly go to war with us!

The Georgian asked the Senate thirty-two questions about the League of Nations, including this one:

"Do you believe in fairies?"

Senator Knox addressed the Senate, too. He declared that the provisions of the Covenant which intended to unite all nations against any aggressor would simply make every future war a World War.

"We are thus thrust fully into the terrible cauldron of European politics," he remonstrated, "and every outbreak in the Balkans—even domestic, if it threaten international war—will call for some expenditure of treasure, for some shedding of American blood, for some loss of American life."

To Knox's mind, the League of Nations was not only dangerous but unnecessary, for it was his considered judgment that war was now farther away than it had been for centuries. We had just finished rescuing civilization, he said. If, by any chance, there ever *was* another—"so surely as the sun rises, if the Hun flood again threatened"—we would stop it.

Attired in his customary striped pants and bow tie, the paunchy Senator expressed a deep fear that if we joined the League of Nations, American boys might even be sent "to the inhospitable South Pacific Isles!"

March 2, 1919. A Letter to a Senator

Early on this Sunday morning, Senator Frank Brandegee of Connecticut went to the Senate Office Building to put in a few extra hours of work.

Thumbing through his mail, he came across a letter from a man he had never heard of before—a man who played a vital role in the course of history, but whose name is unknown. The stranger warned Brandegee that if the opponents of the League of Nations did not soon do something more than orate against it, President Wilson would commit the United States so deeply we would be compelled to join.

Senator Brandegee, an acute, high-strung man who would one day commit suicide, leaped to his feet. He put the letter in his pocket, put on his hat, walked rapidly down Capitol Hill, and struck out along Massachusetts Avenue. Deep in thought, he passed the White House and went on to No. 1765, where he knocked on the door.

The door was opened by Senator Lodge, who later wrote this record of the events that followed:

"Senator Brandegee came to my house soon after breakfast and told me it seemed to him . . . some declaration should be made, securing for it if possible the signatures of more than one-third of the Senate, to the effect that a League of Nations as it was understood was to be proposed, and the outlines of which had been given through the press, could not be passed.

"I was very much struck by the proposition, and he had no difficulty in convincing me of its essential and even vital importance."

The Senators talked over the scheme for several hours. Senator Knox lived close by at 1527 K Street, and late in the morning they walked over to take him into their confidence. He at once gave them his blessings. They asked him to put his legal talents to work by writing a draft of the declaration. He agreed to try his hand.

Brandegee and Lodge left Knox alone, but they came back later in the day, and went over his draft with him.

While the three Senators were putting in this busy Sabbath day, a good many Americans who were idling about their homes had an opportunity to glance through the latest issue of the *Literary Digest*. The magazine had made a careful survey of press opinion on the League of Nations, and it reported: "The majority of our papers regard the experiment as tremendously worth trying."

Said the *Des Moines Register,* a Republican paper: "What the American delegation is proposing at Versailles is the greatest thing the world has ever had proposed since governments were born."

The *Topeka Capital,* likewise Republican, said of President Wilson: "Millions of people are burning candles to his name and success before the altars of the cathedrals of Europe."

March 3, 1919. The Round Robin

Most members of the Senate slept very late this morning, for they were going to be up all night.

Senator Lodge, however, was up and breakfasting at dawn. As

soon as he had finished his coffee, he went to see Senator Cummins of Iowa, an old and venerated man who possessed a nation-wide reputation as a liberal. Lodge wanted him to be among the original signers of the declaration, for if he put his name to it several other Senators would follow suit, and many liberal-minded citizens would wonder about the League of Nations for the first time.

Lodge, who made a science of his study of his fellow-Senators, knew something that was not yet generally recognized: the years were rapidly depriving old Cummins of his fire and faith.

The white-haired Iowan read the declaration, sat and thought a bit, and agreed to sign it provided two modifications were made.

Lodge summoned Brandegee and Knox, and they cheerfully accepted the amendments. All four men signed the declaration.

Lodge, Brandegee, and Knox spent the rest of the day hurrying from Senator to Senator seeking signatures. They approached no Democrats. A few Republicans, led by Senator McCumber, indignantly refused to sign. Others hesitated, but the declaration had been worded very cleverly, and time and again Lodge and Brandegee and Knox patiently explained to colleagues who favored the League of Nations that their signatures on the round robin would not commit them to vote against it. They declared that all the round robin did was put them on record as opposed to the League of Nations in the precise form Woodrow Wilson proposed.

To Lodge, every added signature was a body blow against the League of Nations itself, committing one more Senator to a strategy intended to defeat it. As far as Lodge was concerned, it was entirely beside the point that many of the Senators who signed really did want a perfected League of Nations.

Late in the afternoon, the round robin still lacked the necessary thirty-three signatures. Lodge and his friends started telephoning and telegraphing Senators who were away from Washington, and also Senators-elect who would be sworn in when the next Congress convened.

The Senate was kept in session all through the afternoon and on into the night. Finally, the signatures of 31 sitting Senators and 6 Senators-elect were obtained.

A few minutes before midnight, Lodge entered the Senate chamber with the round robin in his hand. He was not the calm Lodge known to the Senate. He was highly nervous, for the plan could still fail.

The whole purpose of the round robin was to tell the world that a third of the Senate—enough to kill the League of Nations—had announced opposition to it in its present form. This would weaken Wilson's power at home and abroad, and might well kill the League of Nations. The threat to the success of the scheme lay in the possibility that the Senate might vote on the round robin. If it came to a vote, it was certain to be defeated, for over half of the Senate strongly supported the League of Nations. Senate defeat of an anti-League resolution would only serve to strengthen Wilson and the League.

Lodge pinned his hopes on the fact that he was bringing up the resolution at an improper time. "Its consideration was clearly out of order in the condition of the existing business," he admitted after it was all over. He counted on some pro-League Senator objecting to consideration of the anti-League resolution. One objection would prevent a vote.

The chair recognized the Gentleman from Massachusetts.

"Mr. President," he said, "I desire to take only a moment of the time of the Senate. I wish to offer the resolution which I hold in my hand, a very brief one."

Henry Cabot Lodge's voice was steady, but the hand holding the round robin trembled, as he read:

> Whereas under the Constitution it is a function of the Senate to advise and consent to, or dissent from, the ratification of any treaty of the United States, and no such treaty can be operative without the consent of the Senate expressed by the affirmative vote of two-thirds of the Senators present; and
>
> Whereas owing to the victory of the arms of the United States and of the nations with whom it is associated, a peace conference was convened and is now in session at Paris for the purpose of settling the terms of peace; and
>
> Whereas a committee of the conference has proposed a constitution for a league of nations and the proposal is now before the peace conference for its consideration: Now, therefore, be it

> *Resolved by the Senate of the United States in the discharge of its constitutional duty of advice in regard to treaties,* That it is the sense of the Senate that while it is their sincere desire that the nations of the world should unite to promote peace and general disarmament, the constitution of the league of nations in the form now proposed to the peace conference should not be accepted by the United States; and be it *Resolved further,* That it is the sense of the Senate that the negotiations on the part of the United States should immediately be directed to the utmost expedition of the urgent business of negotiating peace terms with Germany satisfactory to the United States and the nations with whom the United States is associated in the war against the German Government, and that the proposal for a league of nations to insure the permanent peace of the world should be then taken up for careful consideration.

Lodge paused, glanced around the Senate and up at the chair, and requested the one thing in the world he wanted least:

"I ask unanimous consent for the present consideration of this resolution."

Senator Swanson of Virginia, a strong advocate of the League of Nations, leaped to his feet and cried:

"I object to the introduction of the resolution!"

Lodge didn't waste a moment. "Objection being made, of course I recognize the objection," he said.

And then he completed the act.

"I merely wish to add, by way of explanation, the following," he said, and he read the rest of the round robin:

> The undersigned Senators of the United States, Members and Members-elect of the Sixty-sixth Congress, hereby declare that, if they had had the opportunity, they would have voted for the foregoing resolution.

Henry Cabot Lodge	F. E. Warren
Philander C. Knox	James E. Watson
Lawrence Y. Sherman	Thomas Sterling
Harry S. New	J. S. Frelinghuysen
George H. Moses	W. G. Harding
J. W. Wadsworth, Jr.	Frederick Hale
Bert M. Fernald	William E. Borah
Albert B. Cummins	Walter E. Edge

Reed Smoot
Asle J. Gronna
Frank B. Brandegee
William M. Calder
Henry W. Keyes
Boies Penrose
George P. McClean
Carroll S. Page
Joseph Irwin France
Medill McCormick
Charles Curtis
Lawrence C. Phipps
Selden P. Spencer
Hiram W. Johnson
Charles E. Townsend
William P. Dillingham
I. L. Lenroot
Miles Poindexter
Howard Sutherland
Truman H. Newberry
L. Heisler Ball

When Lodge was finished, he looked about him. There was no response from the floor or the galleries. The full significance of his deed was not at once understood.

Lodge walked out of the Senate.

March 4, 1919. Filibuster!

After midnight, when Henry Cabot Lodge had departed, Senator Sherman launched a filibuster.

"Let us be the king's fool a while. . . ." he exclaimed. "We make holiday tonight!"

It was in a sense a filibuster against the United States Constitution, for under its provisions the Sixty-fifth Congress would adjourn at noon, and the Sixty-sixth Congress would not meet until December 9. This schedule interfered with the plans of the opponents of the League of Nations.

They wanted to stay in Washington to carry on the fight while Wilson was away in Paris. They determined to filibuster to death eight bills appropriating $3,627,000,761 for Government expenses.

If they prevented passage of the bills before Congress automatically adjourned at noon, Wilson would be compelled to call a special session of Congress to pass them—if he wanted the United States Government to stay in business beyond July 1, when current funds would be exhausted. Once he called Congress into session, they would keep it in session until they had killed the League of Nations.

"If I thought there were any grave questions involved, I would not be addressing the Senate in this mood," explained Senator Sherman.

He playfully proposed an amendment to the Covenant of the League of Nations providing that no United States funds be used to pay off any international debts incurred by Confederate States during the Civil War.

Senator Sutherland hopped to his feet to engage in mock debate concerning Virginia's attitude on the amendment. The honor of Virginia was at stake!

It was difficult to debate with Senator Sherman, for he was very deaf, and the Gentleman from Virginia soon subsided in his chair. Senator Sherman carried on alone. He took up a rumor that Wilson had told members of the Democratic National Committee that the opponents of world organization were blind, provincial little people whose minds were "knots" intended to prevent their bodies from unraveling.

"He intimates that all who differ with him have pygmy minds," protested Senator Sherman in his rasping voice. "I remember one time being in a hospital for the demented, and there was not one of them who did not insist that anybody outside was insane and they were the only sane people there were in the world."

Senator Sherman had read thousands of books in his deafness, and he could talk brilliantly and endlessly on any subject under the sun. He was pounding along like a steam engine at 1:50 in the morning, when long-legged Senator Poindexter walked in and suggested the absence of a quorum.

Bells rang, and sleepy little pages scurried around the cloakrooms awakening Senators sprawled in armchairs and sofas.

Soon the Senate began to fill with seedy, limping men in baggy trousers and wrinkled coats. Some were wide awake and jovial; they had been playing poker. Senator Lodge did not appear.

Senator LaFollette took over after the roll call. As most of the members drifted from the Chamber, he set out to prove that it would be entirely Wilson's fault if the United States Government ran out of money.

"If any measure of vital importance . . . fails before this Congress adjourns . . ." he declared, "then by a stroke of the pen President Wilson can convene the new Congress to meet one minute after the life of this Congress expires."

The Senator from Wisconsin suggested there was a sinister resemblance between Woodrow Wilson and autocrats of Europe who dissolved their legislatures and never called them back into session.

"The country must be made to know the truth!" he shouted. "If that truth is that the President is the one autocrat left in the world who insists on ruling without a parliament, the sooner we know it, the better."

To a deserted Senate, LaFollette then orated upon constitutional government, the Federal Trade Commission, prohibition, Liberty Loans, unemployment, and reconstruction in England.

Eventually he was relieved by Senator France of Maryland, who read "Cooley's Constitutional Limitations" and interminable statistics from the latest census reports. He made an eloquent plea for a special session of Congress:

"I know there are many men in this Chamber who are worn, weak and weary with the burdens which they have borne; but I know that there is not one of them . . . who is not willing to stay here, if need be, until he gives up his life in the cause of the Republic . . . firm in the faith that if he shall fall in her service some other, perhaps better, braver man will seize from his weakened arm and trembling hands her glorious banner and bear it yet ever forward in the vast procession of mankind, whose faces, eastward looking, shine now with the first radiance caught from the glancing rays of a glorious sun rising in splendor on a better age."

The Senator glanced at his watch, and abruptly abandoned his eloquence. "I have not yet reached the body of what I wanted to say, but in view of the increasing daylight, I feel disposed to yield the floor."

It was seven o'clock. Senator Sherman took the floor again, a glass of milk standing on his desk beside a copy of *Huckleberry Finn.*

A persistent supporter of the League of Nations, Senator Thomas of Colorado, made desperate efforts to get the floor away from the filibuster. Once he caught Senator Sherman off balance with a parliamentary inquiry as to what he was talking about.

"I am now addressing myself to the $750,000,000 appropriation, Section 7 of the bill," declared Sherman, who had been reading a report by Roger Babson entitled *Velvet or the Ragbag*. He was wrong. It turned out that, technically, he had been talking about a motion by Senator Cummins to suspend the rules. He was reminded in time by Senator Smoot, and Senator Thomas failed to deprive him of the floor.

The friends of the League of Nations gave up.

Late in the morning, bleary-eyed Senators began to drift in to their seats. Senator Meyers of Montana sought approval of some Army and Navy promotions, but Senator Sherman refused to yield the floor even for a moment.

"I have a carefully prepared address," he stated, "and I do not wish to have it marred by interruptions, even of . . . the confirmation of a great number of deserving patriots."

He proceeded to reminisce about the "old days" when he was a country lawyer settling claims against the railroads for killed cattle: "I have settled many of those claims in my time, and there never yet was a scrub cow killed by a steam railroad in the territory where I operated. They were all of the highest pedigree. Their offsprings' potentialities in the future, were of fabulous value. The quantities of milk they gave were astounding! With a lactometer test the average of butter fat was enough to. . . ."

Shortly before noon, President Wilson came to the Capitol to be on hand in case any measure was approved and required his signature. He sat in the President's room talking with friends.

This was not Wilson's first brush with a filibuster. Senator LaFollette had led one in 1916 against the arming of United States merchant ships. President Wilson, pointing out that the Senate is the only legislative body in the world which cannot act when its majority is ready for action, had said scathingly then:

"A little group of willful men, representing no opinion but their own, have rendered the great government of the United States helpless and contemptible. The remedy? There is but one remedy. The only remedy is that the rules of the Senate shall be so altered that it can act."

Twelve o'clock came, and the Senate adjourned. Wilson at once made a public statement:

"It is plainly my present duty to attend the Peace Conference in Paris. It is also my duty to be in close contact with the public business during a session of Congress. . . .

"It is not in the interest of the right conduct of public affairs that I should call the Congress in special session while it is impossible for me to be in Washington. . . ."

Wilson went down to Union Station, got on a train, and started the long trip back toward Paris. He was applauded by great throngs out of Washington, through Baltimore and Wilmington and Philadelphia and Trenton, and into New York. When he arrived there he was more certain than ever that the people were with him, even if a minority of the Senate was not.

Several days earlier, wanting evidence of Republican support for the League of Nations to strengthen his hand in Europe where Clemenceau, Lloyd George, and the rest might conclude he was a weakling with no strength at home, Wilson had wired to Taft inviting him to speak with him in New York before he sailed. Taft was resting in North Carolina, and his physicians told him to decline the invitation. He accepted it.

The audience packing the Metropolitan Opera House went mad as Wilson and Taft walked out on the stage together, arm-in-arm. All stood as Caruso sang the "Star-Spangled Banner."

Taft urged the nation to support the League of Nations. Looking at Wilson, he said, "Our profound sympathy in his purpose and our prayers for his success should go with him in his great mission."

The band played "Over There," and then Wilson promised he wouldn't come back until it was over, over there.

Openly defying the round robin demand that the League of Nations be separated from the peace treaty, he declared: "When that treaty comes back, gentlemen on this side will find the Covenant not only in it, but so many threads of the treaty tied to the Covenant that you cannot dissect the Covenant from the treaty without destroying the whole vital structure. The structure of peace will not be vital without the League of Nations, and no man is going to bring back a cadaver with him."

He spoke a word of warning to the Senate, too: "The great tides of the world do not give notice when they are going to rise and run; they rise in their majesty and overwhelming might, and those who stand in the way are overwhelmed."

President Wilson slipped away and went down to the docks, where in the darkness of the night the *George Washington* waited to carry him back to Europe. Newsboys along the waterfront were peddling papers full of the story of the filibuster and the round robin. Two more men—Senator Fall and Senator-elect Elkins—had signed the declaration. The *New York Sun* gloated:

"Woodrow Wilson's League of Nations died in the Senate. . . . Henry Cabot Lodge . . . read the death warrant."

March 6, 1919. "The Abandonment of Those Who Died"

All Europe speculated about the meaning of the round robin, weighing it against the significance of Taft's speech. Did the United States intend to desert the League of Nations its President had proposed? Was Woodrow Wilson a man without a country?

Presidents and prime ministers debated how much attention they should pay to Wilson, and some decided to forget all about the League of Nations. They all agreed his power and prestige had dwindled, and they prepared to drive some hard bargains. They studied with new interest a secret memorandum available in Paris. Drawn up by an American lawyer, it purported to state Wilson's weaknesses and to explain how they could be exploited.

Most Americans in Paris were gloomy. Henry White wrote to Representative Rogers: "It seems to me that a frightful responsibility will rest upon any set of men who are instrumental in preventing the trial, at least, of an experiment to settle international differences in some other way than by methods involving such frightful sacrifice of human life and tending toward the destruction of civilization."

The *New York Tribune* correspondent cabled to his paper: "I have talked with many Republicans who are here. . . . Without exception they recognize the greatness of the American mission's opportunity and duty in Europe; with no dissenting voice they assert that to abandon the League of Nations with its European responsibilities now will be little less than the abandonment of those who died in Europe to establish American ideals in the world."

March 7, 1919. A Letter to Lodge

Henry White was terribly worried, for it seemed more and more likely that the League of Nations—and the peace of the world—was in great danger unless something was done about Henry Cabot Lodge.

The wise old diplomat, who had been corresponding with his friend regularly ever since he had reached Paris, sat down in his room in the Hotel Crillon to write what he thought might be the most important letter of his life.

"Dear Cabot . . ." he wrote. "In view of the fact that more than seven million, two hundred and forty-odd thousand men have been killed in this war; that five million more men have been entirely incapacitated for any sort of usefulness during the rest of their lives, either by blindness or the loss of both arms or legs or one of the innumerable reasons which you can imagine, I cannot but feel that a strenuous effort must be made to try to prevent a return to the barbarous methods hitherto prevailing, which will, of course, be even more barbarous hereafter in view of the constant scientific improvements in weapons for the destruction of human life. . . .

"I am far from maintaining that the Covenant, as drawn, is perfect, nor do I believe that anyone who had to do with its preparation is of that opinion, but I remember that our late dear and lamented friend, Theodore Roosevelt, used to say that he always tried to get the best that he could obtain in respect to a measure of importance, instead of holding out for perfection, which, in matters requiring the assent of a great many persons of different ways of thinking, is practically impossible to attain."

White tried to answer all the criticisms Lodge had voiced in his speech of February 28. He declared he had not found a single member of the Peace Conference who had any idea that the League of Nations would do the startling things Lodge seemed to fear it would do.

Then, despite this effort to show that Lodge's fears were unfounded, White suggested a way to eliminate the causes of his fears. White asked Lodge to send him any amendments he wished put in the Covenant.

"I shall be particularly grateful," he told Lodge, "for the exact phraseology you would propose. . . ."

March 9, 1919. A Cable to Lodge

Henry White decided that by the time Senator Lodge answered his letter, the League of Nations might be in final form. Then it would be too late to seek amendments.

He sent this wire to Lodge in code through the State Department:

"SHOULD BE GRATEFUL IF YOU WOULD CABLE ME IN CIPHER, THROUGH STATE DEPARTMENT, EXACT PHRASEOLOGY OF AMENDMENTS MODIFYING LEAGUE OF NATIONS COVENANT WHICH SENATE CONSIDERS IMPORTANT. OUR DESIRE IS TO MEET SENATE'S VIEWS AS CLOSELY AS POSSIBLE TO OBTAIN ACQUIESCENCE THEREIN OF OTHER NATIONS ANXIOUS FOR RECOGNITION OF THEIR OWN SPECIAL INTERESTS WHICH THEY WILL IMMEDIATELY INSIST UPON IN THE COVENANT IF WE DEMAND EXCEPTIONS IN FAVOR OF OURS. WROTE YOU FULLY TWO DAYS AGO BUT FEEL USE OF CABLE DESIRABLE, TIME BEING SO IMPORTANT."

March 14, 1919. "No Matter What I Do . . ."

All the long, slow way across the Atlantic, Woodrow Wilson tried to plan his strategy. Walking the deck; conferring with assistants;

standing in the ship's bow; at breakfast, lunch, and dinner; turning in his bunk at night, he pondered.

The Covenant was still open to amendment. Its authors knew it needed improvement, and they sought constructive criticism. But most of the suggestions made in the United States seemed unnecessary, and Wilson hated to seek needless amendments. Every demand he made for American revisions would be met by demands for concessions to Britain, France, Italy, Japan, and other nations.

However, many American supporters of the League of Nations, among them Taft, had strongly advised Wilson to amend the Covenant to satisfy the critics. Senator Hitchcock had told him that a few amendments would win over some of the Senators who had signed the round robin.

Actually, Wilson was rapidly reaching the conclusion that no amendments would appease the real enemies of world organization. Once during the voyage he remarked:

"No matter what I do, they will continue the attack."

Colonel House met the ship at Brest, and a long conference was held in the President's cabin. Wilson was appalled to learn that it was now generally assumed in Paris that creation of the League of Nations would be postponed until after the peace treaty was signed. Many delegates thought the League was dead. Many still felt there would be no lasting peace without it. Colonel House had already felt compelled to make several concessions to other nations due to the weakened position of the United States delegation.

At the end of the conference, Mrs. Wilson found her husband white-faced and shaken.

March 15, 1919. "I Cannot Now Speak for the Senate"

This bold statement was issued by the United States delegation a few hours after Woodrow Wilson, in a fighting mood, reached Paris:

"The President said today that the decision made at the Press

Conference at its plenary session, January 25, 1919, to the effect that the establishment of a League of Nations should be an integral part of the Treaty of Peace, is of final force and that there is no basis whatever for the reports that a change in this decision was contemplated."

Wilson did indicate a willingness to make constructive changes in the Covenant. He spoke of it as something still malleable and in the making.

Wilson told a delighted Henry White that he wanted to have any suggestions for amendments that he might have in mind. He said he was willing to make any reasonable changes that would win greater support back home.

The diplomat felt that perhaps he would really be able to bridge the gulf between Wilson and Lodge. Impatiently, he awaited word from his Senate friend.

The moment Lodge had received White's cable, he had consulted Knox and Brandegee, and then Elihu Root. He determined his course, and now he cabled this reply back to Paris:

"HAVE CONSIDERED YOUR CABLE MARCH 9. THE PRESIDENT EXPRESSED NO WILLINGNESS TO RECEIVE ANY COMMUNICATION FROM THE SENATE WHILE THAT BODY WAS IN SESSION. IF HE NOW WISHES TO HAVE AMENDMENTS DRAFTED WHICH THE SENATE WILL CONSENT TO, THE NATURAL AND NECESSARY COURSE IS TO ASSEMBLE THE SENATE IN THE CUSTOMARY WAY. MANIFESTLY I CANNOT NOW SPEAK FOR THE SENATE OR CONSULT ITS MEMBERS, NOR CAN THEY CONSULT WITH EACH OTHER, NOR CAN THE PRESIDENT CONSULT THEM WHILE THEY ARE AT THEIR HOMES IN 48 STATES."

The telegram was a stinging slap in White's face. It completely ignored the long personal correspondence between Lodge and White. More, it seemingly closed the door on all hope of compromise between Lodge and Wilson.

The diplomat sadly filed the telegram away beside the secret memorandum from Lodge, dated December 4, 1918, advising the heads of European nations as to "the real feeling of the people of the United States and certainly the Senate of the United States" concerning the League of Nations.

The fact was, Lodge could not state his demands for revision of the League of Nations in specific language.

If he did, and if his proposals were adopted, he would be deprived of his only sure weapon: the demand for revision.

He would no longer be able to carry on the pretense of wanting an amended, perfected League of Nations. He would be compelled to support it, or to fight it openly.

And from the very beginning, Lodge had known he would lose in an open fight.

March 16, 1919. Taft's Offer—Wilson's Acceptance

A cable was received by Wilson from Joe Tumulty stating that Taft had some specific amendments to propose if the President would like to consider them.

Tumulty made it clear that Taft did not consider his amendments necessary to the improvement of the Covenant, explaining:

"... THESE SUGGESTIONS DO NOT LOOK TO THE CHANGE OF THE STRUCTURE OF THE LEAGUE, THE PLAN OF ITS ACTION OR ITS REAL CHARACTER, BUT SIMPLY TO REMOVING OBJECTIONS IN MINDS OF CONSCIENTIOUS AMERICANS, WHO ARE ANXIOUS FOR A LEAGUE OF NATIONS, WHOSE FEARS COULD BE REMOVED WITHOUT ANY CONSIDERABLE CHANGE OF LANGUAGE."

Wilson immediately wired back:

"APPRECIATE MR. TAFT'S OFFER OF SUGGESTIONS AND WOULD WELCOME THEM. THE SOONER THEY ARE SENT THE BETTER."

March 18, 1919. Taft's Recommendations

Taft cabled Wilson that "the ground will be completely cut from under opponents of the League in the Senate" if he obtained a reservation protecting the Monroe Doctrine, and four amendments including one protecting domestic issues from League interference. The cable concluded:

"MONROE DOCTRINE ALONE WOULD PROBABLY CARRY THE TREATY, BUT OTHERS WOULD MAKE IT CERTAIN."

March 19, 1919. "We Have Work to Do"

Senator Lodge was openly accused of offering only destructive criticism of the Covenant in a Boston debate with A. Lawrence Lowell, President of Harvard and one of the leaders of the League to Enforce Peace.

The audience applauded loudly when President Lowell tried to pin Lodge down:

"As our Senior Senator, and as the leader of the Republicans in the Senate, we have a right to ask Mr. Lodge two questions: first, whether he will, or will not, vote for the Covenant of Paris, provided it is amended as he wishes; and second, what amendments thereto he desires. . . .

"I believe that if Senator Lodge in his position will formulate his amendments and send them to Paris, and say: 'I will vote for this Covenant if those amendments are adopted,' they will be adopted and the Covenant will pass."

Lodge repeated his fears for the Monroe Doctrine, and domestic affairs, but he would only speak of amendments to the Covenant in the most general terms. When Lowell pressed him, he finally invoked the name of Theodore Roosevelt to bolster his position.

"Two weeks before his death I was with Theodore Roosevelt for some hours, seeing him for two mornings in succession," said the Senator. "The draft of the Covenant of the League of Nations now before the country was not then before us, but we discussed fully the League of Nations in all its bearings. We were in entire agreement.

"The position that I have taken, and now take, had his full approval. The line I have followed in the Senate and elsewhere was the one he wished to have followed."

Right after the debate, Senator Lodge told a constituent, "The audience was with him. We have work to do."

March 22, 1919. Wilson Seeks Four Amendments

The League of Nations Commission convened once more for the final consideration of the Covenant.

A minute analysis of Lodge's speeches and of the main lines of all American opposition to the League of Nations, together with the advice of Taft, Hitchcock, and other friends of world organization, had convinced a reluctant Wilson that to diminish opposition he should try to amend the Covenant in four important ways:

1. To protect the Monroe Doctrine.
2. To protect domestic affairs.
3. To provide withdrawal from the League of Nations.
4. To reserve the right to refuse mandates.

Wilson anticipated a bitter struggle over the proposals. He knew that to get them into the Covenant, he would be compelled to make many concessions to other nations.

"I am yielding to men, to the judgment of men, who have little knowledge or appreciation of the world situation, but who, alas! control votes," he told his fellow-delegates. "These changes we shall put through, but I fear we will find in the end that we have jumped out of the frying pan into the fire. Certainly the way will be opened for a flood of amendments which will surely delay us and may disfigure our solemn agreement—so patiently, so painfully arrived at."

The dreams and desires of every people, some in the interest of all, some in the interest of narrow nationalism, were gathered in Paris with their spokesmen. The differences between the good and the bad were often clouded; the differences between fact and opinion were often obscure. And through it all there were deals and bargains and compromises, secret treaties and promises and pledges.

Yet the peace would fail if the men in Paris failed to sift the good from the bad, if they failed to put the sound proposals into the Peace Treaty and the unsound proposals into the waste basket.

It fell to Wilson to bear the brunt of the battle, but his position was woefully weakened the moment he made his demands for the provisions demanded by his own countrymen.

March 26, 1919. All but the Monroe Doctrine

When this day was done, Wilson had won three of the four amendments. One made it still more clear that the League of Nations would not interfere in domestic issues. Another stated that mandates would be entrusted only to nations "willing to accept" them. A third stipulated that any member nation could resign after two years' notice.

The withdrawal amendment was added only after a long fight. France and the other neighbors of Germany were strongly opposed to a move implying that the United States might soon desert the League of Nations. Wilson was on exceedingly weak ground, for he had previously opposed a withdrawal clause; some of the men who fought him now remembered that they had heard him joke about the fact that he, a Southerner, opposed the right of secession.

The struggle was so furious that Wilson decided to postpone all mention of the Monroe Doctrine amendment. It was bound to produce an even greater uproar.

March 28, 1919. "Treaty Will Be Promptly Ratified"

This telegram flashed across the Atlantic Ocean:

"PRESIDENT WILSON, PARIS:

"FOLLOWING IS SENT AT THE REQUEST OF MR. TAFT:

"'FRIENDS OF THE COVENANT ARE SERIOUSLY ALARMED OVER REPORT THAT NO AMENDMENT WILL BE MADE MORE SPECIFICALLY SAFEGUARDING MONROE DOCTRINE. AT FULL MEETING OF EXECUTIVE COMMITTEE OF LEAGUE TO ENFORCE PEACE, WITH THIRTY MEMBERS FROM EIGHTEEN STATES PRESENT, UNANIMOUS OPINION THAT WITHOUT SUCH AMENDMENT REPUBLICAN SENATORS WILL CERTAINLY DEFEAT RATIFICATION OF TREATY, BECAUSE PUBLIC OPINION WILL SUSTAIN THEM. WITH SUCH AMENDMENT, TREATY WILL BE PROMPTLY RATIFIED.

"'WILLIAM H. TAFT

"'A. LAWRENCE LOWELL.'

"TUMULTY"

Wilson was busy sparring with the men of other nations over their own demands. Clemenceau, physically weakened but politically strengthened by the bullet still lodged in his body, was giving him a rough time. When Wilson opposed him, Clemenceau would say, "Before the accident, I was only a tired old man. Now I am a martyr—and you must pay attention to me!"

The Frenchman was under severe attack in the Paris press for failing to secure the Rhineland for France and now he was out to weaken Germany in every possible way. He had spent four years as a journalist in the United States and, actually, he was more afraid than most of his countrymen about the future. He had seen the Senate, and he knew what it might do to the League of Nations—the instrument Wilson insisted would curb Germany and all other aggressors.

Lloyd George, too, was not exactly pleasant company for Wilson. He expanded prodigious amounts of his boundless energy demanding that the United States Navy be no bigger than the British Navy, and looking out for the interests of the Dominions. Whenever Wilson put his finger on a flaw in the demands of Clemenceau and Lloyd George, they would innocently remark that the ill-advised demands of their countrymen were fully as important as the ill-advised demands of his countrymen.

Most of the demands of the Italian delegates were backed up by the terms of the secret Treaty of London before they had entered the war. When Wilson protested, the British said the treaty had to be honored. Then the Italians started demanding the Yugoslav port of Fiume as additional booty.

The Japanese also had secret agreements with Great Britain, guaranteeing them control of the former German-held province of Shantung in China, jutting into the Yellow Sea opposite Korea, and German islands in the Pacific north of the equator. The Japanese had lost only three hundred men in the World War, but they were intent upon getting the promised payment. They also had been seeking a provision in the Covenant guaranteeing equality of all nations regardless of race. The Australians opposed the provision, and Wilson, too, took a stand against it; his position was backed by a wire from Elihu Root, whom Colonel House had consulted. Root had cabled:

"DON'T LET IT IN, IT WILL BREED TROUBLE. IN ANY EVENT, YOU'RE GOING TO HAVE HARD SLEDDING, BUT WITH THE RACIAL PROVISION, YOU WILL GET NOWHERE IN THE SENATE. AND THE PEOPLE . . . ? ON THE PACIFIC COAST, AT LEAST, THEY WOULD THINK THERE LURKED BEHIND IT A PLAN FOR UNLIMITED YELLOW IMMIGRATION."

All the small nations, with all the things they wanted, were in constant pursuit of Wilson. In a typical day, he conferred with twenty-one people representing seventeen different nationalities. Sometimes the little nations sided with Clemenceau or Lloyd George against Wilson. The Poles and the Czechoslovaks and the Yugoslavs and the Belgians—the little neighbors of Germany—cheered and applauded all Clemenceau's demands for an all-powerful League of Nations. The Polish delegate, when he saw that American sentiment made a League of Nations with its own army impossible, said sadly:

"I had hoped that our distinguished and most welcome visitors from across the seas, broad as well as narrow, would carefully weigh the unanimous opinion of those unfortunate peoples who dwell so near the cave where the wolf pack lowers."

April 3, 1919.
"Grayer and Grayer, Grimmer and Grimmer"

Wilson was struggling all day every day with Clemenceau and Lloyd George and Orlando, and he was meeting every night with the League of Nations Commission. Then, around midnight, his American aides would come to his room to confer with him. They would find him utterly exhausted, his face drooping and one side of it twitching. Ray Stannard Baker, who was one of them, wrote, ". . . day after day . . . we saw him growing grayer and grayer, grimmer and grimmer, with the fighting lines deepening in his face."

On this day, he suffered a violent attack of influenza.

There was no pause in the struggle—in America. Beveridge was writing another of his strategy letters to Lodge:

"Before long, within the next five or six weeks, we must sound the battle-cry, *'Get out of Europe and stay out.'* "

April 5, 1919. The Press, the Civilians, the Soldiers

The most important newspapers in the United States were revealed to be overwhelmingly in favor of the League of Nations in a poll conducted by the *Literary Digest.* A total of 718 papers reported they were for it unconditionally, 478 more were for it conditionally, and only 181 were against it.

Most of the people in the communities where the newspapers were published supported the plan for peace, the editors told the *Literary Digest.*

Soldiers, too, were very much for it, announced Secretary of War Newton D. Baker.

"As I have talked with the soldiers, both abroad and at home," he declared in Washington, "I found them not disposed to discuss abstract questions, but burning with hope that America can lead the world into a League of Nations formed for the purpose of substitution of right and justice for force in international controversies....

"The men who fought for American ideals in the World War know best the tragedy which has laid waste the fairest civilizations of the Old World.... Throughout all their fighting they felt that their sacrifice was being made to put an end to that sort of tragedy."

April 8, 1919. "The People of the Country Desire a League"

Senator Lodge frankly admitted that the people favored the League of Nations in a letter to Henry White.

"I think a majority of the people of the country desire a League," he wrote, "but there is an active minority against any League and

I think the majority of the people today, in the course of discussion, although they want a League, will insist on some very vital amendments covering particularly the Monroe Doctrine. . . ."

April 10, 1919. The Lost Speech

The friends and the foes of the League of Nations had all insisted Wilson must obtain a provision protecting the Monroe Doctrine.

Senator Lodge had demanded it in many speeches.

Taft had urged it repeatedly, and so had Senator Hitchcock. Elihu Root, Charles Evans Hughes, Henry White, and countless other leading American figures had likewise proposed it.

So, on this day, a grim and gloomy Wilson went after this amendment:

> Nothing in the Covenant shall be deemed to effect the validity of international engagements, such as treaties of arbitration or regional understandings like the Monroe Doctrine, for securing the maintenance of peace.

To Wilson, the amendment was absurd. He had originally conceived of the League of Nations as an expansion, from hemisphere to world proportions, of the principles of the Monroe Doctrine—as a guarantee of the freedom and security of all nations. The first time he ever addressed Congress on world organization, on January 22, 1917, he had said, "I am proposing, as it were, that the nations should with one accord adopt the doctrine of President Monroe as the doctrine of the world." And now he was supposed to ask that what he considered the fundamental principle of the League of Nations should be protected from the League of Nations!

To all Europe—except England—the Monroe Doctrine had always seemed a brazen piece of "Yankee Imperialism." To ask Europe to endorse a doctrine fencing them out of the Western Hemisphere was not calculated to delight them.

The Chinese, too, opposed the amendment. Wellington Koo was afraid that if the Covenant specifically preserved the Monroe Doctrine, it might encourage the Japanese, who seemed to be nursing ambitions about some kind of a sphere of influence of their own in Asia. Baron Makino, the calm, imperturbable Japanese delegate, supported the amendment.

The French assumed a devastatingly logical position when Wilson proposed the amendment. To assurances that a provision protecting the Monroe Doctrine really wouldn't alter the Covenant because both were based on precisely the same principle, they countered with the declaration that in that case, the provision was obviously unnecessary. Privately, the French asked representatives of other European nations, "Why are we expected to make every concession to American prejudice when the President will make none to European traditions? We have gone to the length of accepting the doctrine of Monroe for the whole of the earth, but now because American pride demands it, we must make public confession of America's right to give orders. No!"

And the French, playing poker with straight faces, renewed their demands that they be given the Rhineland and the Saar Basin, and a specific guarantee of military aid from England and the United States in case of German aggression. "Oh, so the League of Nations protects us in case of German aggression," they asked with superb sarcasm. "So it doesn't need to be mentioned specifically? Then why need the Monroe Doctrine be mentioned specifically? Everyone knows the League of Nations protects it."

And Italy again demanded Fiume and Dalmatia.

Japan pressed her claims for Shantung.

Only three days out of his sick bed and still very weak, Wilson showed no willingness to give way. Three days before, the demands of the other nations—brought to him by Colonel House—had seemed to him so impossible that he had threatened to go home. Now, to get the Monroe Doctrine amendment, he was willing to bargain, but he refused to undermine the whole peace. The struggle went on for hours.

It was well after midnight when Wilson, desperate, feeling that if he failed to get a provision covering the Monroe Doctrine he would fail to get a League of Nations, frankly put himself at the mercy of the group. He stood up, and started off in an apologetic sort of way by saying:

"You see, the whole object of this mentioning of the Monroe Doctrine is to relieve a state of mind and misapprehension on the other side of the water."

Gathering his strength, he went on to plead for the amendment with what one who was there called "witching eloquence." Spellbound by the magic of his words, the official reporters stopped to listen, their pencils idle. Only a few sentences were taken down, so that mere fragments of the speech remain and no full record of it exists anywhere.

There was a long silence when Wilson sat down, and then the Monroe Doctrine amendment was adopted; the cause was carried.

April 12, 1919. "It Is All Ours!"

The supporters of the League of Nations were delighted by Wilson's success, but their delight was short-lived.

Senator Lodge, who had started and led the demand for the Monroe Doctrine amendment while flatly refusing to state what form he thought the amendment should take, bluntly denounced the amendment.

The moment its terms became known, he castigated the authors of the Covenant for daring to call the Monroe Doctrine an "international engagement." It was no such thing, he protested.

"It is all ours!" he cried. "And now it is to be carried into this League of Nations. It is already interpreted by England, although it is wholly our affair, and it is to be determined in the future by the League of Nations!"

Those who had witnessed the fight at Paris for the Monroe Doctrine, those who really knew its price, shook their heads.

Senator John Sharp Williams said bitterly of Lodge:

"His objection to the exclusion of mention of the Monroe Doctrine increased to virulence when he was faced with the inclusion of it."

April 19, 1919. "Pretentious Hypocrisy"

One American denounced Woodrow Wilson for *all* the amendments he had gotten into the Covenant to meet American criticisms.

It was a man who, like Lodge, had demanded the amendments. It was a man who had helped Elihu Root frame a letter suggesting amendments. It was a man who, after Root released the letter, had declared late in March, "The situation has now been changed so simply and so convincingly that none can fail to realize precisely what must be done in Paris to win the approval of America. . . ."

That man was Colonel Harvey.

Now that the amendments were in the Covenant, he raged in his *War Weekly:*

"When a man urges acceptance of a scheme which he declares to have been so carefully thought out and so perfect as to be unsusceptible of improvement, and then eagerly assents to its being turned inside out and radically remade, things stricken out which he deemed indispensable and things inserted which he considered inadmissible, and as zealously as before urges its adoption in the new form which completely stultifies the old, he discredits himself save as a self-seeker equally ready to cry 'Good Lord!' or 'Good Devil!' so long as he can get something or anything adopted as of his devising."

Colonel Harvey offered this advice:

"For such pretentious hypocrisy there can be but one fitting fate—rejection; but one fitting place—the scrap-heap."

April 23, 1919. The Fight over Fiume

When the Allied nations capitulated to Wilson's demands for American amendments, they resolved to fight as relentlessly as he for their own claims.

Italy put up a fight for Fiume. Not a single nation represented at Paris considered the Italian demand for the Yugoslavian port justified, but since they wanted to press their own claims, they left it to Wilson to oppose the Italians openly. Wilson had already won the concessions demanded by *his* countrymen.

The entire American delegation considered Italy's demand unfair. Wilson, knowing he would often have to rely entirely on the advice of the many experts he took to Paris, had told them before the Peace Conference, "Tell me what's right and I'll fight for it. Give me a guaranteed position." They gave him a guaranteed position on Fiume. He fought for it.

When Orlando would not give up, Wilson appealed over his head to the Italian people—a move unprecedented in the history of diplomacy but characteristic of his faith in the common people. He begged the people of Italy not to ask America to make a settlement inconsistent with the sacred principles for which the World War was fought:

"Only upon these principles, she hopes and believes, will the people of Italy ask her to make peace."

April 24, 1919. Fiume . . . and Two Men . . .

Orlando wept and stormed, and bolted the Peace Conference. As he and his fellow-delegates boarded a train in Paris to go back to Rome, the British Secretary of Foreign Affairs, Balfour, handed them a confidential memorandum asserting the opposition of both Great Britain and France to Italy's claims. It said:

"After the most prolonged and anxious reflection, we cannot bring ourselves to believe that it is either in the interests of Yugoslavia, in the interests of Italy herself, or in the interests of future peace—which is the concern of all the world—that this port should be severed from the territories to which, economically, geographically, and ethnologically it naturally belongs.

"Can it be that Italy on this account is prepared to separate herself from her Allies?"

The memorandum sounded a prophetic warning: "Germany, even when she began to entertain misgivings about the issues of the campaign, felt sure that the union of her enemies would never survive their triumphs. She based her schemes no longer on the conquest of Europe, but on its political, and perhaps also on its social, disintegration. The Armistice might doubtless produce a brief cessation of hostilities; but it would bring no repose to a perturbed and overwrought world. Militant nationalism would lead to a struggle between peoples. . . .

"This or something like this is the present calculation of a certain section of German politicians. Could anything more effectually contribute to its success than that Italy should quarrel with her Allies? . . .

"For these reasons, if for no other, we beg our Italian colleagues to reconsider their policy."

While an alarmed world watched the efforts to construct a sound peace verge on collapse, two men eagerly sought to exploit the controversy for their own ends.

Senator Lodge sent public telegrams to various Italian-American leaders in Boston saying, "IF ITALY IS OF THE OPINION THAT IT IS NECESSARY TO HER SAFETY AND FOR HER PROTECTION THAT SHE SHOULD HOLD FIUME, I AM CLEARLY OF THE OPINION THAT IT SHOULD BE HERS. . . ." The telegram convinced most of America's five million Italian-Americans (hundreds of thousands of them Lodge's constituents in Massachusetts) that Lodge was their friend, Wilson their foe.

And in Italy Benito Mussolini, the leader of a little-known band of cutthroats who called themselves fascists, seized upon "FIUME!" as the most stirring nationalist slogan of his campaign to win a following in Italy.

April 29, 1919. Senator Borah Agrees

The full text of the amended Covenant was published in the morning papers, under bold headlines announcing that it had been accepted by the Peace Conference by unanimous vote.

All told, President Wilson had succeeded in securing amendments covering the four most important demands made by Senator Lodge in his speeches, all of the recommendations of Taft, six of seven proposals made by Charles Evans Hughes, and the majority of Elihu Root's suggestions. These covered all the suggestions made by Senator Hitchcock and by the League to Enforce Peace.

Senator Lodge, who was on the job in Washington even though Congress was not in session, was startled by the extent of the amendments. He hurried into conference with Senator Curtis of Kansas, Republican whip in the Senate. To stifle any chorus of premature praise, they rushed off a telegram to their colleagues, who were scattered all over the United States in their homes:

"WE SUGGEST THAT REPUBLICAN SENATORS RESERVE FINAL EXPRESSION OF OPINION RESPECTING THE AMENDED LEAGUE COVENANT UNTIL THE LATEST DRAFT HAS BEEN CAREFULLY STUDIED AND UNTIL THERE HAS BEEN AN OPPORTUNITY FOR CONFERENCE."

Capitol Hill reporters soon came knocking on Lodge's door to hear his opinion of the Covenant. He refused to see them. After lunch he issued a brief statement: "I am not prepared to make a statement in regard to the new draft at this moment, because I desire to examine it carefully and compare it with the former draft, and also to confer with my colleagues, for it is obvious that it will require further amendments if it is to promote peace and not endanger certain rights of the United States which should never be placed in jeopardy."

Later in the afternoon, Lodge held a private conference with Borah. A few days before, the two Senators had joined forces in a conference in Lodge's home on Massachusetts Avenue. Lodge, who had just returned to Washington from New England, had told Borah that in his opinion sentiment was overwhelmingly for the League of Nations.

Lodge had declared that the man in the street—"the farmers, the shopkeepers, the men in small business, clerks and the like, in short the people generally"—did not understand the League of Nations but tended to support it. He said he was convinced that "the vocal classes of the community, most of the clergymen, the preachers of sermons, a large element in the teaching force of the universities, a large proportion of the newspaper editors, and finally the men and women who were in the habit of writing and speaking for publication" were all advocates of the League. And he had said that a large number of Republican Senators would undoubtedly vote for it after it had been somewhat revised.

"With these conditions existing," recorded Lodge later of his meeting with Borah, "it seemed perfectly obvious to me that any attempt to defeat the treaty of Versailles with the League by a straight vote in the Senate, if taken immediately, would be hopeless, even if it were desirable. . . .

"I told him that in any event there was only one thing to do and that was to proceed in the discussion of the treaty by way of amendment and reservation.

"He told me that he agreed entirely with my description of the situation, that he did not believe the treaty could possibly be beaten at that time by a direct vote, that he was against the treaty in any form whatever, whether with reservations or amendments or not, but that thinking I was right in my judgment of the conditions and the situation generally he would support any amendments or reservations which I and those who agreed with me should offer, although, of course, so far as he was personally concerned, after having voted for the reservations or amendments in the belief that they would make the treaty better and the League safer, on the final vote he would vote against the acceptance of the treaty by the Senate."

Lodge's winning of Borah's support for the drive to defeat the Covenant by revision was of vital importance. Lodge needed the support of two groups in the Senate if he was to control enough votes to alter the Covenant—the men who wanted an amended League of Nations, and the men who wanted no League of Nations, amended or not amended.

Lodge, leader of the first group, maintained publicly that he really wanted an amended League of Nations.

Borah, leader of the second group, maintained publicly that if the Saviour should revisit the earth and declare for the League of Nations, he, Borah, would still oppose it.

Privately, however, Lodge and Borah were now in full agreement on strategy.

April 30, 1919. Lodge and Borah Were Right . . .

The telegram from Lodge and Curtis failed to prevent two Senators from praising the revised Covenant.

"In my opinion," said Senator Charles McNary of Oregon, "the Covenant has been amended to meet all legitimate objections raised against it."

Senator Reed Smoot of Utah, too, declared he was "pleased" with the amendments.

Even the *Chicago Tribune* gloomily admitted the League of Nations seemed destined for Senate approval. Its Washington correspondent reported that not more than 15 Senators were openly opposed to it. The League to Enforce Peace confidently announced that only 12 were flatly opposed. The latter estimate, stating that 64 Senators were definitely for the Covenant, was based upon newspaper interviews, personal interviews, letters, and speeches made by the Senators.

Other evidence that Lodge and Borah were right about the sentiment of the nation came in the announcement that thirty-two state legislatures—including Lodge's own Massachusetts—had now passed resolutions advocating United States' entry into the League of Nations.

Added to previous surveys of the general press support were *Literary Digest* and League to Enforce Peace tabulations revealing that farm, labor, and religious newspapers were all overwhelmingly for the League of Nations.

The American Agricultural Association, the National Grange, the National Board of Farm Organizations, the Farmers' Educational and Cooperative Union of America, and the Farmers' Reconstruction Conference were all for the League of Nations. So were such organizations as the National Retail Dry Goods Association, the American Manufacturers' Export Association, the National Association of Builders' Exchange, the National Association of Merchant Tailors of America.

So were the Daughters of the American Revolution, the National American Women's Suffrage Association, the General Federation of

Women's Clubs, and the Victory Committee for Women, composed of heads of all organizations that had done active war work.

Many religious groups had gone on record as favoring the League, including the Federal Council of Churches, the National Society of Christian Endeavor, the Church Peace Union, the General Assembly of the Presbyterian Church, the Northern Baptist convention, the Evangelical Lutheran Church in America.

"Practically all Americans of the type that politicians call 'church folks' were for it," commented Mark Sullivan.

May 1, 1919. "The Mechanism to Perfect Our Work"

There was tension at the White House all morning, for a cable had come from Admiral Grayson:

"JAPANESE SITUATION HANGING BY A THREAD. . . . THESE ARE TERRIBLE DAYS FOR THE PRESIDENT PHYSICALLY AND OTHERWISE."

Then word came that the crisis was passed. Their claims buttressed by the secret treaties with England, by conquest, and by possession, the Japanese had vowed never to yield on Shantung when they lost their fight for a racial equality clause in the Covenant. And Wilson, weakened by his fight for American amendments, weakened by the support his American foes gave Italy in the one dispute that really boiled over, finally compromised.

Even so, he drove a stiff bargain. It was stipulated that Japan would retain only Germany's old economic holdings in Shantung, together with the right to establish a settlement under restricted conditions. The Japanese agreed to turn over full sovereignty to China.

Wilson did not like the Shantung settlement. He did not like a good many other Paris compromises. Many of them were obviously unfair to one nation or another. However, Wilson was convinced that the League of Nations would make it possible to correct the wrongs in the course of time—by peaceful methods.

If he had held out against all the demands of all the nations he would have broken up the Peace Conference. Once he did threaten to go home, actually cabling for the *George Washington* to come after him; this sufficed to win a retreat from Clemenceau. Again, Wilson said, "Do you wish me to go home?" Clemenceau replied, "I do not wish you to go home, but I intend to do so myself." And he stalked off like Orlando—with the important difference that he only had to go around the corner, and could come back the next day.

Finally, Clemenceau won an agreement that France would stay in the Rhineland and the Saar Basin for fifteen years; the sum of the reparations to be paid by Germany was left open; and it was agreed that the United States and England would sign a separate treaty with France promising to go to her assistance if she was attacked by Germany.

The dilemma Wilson faced when confronted by the demands o_ the Allies was described by Colonel Stephen Bonsal, aide and interpreter to Wilson and Colonel House, in his diary:

"What should he do? Wash his hands of the whole matter and go home? In this case there would be no treaty, and a state of anarchy not only in Europe but throughout the world would follow. The predatory powers would pitch in and take what they want, and the democracies we thought to help, and most certainly promised to help, would be despoiled. Or should the President consent to a treaty that will reveal some compromises in principle but at least one that will contain the Covenant, a bright star of hope and guidance in the dark heavens by night and a rainbow of promise in the troubled skies by day?"

Colonel House told the diarist: "I think the President will reject the counsel of despair. He will not run away."

Colonel Bonsal read Colonel House a quotation from Gladstone, and House said he would show it to Wilson. The great Britisher had said once in a moment of diplomatic distress: "Men ought not to suffer from disenchantment; they ought to know that ideals in politics are never realized."

Colonel House's prediction came true: Woodrow Wilson did not run away. He stayed and fought, and when he thought he had to compromise, he compromised. If the compromises seemed sometimes to come a bit too quickly, it was mostly because there clearly had to be a plan for the peace soon or Europe would fall apart. It had lived in a state of suspension ever since November 11.

Wilson's antagonists in Paris did not share the view held by his antagonists in America that he had compromised too much. Clemenceau said when it was all over: "Wilson talked like Jesus Christ but acted like Lloyd George." Clemenceau was driven from office in the next election; the people of France thought he had compromised too much with Wilson.

Several times Wilson remarked to House how glad he was that he had withstood the demands of his opponents in America who wanted the League of Nations separated from the rest of the peace settlement.

"While I hope for the best, the Treaty, like all human documents, may prove imperfect," he would say. "It may not live up to our ideal, but with the Covenant an integral and inseparable part of the Treaty, the mechanism to perfect our work, to adjust it to the needs of situations which may arise, will be close at hand."

May 7, 1919. The Germans at Versailles

A German delegation headed by Count Brockdorff-Rantzau, a proud man whose face was virtually hidden by thick spectacles and a heavy beard, was handed the completed Versailles Treaty on this fourth anniversary of the sinking of the *Lusitania*.

A state of war still existed, and the Germans were guarded behind barbed wire until the moment of the ceremony. Then old Clemenceau faced them to say: "The time has come when we must settle our accounts. You have asked for peace. We are ready to give you peace."

Count Brockdorff-Rantzau, without standing up, without even looking up, read a long protest against the whole peace settlement. "It is demanded of us that we confess ourselves to be the only ones guilty of the war," he read bitterly. "Such a confession in my mouth will be a lie." He snarled the last word.

Then the Germans silently returned to the Fatherland.

The Allied delegates waited in Paris, and there was talk of a blockade if the Germans refused to sign the treaty. Meanwhile, the Allies began to make plans for the actual creation of the League of Nations, and took up other unfinished business.

May 8, 1919. Would the Germans Sign?

The feeling in Paris was tense, strained. The wounds wrought by some of the settlements written into the Versailles Treaty were deep. There was restlessness and doubt.

Would the Germans sign? Would the Americans?

Would the peace endure?

"The President has evidently pretty well made up his mind not to go home until he has either signed the Treaty or there is no immediate hope of getting it signed," wrote Henry White to William E. Phillips of the State Department, informing him that Wilson had called Congress to meet on May 19.

"I cannot help feeling that he will be attacked in many directions the moment the session opens, and that in his absence there will be no one in a position either from full knowledge of what has taken place or from proper authority to do so, to defend him, and that the opposition will have taken a pretty good hold of the country before he returns."

May 17, 1919. A Young Man Named William C. Bullitt

A young man named William C. Bullitt, who had been attached to the United States Peace Delegation, staged a dramatic resignation. He made public a letter addressed to President Wilson denouncing the compromises in the Versailles Treaty and declaring they undermined the peace.

"I am sorry that you did not fight our fight to a finish and that you had so little faith in the millions of men like myself in every nation who had faith in you," he told Wilson.

Young Bullitt called a press conference and announced that he (aged 29) was going to the Riviera to lie on the sands and watch the world go to hell.

The startled *New York Times* dismissed Bullitt in a scathing editorial declaring, "It is a hard, long game we are playing, with rebuffs and setbacks, as it seems, for everybody. But the only hope for most of us is to be among those who see it through."

In Washington, Senator Lodge made a note of the name "William C. Bullitt" for future reference.

May 19, 1919. The New Congress Convenes

Congress convened at noon in Washington, and the Republicans took command for the first time since the inauguration of Woodrow Wilson in 1913.

Senator Henry Cabot Lodge prepared to become majority leader of the Senate, and chairman of the powerful Foreign Relations Committee.

President Wilson sent a message from Paris: "I deeply regret my inability to be present for the opening of the extraordinary session of the Congress. It still seems to be my duty to take part in the counsels of the Peace Conference and contribute what I can to the solution of the innumerable questions to whose settlement it has had to address itself; for they are questions which affect the peace of the whole world and from them, therefore, the United States cannot stand apart. I deemed it my duty to call the Congress together at this time because it was not wise to postpone longer the provisions which must be made for the support of the government."

The Germans were stalling. They had not yet accepted the Versailles Treaty. They knew that the Allies, no longer held together on the field of battle, might fall apart if the peace settlement was long delayed. They knew that if controversy developed among the Allied peoples, Germany might get a softer peace.

The Allied delegates in Paris, too, knew the great dangers involved in any controversy among their own people. They had agreed to keep the terms of the Versailles Treaty secret until the Germans signed it. This provided the American opponents of the planned peace with a new opportunity to shout: "Secret diplomacy!" It gave them a new chance to imply that Wilson and his "accomplices" had done terrible things.

Senator Hiram Johnson set about preparing a resolution ordering the State Department to turn over a copy of the Versailles Treaty to the Senate. He omitted the protective phrase, usually placed in such resolutions demanding documents from the Executive, stating that it should be complied with only "if not incompatible with the public interest."

May 21, 1919.
Senator Knox's Multimillionaire Constituents

There was a gloomy gathering after dinner at the home of Senator Brandegee at 1521 K Street in Washington.

Colonel Harvey was there from New York, and there were Senators back from distant states for the new Congress. All dolefully reported that they had found sentiment to be overwhelmingly for the League of Nations, and that the League to Enforce Peace was drumming up more and more support every day.

The League to Enforce Peace was carrying on a masterly campaign, done in the spirit of '76 and after. It had prepared some brilliant articles called "The Covenanter"—patterned after the Federalist Papers—for publication in many important newspapers. It was holding "Ratifying Conventions" in fifteen great states in May, June, and July—the first opening on this very day in Vermont. It now had 10,000 men and women holding official positions all over the country, 50,000 more volunteer workers, and 300,000 members chosen for their influence in their home communities. It was not only organized in all forty-eight states, but in a third of the nation's counties; it was putting powerful political pressure on many Senators. Thousands of resolutions urging ratification of the Covenant were being passed by business and professional associations, labor unions, college faculties, farm groups, clergymen, clubs and societies of all sorts, and by huge mass meetings.

The opponents of the League of Nations were doing nothing, by comparison. *Harvey's Weekly* was fighting valiantly week after week, and a few Senators had delivered a few speeches here and there outside Washington. There had been a couple of mass meetings in the Middle West. They had the support of a few powerful newspapers, including the *Chicago Tribune* and the Hearst chain.

They had no grass-roots strength. They seemed to face utter defeat unless they launched a high-powered campaign—posters, pamphlets, stump tours, mass meetings. Yet they had no funds to support such a campaign. They had nothing to match the thousands of dollars pouring in to the League to Enforce Peace in small amounts from thousands of supporters all over the land.

The men tried to think of a way to raise some fast money. It appeared hopeless. Many sources and schemes were proposed, but all were rejected as impractical.

Late at night, the meeting started to break up when Colonel Harvey remarked that he had to return to New York early the next day to attend a dinner at the home of Henry Clay Frick, the steel multimillionaire.

Senator Knox suggested that Colonel Harvey appeal to Frick for financial aid. He said he believed Frick would support the fight against the League of Nations, if it was put to him properly. Knox promised he would approach Andrew Mellon, if Harvey managed to obtain a contribution from Frick. The vast coal, coke, iron, steel, and banking enterprises of Frick and Mellon were represented by Knox's law firm in Pittsburgh, and the Senator explained that the two financiers often acted together in public affairs.

Colonel Harvey agreed to tackle Frick.

May 22, 1919. "A Crazy Thing to Do"

The dinner at Henry Clay Frick's was in honor of General Leonard Wood—strong candidate for the Republican nomination for the presidency in 1920. Forty of New York's most famous men were present.

Colonel Harvey lingered when the other guests began to depart, and soon he was alone with Frick, and soon they were talking about the League of Nations.

"Those whom I come into contact with seem to feel that this country ought to join and I am being constantly urged to support the movement," said the sixty-nine-year-old steel king. "But the fact is that I have been so busy of late that I haven't followed the discussion as closely probably as I ought. I went to the opera house and listened to the President and Mr. Taft and I must confess that, while Mr. Taft's speech seemed to me very good, Mr. Wilson's was not convincing. I should like to hear the other side if there is one, and I judge from the little I have read about it that there is."

Colonel Harvey proceeded to set forth the "stock arguments" as succinctly as he could. Frick interposed many questions, and finally said:

"As I understand it, then, the proposition is to pledge the United States, now the richest and most powerful nation in the world, to pool its issues with other countries, which are largely its debtors, and to agree in advance to abide by the policies and practices adopted by a majority or two-thirds of its associates; that is, to surrender its present right of independence of action upon any specific question whenever such a question may arise."

Colonel Harvey must have known the Covenant backwards and forwards. He must have known that under its provisions the United States would have to abide by no policies and practices determined against its own wishes—since important decisions could be reached only with the unanimous approval of all member nations. Yet he replied: "That is substantially it."

"Well, I am opposed to that!" exclaimed Frick. "Of course I am. I don't see how any experienced business man could fail to be. Why, it seems to me a crazy thing to do!"

"That is what Senator Knox and the rest of us think. Now the question is, will you help us to beat it?"

Colonel Harvey frankly told about the meeting at Senator Brandegee's house, and Frick wanted to know why Senator Knox thought he should be approached ahead of Mellon. "Come now, do you consider that a compliment or a reflection?" he demanded.

"Oh, a compliment surely," said Harvey. "In fact, my only objection was that Mr. Mellon might feel aggrieved."

"I don't think you need to worry about that," chuckled Frick. "I'll go along. How much do you want?"

The Colonel named a sum.

"That won't go far."

"Only for a starter of course," shot Harvey.

It was agreed. Colonel Harvey joyfully shook Frick's hand. He had walked to the door, and had his hand on the knob, when he heard a patter of footsteps and Frick came running after him. The old man's eyes gleamed and he raised an admonishing finger.

"Be sure you put up a good fight," he cried. "Now that we are in, we must win, you know!"

May 25, 1919. "It Was Both Deep and Full"

Henry Clay Frick sent a large check to the men fighting the League of Nations, and Colonel Harvey proudly notified Senator Knox of his success.

"Thanks for your note," replied Senator Knox. "I had already received a letter from Mr. Frick announcing what he had done and I wrote to Pittsburgh and obtained the same amount from Mr. Mellon. I told Medill today and he says he can now go to Chicago and raise about twenty."

The sum put up by Frick and matched by Mellon remains unrevealed. A hint, at least, of its dimensions is contained in a story involving Senator Boies Penrose, the Pennsylvania colleague of Senator Knox. Penrose went to Mellon one day in the midst of another campaign, and said, "We've got to have $250,000 to make this fight."

"Can't you get along with $150,000?" asked Mellon.

"Oh, I suppose I can if I have to."

Mellon gave Penrose a check for $150,000, and later in the day boasted to a friend, "Well, I just made $100,000!"

The financial worries of the opponents of the League of Nations were definitely over.

"The desired reservoir had been found and it was both deep and full," commented Colonel Harvey. "All anxiety respecting sinews of war was dispelled. Rejoicing pervaded the camp of the Irreconcilables, efforts were redoubled all along the line and the redoubtable little band pushed on. . . ."

May 26, 1919.
Scapegoat No. 4—"A Colored League of Nations"

Senator Jim Reed of Missouri stood in the Senate chamber and brandished a chart in the faces of the Southern Democrats.

"Ninety per cent of them are a mixture of Negroes and Spanish mulattoes!" he stormed. "Yet, you men of the South, you lily-whites, you gentlemen who say that white men alone should control in your own states are willing to allow this meagre population, ninety per cent of whom are Negroes and mulattoes . . . to have a vote equal to the total vote of the United States in the League of Nations.

"Go back to your people and justify yourselves if you can!"

Jim Reed was a grim man with tight, thin lips, a sallow face, and a rough thatch of gray hair. He usually wore a white jacket, and a flowy, old-fashioned, polka dot tie. Frankly a demagogue, he admitted to intimates that whenever he spoke on a controversial matter he saw red and tinctured his utterances with gall and bitterness.

"This is a colored League of Nations!" he shouted, consulting his chart and asserting that Brazil, Bolivia, Siam, Haiti, and thirteen other proposed members of the League of Nations were conglomerates of "black, yellow, brown and red races" and "mongrel breeds."

Senator Hitchcock leaped to his feet.

"It was the Senator from Missouri," he pointed out, "who made the statement that this was a league which was to be dominated by the British Empire."

"Exactly," snapped Senator Reed.

"Then he said it was going to be dominated by the monarchs of Europe and Asia," persisted Hitchcock. "Now he says it is going to be dominated by the little half-baked countries that he is proceeding to name."

"Oh, Mr. President—"

"I should like to know which the Senator means."

"Well, I will tell the Senator where I stand," replied Reed, "and he will find that I am standing on the rock of truth. . . ."

While Senator Hitchcock fumed in his seat, Senator Reed yelled:

". . . when the members of the League of Nations meet about the council table there will be fifteen men representing white nations and seventeen men representing black, brown, yellow and red races. . . ."

The Gentleman from Missouri proceeded to inform the Senate that if the United States entered the League of Nations it would thus deliver itself into the hands of "the depraved, the wicked, the vicious." He described his seventeen "dark" nations one by one—Liberia was a "joke nation" inhabited by cannibals, Haiti was a nation of "baby murderers," the Siamese were a "degenerate" race.

Instead of predicting that the "cannibals" and the "mongrels" would control the League of Nations by voting together, Senator Reed concentrated his fire on the unanimity provision of the Covenant.

". . . the Negro Republic of Haiti can cast a vote that will block the machinery of the League," he protested, ". . . the United States with its population of 110,000,000 is given no greater voting strength than the smallest of the nations concerned."

Senator Hitchcock rose again: "I ask the Senator whether he did not complain on a former occasion that the United States was going into an enterprise where the majority might decide against it?"

Senator Reed: "Yes."

Senator Hitchcock: "And is not the Senator here now condemning the League because it requires a unanimous vote?"

Senator Reed: ". . . I condemn any league—"

Senator Hitchcock: "I guess that is right."

Senator Reed: "—that proposes to put the vital interests of the United States within the power of a majority of foreigners. . . ."

Senator Hitchcock lapsed into hopeless silence.

Senator Reed switched from "black" to "yellow," and turned from the Southerners to the Westerners. He warned them that the "Yellow Peril" would flood our shores if we joined the League of Nations:

"If you erect a league of nations you will have taken a long step toward a declaration that American doors shall be opened to the peoples of all lands and we shall have Chinese and Japanese knocking at our gates, and along with them all the races of Asia. . . ."

June 7, 1919. "I Don't Care Who Gets the Credit"

Most Democratic supporters of the League of Nations, and a good many Republican supporters, were becoming convinced that the primary reason for Henry Cabot Lodge's opposition was his fear that success for the League of Nations would sweep Woodrow Wilson back to the White House for a third term in the 1920 elections.

William Howard Taft was waging a valiant fight against the tendency among many Republicans to go along with Lodge in his demands for amendments. The trend was developing even among Republicans who favored the League of Nations; they felt it would be a political disaster if Wilson led the United States into it—unless it was so revised by Republicans that it became partly their own.

William Howard Taft seemed violently opposed to this partisan position. The former President was working as hard as any American for the Covenant.

Morning papers all over the country carried an article by him in favor of the plan for peace.

At lunch, he told the Albany Chamber of Commerce that the League of Nations was not Wilson's but the world's: "I don't care who gets the credit for the League of Nations if it goes through."

In the evening, Taft appeared before the New York State Ratifying Convention called by the League to Enforce Peace. There he declared: "We should be for or against the League without respect to whether we are Democrats or Republicans. We should be for or against the League without regard to whether we think it will bring credit to our party or credit to any man. Personal and partisan considerations of this kind are reasons which should have no influence with us in determining an issue so fateful in the world's history and so likely to affect the future welfare of the people of the United States and of all mankind.

"When, therefore, you come to consider the question whether you are in favor of the treaty or not, you should search your hearts and souls and your consciences to see whether you are approaching it in the proper patriotic and humane spirit, or whether you are against it because Mr. Wilson is for it and you may fear that he will gain credit for its adoption, or because you may suppose that his party may gain party credit for it. These are small reasons for supporting or opposing the League."

June 9, 1919.
Germany, the *Chicago Tribune,* and Senator Borah

Excitement mounted day by day over Hiram Johnson's resolution demanding that the Versailles Treaty be produced. Senator Borah enlivened the debate with a sinister charge that "special interests" in New York possessed a copy—even if the Senate did not. Lodge chimed in to declare he had actually seen a copy in Manhattan.

A Special Senate Investigating Committee was established to find out how any copy had reached this country. The Senate finally passed the Johnson resolution—after adding the customary "if not incompatible with the public interest" clause. Wilson was notified at once, and now Senator Hitchcock stood up to read to the Senate this cabled reply from the President:

"I HAVE FELT THAT IT WAS HIGHLY UNDESIRABLE OFFICIALLY TO COM-

MUNICATE THE TEXT OF A DOCUMENT WHICH IS STILL IN NEGOTIATION AND SUBJECT TO CHANGE. ANYONE WHO HAS POSSESSION OF THE OFFICIAL ENGLISH TEXT HAS WHAT HE IS CLEARLY NOT ENTITLED TO HAVE OR TO COMMUNICATE. I HAVE FELT AS HONOR BOUND TO ACT IN THE SAME SPIRIT AND IN THE SAME WAY AS THE REPRESENTATIVES OF THE OTHER GREAT POWERS IN THIS MATTER, AND AM CONFIDENT THAT MY FELLOW COUNTRYMEN WILL NOT EXPECT ME TO BREAK FAITH WITH THEM."

Hitchcock sat down, and Borah stood up.

"I have in my possession this morning a copy of the treaty, which I am going to ask permission of the Senate to print as a Senate document," Borah announced dramatically, waving a sheaf of papers at the startled Senate. "I am permitted to make this treaty public by the consent of those who gave it to me. The particular copy which I am offering this morning was brought to this country by Mr. Frazier Hunt, the staff correspondent of the *Chicago Tribune*."

The German peace delegates had let the text leak out in the hope of stirring up opposition to it.

The *Chicago Tribune* had procured a copy.

And now Senator Borah sought to make it public by asking that it be printed by the Senate.

Senator Thomas of Colorado promptly objected.

One objection was enough to block Borah's request, but he and his delighted friends were determined to release the text of the treaty. There was a parliamentary scramble, with heated debate over the propriety of releasing the text in the face of the President's message revealing his pledge to the Allies. "Pro-German!" shouted several Senators at several other Senators. Senator Brandegee sat at his desk in the midst of the melee for a while, and then thoughtfully got up and suggested that Borah's copy should be compared to copies in the State Department to establish its authenticity.

Borah grinned at Brandegee, and started to read the copy in his hands as prima facie evidence of its validity. Senator Swanson tried to stop him by raising a point of order.

"The Senator says he lays before the Senators a treaty," he said, and he quoted a Senate rule requiring that all treaties laid before the Senate must be kept secret until the Senate votes otherwise.

"I don't contend that this instrument is a signed treaty which has been transmitted to the Senate by anyone," bellowed Borah. "I claim that it is a copy of the proposed treaty . . . which has not yet been signed either by the German Government or by anyone else so as to constitute it in any sense a treaty as referred to by the rule."

After a long, acrimonious debate on this fine point, the Senate voted 42 to 24 that Borah was not breaking the rule.

Borah started to read again. Senator Phelan of California brought him to a halt with a reference to another rule. He said Borah was violating it by speaking more than twice on the same matter without permission. More wrangling. The Senate decided Borah had spoken only once on his "proposed treaty." Borah read on.

The pile of papers on Borah's desk indicated that the treaty was surprisingly long. There was some whispering and gesticulating; it looked like it would take Borah two or three weeks to read the whole thing. Some were for letting him keep at it, but Senator Knute Nelson of Minnesota got up and suggested that the Senate reconsider the motion denying Borah the privilege of simply printing the "proposed treaty." A vote was taken, and the motion carried, 41 to 26.

The proposed Versailles Treaty was printed as a Senate document, and became available to the world.

President Wilson's agreement with the Allies was broken.

June 20, 1919. Scapegoat No. 5—Catholicism

Senator Lawrence Y. Sherman devoted the afternoon to telling his colleagues that he had ferreted out a fate worse than war concealed in the Covenant.

Vice President Marshall once said: "Senator Sherman had none of the graces of polite society, but he had a tongue swung in the middle and sharp as a Damascus blade."

Wildly waving his Damascus blade, the little Gentleman from

Illinois went shrieking after the Pope. He undertook to prove that His Holiness would rule the League of Nations.

Sherman prefaced his remarks by solemnly stating that he was not a member of any church, and that his motives were high, patriotic, and unselfish. "I shall have criticism. I shall bear it," he said with a brave and noble air. "I shall be maligned. I shall endure it."

In contrast to Senator Reed's list of 32 members of the League of Nations—17 of them colored, Senator Sherman produced a list of 40 members of the League of Nations—24 of them Catholic.

He submitted his list as proof that the Vatican would run the League of Nations. He warned that the Holy Father would probably try to enforce Catholicism on the world: "The temptation to enforce that belief might break down every barrier built up by centuries of struggle and sacrifice," he cried. "Shall the United States commit itself to the mercy of a power from which our ancestors delivered us? ... The Covenant of the League of Nations bears within its folds a reactionary power more fatal and insidious than a Prussian helmet, more dangerous than future war!"

Picturing a scheming Pope sitting in the Holy City and spinning a web around the world, Sherman shouted: "I believe it a matter of profound apprehension that one man at the head of a great religious organization controls ... or seeks to control the conduct of the delegates of the twenty-four member nations. And this power is proposed to govern the world!"

Senator Sherman had a habit of setting up the Holy Father as a straw man and then knocking him down. Once he had inserted an article in the Congressional Record accusing the Pope of having a secret understanding with the Kaiser. Now he pounced upon the fact that Woodrow Wilson had visited the Pope while in Rome as proof that Wilson (usually ridiculed as a dull-witted Scotch-Presbyterian) was up to something sinister.

"While the evidence is circumstantial," said Sherman darkly, "it all tends to connect President Wilson with influences ... inimical to the future welfare of the United States."

June 21, 1919. "In Expectation of Getting an Invitation"

The scapegoating expeditions into fertile fields of prejudice and passion, staged every now and then by Senators Sherman and Reed and men like them, were a vital part of the fight against the League of Nations. But the crucial campaign was the drive to revise the Covenant. It was to this that Lodge devoted all his time and talent.

Following his private meeting with Borah on the day the amended Covenant was made public, Lodge conferred with other Senators who were in open and absolute opposition to the League of Nations. All agreed to support amendments and reservations, even though they would vote against the Covenant in the end no matter how many of their amendments and reservations were accepted.

Senator Lodge also went after the support of those who were not in outright opposition to the Covenant. The same day that he conferred with Borah, he both wrote and telephoned to Elihu Root, who became the center of a struggle between pro-League and anti-League Republicans. Executive Chairman A. Lawrence Lowell of the League to Enforce Peace wrote to Root pointing out that most of the amendments he had suggested had been put into the Covenant, and declaring: "The lesser Republicans over the country are holding back, waiting for direction; and if you, who have more influence than any other man, were to come out and say that the Covenant as amended is now satisfactory, they would fall in behind you in crowds, for they are timid and waiting for direction."

For a time the Republican Party seemed in danger of falling apart over the League of Nations issue. Twenty-eight prominent party members, including two former Cabinet members, a Governor, and the President of the New York Chamber of Commerce, united in a protest to the Senate against "political partisanship" in the consideration of the merits of the Covenant. They urged that "treaty and Covenant be promptly ratified by the Senate without attempting to embarrass it by amendment."

Senator Borah promptly warned that if the Republican Party wouldn't fight the League of Nations, a new party would be formed for the purpose. Elihu Root finally made up his mind.

Around noon on this day, some reporters spotted him in the Senate wing of the Capitol. They surrounded him and wanted to know what he was up to. He said he had come "in expectation of getting an invitation to luncheon from some Senatorial friends."

He got the invitation. He lunched with Senators Lodge, Knox, and Brandegee.

June 22, 1919. The Root Reservations

A very clever letter was composed by Root, Lodge, Knox, and Brandegee at the luncheon. It was addressed to Lodge, and it was signed by Root, and it was published in the morning newspapers.

The letter appealed to supporters of the League of Nations, stating that the Covenant contained "a great deal of value that the world ought not to lose." Then it appealed to opponents of the League of Nations, parroting George Washington concerning "entangling alliances." And then it demanded reservations.

Root proposed that instead of actually revising the Covenant by amendments, the Senate simply write a resolution of ratification containing reservations. The reservations would interpret the Covenant as far as we were concerned; they would limit America's participation in the League of Nations.

This didn't sound like revising the Covenant at all, and it made the whole thing a bit obscure and difficult to grasp. Yet, actually, it was a proposal that we enter the League of Nations on our own terms—terms different from those applying to any other nation.

Root suggested that the United States refuse consent to Article 10—although he had suggested no such thing in March when he submitted his amendments to the State Department. He also said there should be no qualification of our right to withdraw from the League of Nations. And then, in what amounted to a demand that America go America's way without any international considerations of any sort, he urged a reservation stating that nothing in the Covenant "shall be construed as to imply a relinquishment by the United States of America of its traditional attitude toward purely American questions, or to require the submission of its policy regarding questions which it deems to be purely American questions to the decision or recommendation of other powers."

The letter was a huge victory for Lodge. He wrote a chipper note to Henry White: "Root's letter has consolidated feeling in the Senate and is producing immense effect upon public opinion throughout the country."

Charles Evans Hughes and other prominent Republicans endorsed Root's proposals. Will Hays, Chairman of the Republican National Committee, said Root had turned "what threatened to be a Republican liability into a Republican achievement."

Taft bluntly asserted that Root's switch from his position of March was "indefensible."

Republicans commenced wondering what to do about the errant Taft.

June 25, 1919.
"Reservations Will Put the United States . . . Out"

Europe was on the brink of a new bloodletting the day Root's letter was published in the United States. Forces under Marshal Foch were poised for a strike across the Rhine into a Germany apparently determined to defy the world.

And then the Germans capitulated.

The Allies were waiting for a German delegation to arrive in Paris to sign the Versailles Treaty as word came of the Root reservations. Wilson had been busy resisting last minute efforts by several nations to get amendments into the treaty; he was so convinced that the negotiating and the bargaining and the bickering must come to a halt that he even opposed modifications of provisions he disliked.

He took a firm stand against the Root demands, wiring Tumulty:

"MY CLEAR CONVICTION IS THAT THE ADOPTION OF THE TREATY BY THE SENATE WITH RESERVATIONS WILL PUT THE UNITED STATES AS CLEARLY OUT OF THE CONCERT OF NATIONS AS A REJECTION. WE OUGHT EITHER TO

GO IN OR STAY OUT. TO STAY OUT WOULD BE FATAL TO THE INFLUENCE AND EVEN TO THE COMMERCIAL PROSPECTS OF THE UNITED STATES, AND TO GO IN WOULD GIVE HER A LEADING PLACE IN THE AFFAIRS OF THE WORLD. RESERVATIONS WOULD EITHER MEAN NOTHING OR POSTPONE THE CONCLUSION OF PEACE, SO FAR AS AMERICA IS CONCERNED, UNTIL EVERY OTHER PRINCIPAL NATION CONCERNED IN THE TREATY HAD FOUND OUT BY NEGOTIATION WHAT THE RESERVATIONS PRACTICALLY MEANT AND WHETHER THEY COULD ASSOCIATE THEMSELVES WITH THE UNITED STATES ON THE TERMS OF THE RESERVATIONS OR NOT."

June 28, 1919. "The Treaty of Peace Has Been Signed . . ."

Cannons started to boom all around Paris in the middle of the afternoon.

The salute spread to all French cities, and then to forts and battleships all over the world.

The men and the women and the children of the world celebrated all over again, but there was a sad note of restraint mingled with the brave hope in the opening words of the message the President of the United States sent to the American people on this day of days:

"The treaty of peace has been signed. If it is ratified and acted upon in full and sincere execution of its terms it will furnish the charter for a new order of affairs in the world."

A *New York Times* correspondent scoured Capitol Hill in Washington without finding a single Republican Senator who did not think the Versailles Treaty would have to be revised.

July 4, 1919. To Soldiers and Sailors on the High Seas

The President of the United States was midway between the Old World and the New World when the soldiers and sailors who were aboard the *U.S.S. George Washington* gathered with him to celebrate Independence Day.

There on the sea and under the sun, the President stood on the after hatch and spoke to them of freedom.

"Some people talk as if liberty meant the right to do anything you please," he said. "Well, in some sense you have that right. You have the right to jump overboard. . . . You can jump off the top of the mast, but when you get down your liberty will be lost. . . .

"The sailor, when he is sailing a ship, talks about her running free in the wind. Does he mean that she is resisting the wind? Throw her up into the wind and see the canvas shake, see her stand still, 'caught in irons,' as the sailor says. But let her fall off: she is free. Free, why? Because she is obeying the laws of nature, and she is a slave until she does. And no man is free who does not obey the laws of freedom.

"The laws of freedom are these: Accommodate your interests to other people's interests, that you shall not insist on standing in the light of other people, but that you shall make a member of a team of yourself and nothing more or less, and that the interests of the team shall take precedence in everything that you do to your interest as an individual."

President Wilson let his gaze wander from the soldiers and sailors to the Stars and Stripes flying high on the mast, and he said:

"This is the most tremendous Fourth of July that men ever imagined, for we have opened its franchises to all the world."

July 8, 1919. "American Blood to Subdue Ireland!"

The campaign by the opponents of the League of Nations was gathering strength on the eve of Woodrow Wilson's return to America.

Senator Hiram Johnson was in Boston to speak at a meeting under the auspices of a new organization called The League for the Preservation of American Independence. The affair was lavishly advertised in Boston newspapers, with slogans like these:

"AMERICANS, AWAKE!"

"SHALL WE BIND OURSELVES TO THE WAR BREEDING COVENANT?"

"THE EVIL THING WITH THE HOLY NAME!"

"FLOUTS WASHINGTON'S WARNING!"

Hiram Johnson was in the prime of life, and he was full of fire. His clear gray eyes and stiff, short, gray hair combined with his square jaw and his solemn manner to give an awesome impression of power. Masterful, demanding, he went after the support of the Boston Irish.

Singling out Article 10 for attack, he shouted: "Under this article the British Empire can demand American blood to subdue Ireland!"

Thousands of Irish throats roared a thundering protest.

Hiram Johnson waved and bowed, and hurried away toward Providence, Rhode Island, to deliver another tirade.

July 9, 1919. "The Heart and Purpose of This People"

"To the shouting, flag waving crowd it was not only the President coming home, it was the crowning incident of the war. . . ." said the *New York Tribune* of the greeting given Woodrow Wilson.

"They saw in him the symbol of the victory and the peace, therefore the children shouted and white haired women leaned from the boardinghouse windows with tears streaming down their cheeks to throw him a 'God bless you,' and soldiers in khaki straightened up with a salute which said they, too, had done their part to bring this day.

"Experienced persons said there had never been a demonstration like it."

Wilson rode up Fifth Avenue through the shouts and cheers, and told a thrilled throng at Carnegie Hall: "I have never had a moment's doubt as to where the heart and purpose of this people lay."

At the end of his short speech, he was nearly overwhelmed by a rush of persons to the platform seeking to shake his hand or touch his coat.

July 10, 1919. "Soap Bubbles of Oratory"

The President held a press conference at the White House in the morning, and he tried to tell the reporters why he opposed reservations.

He said that they "presented a grave difficulty in that every nation joining the League would have to assent to them, and while this slow process was going on the United States would be at war with Germany." He said he believed that "even what seemed to be innocuous amendments or reservations may cause great trouble, since it can never be stated that other nations will view a point as this country would. There were occasions at Paris when every other nation took a view opposite to the American commissioners."

At noon Wilson went up on Capitol Hill to lay the Versailles Treaty before the Senate. He avoided details in his address, but he said: "My services and all the information I possess will be at your disposal and at the disposal of your Committee on Foreign Relations at any time, either informally or in session, as you may prefer; and I hope that you will not hesitate to make use of them."

He spoke of the future, of the role America could play in the world if she maintained the great position she had won, a position which only her own action could blemish or destroy.

"The stage is set, the destiny disclosed," he said. "It has come about by no plan of our conceiving; but by the hand of God who led us into this way. We cannot turn back. We can only go forward, with lifted eyes and freshened spirit to follow the vision. It was of this that we dreamed at our birth. America shall in truth show the way. The light streams down the path ahead, and nowhere else."

Only a handful of men on the Republican side of the Senate, led by Porter McCumber of North Dakota, joined in the applause. The others stayed silent. Some did not rise to their feet as Wilson left.

There was a meeting at once in the cloakrooms. Lodge called in a number of the irreconcilables, including Borah, Brandegee, Fall, and McCormick. When the meeting broke up, and reporters caught them in the corridors, they all had pat little comments to make on the President's message.

"Soap bubbles of oratory and soufflé of phrases," snapped Brandegee.

"Soothing, mellifluous and uninformative," added McCormick.

"Utterly lacking in ringing Americanism," said Warren G. Harding.

Senator Truman Newberry said he was interested in the President's English, but disappointed in his advice.

July 11, 1919. "A Pity It Isn't Likely to Live"

A survey of the press by the League to Enforce Peace showed that in one week, 1100 out of 1200 editorials on the League of Nations were in favor of it.

The great majority of the American people wanted the treaty passed "at once," admitted Elihu Root in a letter to Adelbert Moot of Boston. Root added that the Senate should not be guided by ignorant popular sentiment, however.

Judge printed a cartoon showing Wilson in bed, a nurse holding the infant League of Nations, and two elderly statesmen looking at it anxiously. Said one, "What a lovely child!" Said the other, "Yes, a pity it isn't likely to live."

July 12, 1919. A Council of War

The Washington correspondent of the *New York Tribune* reported: "Republican members of the Senate Foreign Relations Committee at a meeting tonight discussed plans for their fight on the peace treaty and the League of Nations."

July 13, 1919. "Lines Were Consolidated"

The *New York Tribune* correspondent sent another report from the Washington battle front:

"Republican lines were consolidated in a dozen scattered conferences today at the houses of various Senate leaders."

July 15, 1919.
The Packing of the Foreign Relations Committee

Chairman Henry Cabot Lodge called the Foreign Relations Committee to order at ten o'clock in the morning, in Room 310 of the Senate Office Building.

The Foreign Relations Committee could attempt to smother the Versailles Treaty, simply by failing to send it out to the Senate. However, Chairman Lodge had determined to depend on amendments and reservations at TR's bedside way back in 1918, and by the time the Versailles Treaty came before his committee, he knew that it would be impossible to kill it in committee anyway. The Senate, by a majority vote, could order his committee to relinquish the Versailles Treaty if he tried to bottle it up—and the Senate would do so, since a majority favored the treaty.

The Gentleman from Massachusetts was in no hurry. He needed more time to gain support in the Senate and in the country for the revision of the treaty. And so he calmly told the members of the committee that he was going to read the entire Versailles Treaty to them before they started to consider it. This would consume at least two weeks of valuable time, but the pro-League members of the committee were unable to force Lodge to start action on the treaty at once.

By painstaking parliamentary moves, Lodge had gained control of a majority of the committee.

The party membership of Senate committees must be in proportion to the party membership of the Senate. In the Sixty-fifth Congress, controlled by a wide Democratic majority, there had been 10 Democrats on the Foreign Relations Committee, and only 7 Republicans.

Now, however, there were 48 Republicans, 47 Democrats, and 1 Progressive in the Senate. This narrow margin would have justified a proportion of 9 to 8 in the committee. But Senator McCumber, Republican of North Dakota, was a member of the committee, and his presence threatened Lodge's control of the Republican membership. Lodge therefore insisted that *both* minority parties deserved representation on the committee—and Hiram Johnson, whose party label was Progressive, was given a seat. Naturally, his seat was taken from the Democrats, not from the Republicans. That left 7 Democratic seats, against 9 Republicans.

Two of the old Democratic members of the committee were no longer in the Senate, and Joe Robinson of Arkansas was ousted from the committee to make way for Hiram Johnson. The remaining Democrats were all left-overs from the last session—ex-Chairman Hitchcock, John Sharp Williams of Mississippi, Claude Swanson of Virginia, Attlee Pomerene of Ohio, Key Pittman of Nevada, and John Shields of Tennessee. There were six Republican left-overs—Lodge, McCumber, Borah, Brandegee, Fall, and Knox. Thus the Republicans were able to appoint three new members.

It is considered a Senate honor to sit on the Foreign Relations Committee, and memberships are generally handed out as rewards for long and faithful service. Lodge, determined that only men who would follow his leadership should get the Republican seats, forced the appointment of George H. Moses of New Hampshire, outspokenly against the League of Nations, Harry S. New of Indiana, a professional politician whose gospel was party regularity, and Warren G. Harding of Ohio.

This almost broke the heart of Frank Kellogg of Minnesota, Senate veteran who was deeply interested in foreign affairs. Taft was outraged. Declaring he had hoped for non-partisanship in the Senate consideration of the League of Nations, he bluntly charged:

"It is unfortunate that this action of the Republican committee on committees in the Senate should give color to a different view by a provision that the Foreign Relations Committee should have Republicans enough to give them a majority without the vote of Mr. McCumber, known to be favorable to the treaty, and by a careful selection of Republicans for that majority whose opposition to the treaty has been pronounced. Senator Kellogg would naturally have been taken before Senator Moses, a new Senator, and one whose term expires in two years. Senator Kellogg, however, had ventured to make a speech in favor of a league of nations, even before the Covenant was agreed upon, and had refused to sign the 'round robin.' "

Another Senator who had longed for a seat on the Foreign Relations Committee was Le Baron Colt of Rhode Island. He had been a member of the Senate since 1913, and was Chairman of the Senate Committee on Immigration. One evening, dining at the Shoreham Hotel in Washington with an official of the League to Enforce Peace, he discussed the three new members of Lodge's committee:

"They are committed against the treaty," he said in a quiet, deliberate tone. "The new men were carefully picked and made their promises in advance. I was asked to take a place on the committee, but the condition was that I oppose the League of Nations and the treaty.

"I declined to commit myself to any attitude toward a document which I had not seen because it did not exist. So I am just Chairman of the Committee on Immigration, but I am not bound regarding this proposal to establish world order, which is certainly the most important matter this generation has to decide."

The Covenant of the League of Nations was in the hands of men committed to destroy it.

July 17, 1919. Arthur H. Vandenberg's Editorial

William Howard Taft had been the object of an intensive campaign by his fellow-Republicans for some time.

He was the most important supporter of the League of Nations in the party, and it was generally agreed that if he could be persuaded to come out for revision, revision would be inevitable.

Taft had taken a position against further revision of the Covenant after it was amended in Paris in accordance with his suggestions. Early in the summer, a pamphlet written by him and released by the League to Enforce Peace declared that revisions would have to be submitted to other nations, and warned:

"Upon those who insist that substantial amendments must be made to the treaty will therefore fall the responsibility for the indefinite postponement of peace which unconditional ratification of the treaty will at once bring about."

Apparently, however, the former President did not grasp the real character of Lodge's campaign. Like most Americans, he did not seem to understand that Lodge would turn every offer of reservations to his own advantage by demanding more, and still more—until revision brought rejection.

For Senator Spencer of Missouri called the attention of the Senate to a startling editorial in the *Grand Rapids Herald*. It revealed that Taft was privately in favor of reservations, and it hinted that Taft might openly swing his support to the reservationists.

The editorial was signed by Arthur H. Vandenberg, a large, round-faced young man who was little known nationally but who, at thirty-five, was managing editor of the *Herald* and a Republican power in Michigan. Vandenberg declared that when Taft had visited Grand Rapids on a speaking tour arranged by the League to Enforce Peace, the *Herald* had sought his "consent to Senate reservations which should officially tell the world that America will always insist upon just such interpretations as he (and other proponents like him) declares, unofficially, to be appropriate."

Editor Vandenberg revealed that in due time a letter had come from Taft saying: "I send you a suggested series of resolutions which might easily be transformed into reservations."

Taft's suggestions covered the old bugaboos. One concerned Article 10, limiting its application as far as the United States was concerned; others dealt with the protection of the Monroe Doctrine, and domestic matters.

Stated Arthur H. Vandenberg: "If such reservations as these meet with Mr. Taft's approval, Mr. Taft and the *Herald* are at last in concert regarding the proper action which should be taken by the United States Senate."

The young editor made no secret of his own opinion of the Covenant. He said: "In each of these important instances, the Covenant can be construed two diametrically opposite ways; one way, safe for the United States; the other way, absolutely subvertive of perpetuated independent American Government."

He was not quite satisfied with Taft's proposals. He suggested another reservation making it clear that America, and America alone, would decide whether or not she had lived up to her international obligations if she wanted to withdraw from the League of Nations.

Editor Vandenberg did not seem at all impressed by the argument that insistence on American reservations would delay and perhaps destroy the peace. He ignored the likelihood that other nations would be unwilling to welcome the United States into the League of Nations on our own terms unless we permitted them to attach all their own reservations to the Covenant. He simply said:

"Advocates of the League insist . . . that the League Covenant is 'safe for the United States,' because, say they, it does not mean just what these reservations say it means. How, then, can they hope to successfully argue against permitting the Senate to say so officially . . . ?

"If the Covenant does not mean what these reservations declare . . . then the League is not safe for the United States and should not be accepted. . . . If the Covenant does not mean these things, then it does mean that our children may be called to fight the foreign wars of all the world without any right of independent American decision as required by our Constitution; and it does mean that we are transferring sovereign authority over our own immigration laws and our own tariffs and our own Monroe Doctrine to an Old World from which we have been successfully independent for one hundred and forty-three years.

"It would be suicidal negligence to ratify the Covenant without making these moot points clear, without protecting ourselves while we are yet free agents in the world. On the other hand, with these reservations declared, it would be rank provincialism not to participate in the League experiment for the sake of the great peace and good it may be made to accomplish within its legitimate sphere."

July 18, 1919. The Meetings at the White House

It was learned in Washington that Wilson was making a forthright effort to persuade Republican Senators who were friendly to the League of Nations that insistence on reservations threatened the whole structure of the peace.

He was conferring quietly at the White House with mild reservationists like Cummins, Colt, and McNary. Seven had been invited to the White House, one after the other, in two days. Borah hotly denounced these "secret conferences."

Wilson surprised his visitors by failing to defend all the details of the Covenant and the treaty. When they mentioned things like the Shantung settlement, he simply said it could not be helped, that it was the best he could get.

He did not object to the proposed reservations on their merits. He said he would have fought for them if they had been proposed while he was in Paris working on the treaty with all the other nations. But, he said, now it was too late. He dwelt on the dangers involved in opening up the Covenant to reservations—because if we insisted on making some of our own other nations would insist on making some of their own. He told the Senators how the other nations had pressed for amendments, when he had pressed for some in response to American demands.

He warned that insistence on American reservations might very well upset the delicate balance of conflicting interests achieved at the Peace Conference only after weary months of negotiations. The result, he said, might be appalling chaos. On the other hand, the League of Nations provided a way to accomplish a gradual, orderly readjustment of any wrongs written into the treaty.

According to the *New York Tribune,* the violent opponents of the League of Nations were "bitterly disappointed" when their colleagues came back to Capitol Hill from the White House and reported Wilson's attitude. The newspaper explained:

"They had been eager to drive the President to oppose the reservations on their merits, believing they could quickly convince the country they were right in any such controversy."

July 21, 1919. "This Is the Way"

There was no evidence that Wilson was getting anywhere with his visitors. To the contrary, screamed Hearst's *New York Journal* in huge headlines:

"SENATE HAS 35 AGAINST TREATY AS IT STANDS."

If that was true, Senator Lodge had enough votes to compel revision. A maximum of 34 votes was all it would take to vote down the Versailles Treaty in its present form.

Two supporters of the League of Nations paid a visit to Senator Lodge in his office. They were Allen T. Burns, President of the National Conference of Social Work, and James G. McDonald, Chairman of the League of Free Nations Association.

Lodge was amazingly frank. These men were not his Senate tools; they were the heads of powerful, nationwide groups of Americans who earnestly desired the League of Nations. Yet this is the report of their interview, as told later by Mr. Burns to the *Springfield Republican:*

"In our discussion of the treaty situation with Senator Lodge he summarized his attitude and purpose in the following manner: Taking from the shelves of the foreign relations committee room a copy of the general arbitration treaty with Great Britain negotiated by President Taft in 1911, the chairman pointed out the amendments and reservations made by the Senate. Exultingly he remarked: 'And President Taft never saw fit to return the treaty to Great Britain. We shall deal with the Versailles Treaty in the same way. If President Wilson does not see fit to return it to our allies that is his responsibility.' Then with a snap of his jaw and a bang of his fist, 'That is the way to handle such treaties!' "

Meanwhile, the fight went on in the Senate chamber. Senator Pomerene of Ohio scoffed at the men who pouted and stormed about the Monroe Doctrine. "Who does not know that we are nearer to Europe today than we were to Central and South America at the time the Monroe Doctrine was announced?" he demanded. "Who is not conscious of the fact that the dangers to the world peace and to our safety are in Europe today rather than in Central or South America? Why should we be so eager to assert our sovereignty over the Americas from which no evil has come to us, and at the same time blind ourselves to the dangers in Europe which well-nigh overcame the world?"

Like other supporters of the League of Nations, he frankly admitted its imperfections: "That it is not perfect all concede. That it would have been written differently if it had been drafted by the American nation alone there can be no doubt. And, may I add, if it had been left to the handiwork of each of the United States Senators, there would have been ninety-six different treaties. . . .

"If this treaty is rejected, what is to take its place?"

Several of the Senators sitting in the chamber were reading the afternoon newspapers while Senator Pomerene spoke. The papers announced that in England the House of Commons had approved the Versailles Treaty without amendment or reservation.

July 22, 1919. The Fearful Founding Fathers

Senator Beckham, Democrat of Kentucky, gave one of the finest speeches of the entire debate on this hot July afternoon. It was so humble and modest, so kindly, tolerant, generous, that it was soon overwhelmed and swept aside by the bombast of Borah, the spellbinding of Sherman. Yet it was never forgotten by those who stayed in the Senate to listen.

The Senator lauded those who saw perils for their country in the Covenant: "I have never for a moment in my mind doubted the sincerity and patriotism of those distinguished Senators who have different views from mine and who have on numerous occasions so ably and eloquently expressed their opposition to it."

Apologetically, he made it plain that he knew practically everything had been said about the League of Nations that could be said: "I can not indulge the hope of throwing any new light upon the subject or of producing any fact or argument that might change the opinion of anyone."

But he had been delving into the past, reading about the great patriots of the American Revolution and the early days of the Republic, and he had been surprised to find how alarmed the Founding Fathers had been about many of the provisions of the Constitution of the United States.

Perhaps, he said, some of the patriots of today had forgotten that even Thomas Jefferson had feared the Constitution and felt inclined to oppose it. Finally, though, on May 17, 1788, Jefferson had written, "There are, indeed, some faults, which revolted me a great deal in the first moment, but we must be contented to travel onward toward perfection step by step. We must be contented with the ground which this constitution will gain for us, and hope that a favorable moment will come for correcting what is amiss in it."

Ben Franklin, too, when he proposed unanimous adoption of the Constitution at Philadelphia, had said:

"I confess that there are several parts of this Constitution which I do not at present approve, but I am not sure I shall *never* approve them: But having lived long, I have experienced many instances of being obliged by better information or fuller consideration, to change opinions even on important subjects, which I once thought right, but found to be otherwise. . . .

"I doubt too whether any other convention we can obtain may be able to make a better Constitution. For when you assemble a number of men to have the advantage of their joint wisdom, you inevitably assemble with those men, all their prejudices, their passions, their errors of opinion, their local interests, and their selfish views. From such an Assembly can a perfect production be expected?

"Thus I consent, Sir, to this Constitution because I expect no better, and because I am not sure it is not the best. The opinions I have had of its errors, I sacrifice to the public good."

Some of the men hallowed in the story of our land had felt unable to heed the advice of Jefferson and Franklin.

"One of the most conspicuous and eloquent opponents was Patrick Henry," said Senator Beckham. "No one for a moment would ever question the patriotism and courage of that man, whose thrilling oratory first . . . set afire the spirit of independence in the Colonies.

And yet when the time came to make good that independence by the construction of the Thirteen States into a strong Federal Government no man fought more persistently or vigorously against it. He saw, so he thought, only danger and disaster if the Constitution should be adopted."

Thumbing through a life of Patrick Henry, Senator Beckham had found a vivid description of the moment when the Virginia patriot stood in the ratification convention of his state to oppose the Constitution "with that awful solemnity and look of fearful portent by which Mr. Henry could imply even more than he expressed and that slow, distinct, emphatic enunciation by which he never failed to move the souls of his hearers."

Patrick Henry had declared then: "I conceive the Republic to be in extreme danger; if our situation be thus uneasy, whence has arisen this fearful jeopardy? It arises from this fatal system; it arises from a proposal to change our government; a proposal that goes to the utter annihilation of the most solemn engagements of the States; a proposal of establishing . . . a confederacy to the eventual exclusion of our States. This proposal of altering our Federal Government is of a most alarming nature. Make the best of this new Government—say it is composed by anything but inspiration—you ought to be extremely cautious, watchful, jealous of your liberty; for instead of securing your rights you may lose them forever. If a wrong step be made now the Republic may be lost forever. If this new Government will not come up to the expectation of the people, and they shall be disappointed, their liberty will be lost, and tyranny must and will arise. I repeat it again, and I beg gentlemen to consider, that a wrong step made now will plunge us into misery and our Republic will be lost."

Senator Beckham put down the book containing the quotation from Patrick Henry, and he asked the Senate a question:

"Does not that remind us of some of the stirring eloquence to which we have listened on this floor in some speeches against the League of Nations?"

The fears of these Founding Fathers, shared by Monroe and many more, were never realized, Senator Beckham pointed out. The common sense of the people prevailed, and the Constitution was adopted; and as time went on its faults were remedied by amendment. Monroe even lived to become President under the Constitution he had opposed.

"And what would have happened if the solemn warnings had prevailed?" asked Senator Beckham. "Shall we now listen to the prophets of evil?"

July 24, 1919.
"His Motives Were Undoubtedly Good . . ."

Arthur H. Vandenberg's hint that Taft was coming over to the reservationists was confirmed with startling suddenness by the unauthorized publication of a confidential letter he had written to Will Hays.

It was revealed in an Associated Press dispatch that the Chairman of the Republican National Committee had received the text of some proposed reservations from Taft, accompanied by a letter stating that it seemed the better part of statesmanship to devise and accept reservations strong enough to satisfy those who wanted some change, yet mild enough to be acceptable to those who preferred no change.

Taft told Hays that he felt that only by such a compromise was passage of the Versailles Treaty certain.

The former President indicated in a letter to Vandenberg that he had intended to keep his reservations secret and to bring them forth as a basis of compromise after more extreme proposals by Lodge and others had been voted down. He had not authorized Hays to release his letter. Yet there it was, in all the newspapers.

Taft and Wilson had been known as the strongest American supporters of the League of Nations. For all practical purposes, Taft's letter took him from Wilson's side and placed him beside Henry Cabot Lodge.

Professor Ruhl H. Bartlett of Tuft's College, who has made an exhaustive analysis of Taft's correspondence covering the period when he was deciding to support reservations, writes:

"His motives were undoubtedly good, but his action was characterized by confusion of thought and ingenuous hopefulness. His confusion is obvious, for within the space of eight days, July 10-18, he stated that France would object to any modification of Article 10, that France would not object, and that his amendment to the article was and was not an interpretive reservation."

Taft had said of Article 10 in a letter written May 10: "It really is the heart of the League. It is the embodiment of what we fought for, and on it as a foundation rest the other provisions in the League to secure peace. It contains the primal essence of the League, which is the union of force in the world to suppress lawless force. . . ."

One of the reservations Taft now proposed to Will Hays limited Article 10 to a life of only five years, as far as the United States was concerned!

Taft demonstrated in a letter he wrote to Gus Karger on July 10 that he was in no mood deliberately to line up with Lodge and Root in their demands for reservations. He declared that their attitude toward Article 10 "is German, is domineering, is bullying, is offensive."

Lodge and Root, delighted as they were by Taft's flounderings, could not refrain from cynical comment among themselves. Root wrote to Lodge that he thought Taft's amendments lacked precision. Lodge wrote back asking Root if he had ever "seen anything of Taft's that had precision."

July 25, 1919.
The Twilight of the League to Enforce Peace

The supporters of the League of Nations were thrown into complete confusion by Taft's action.

The League to Enforce Peace had contributed much to the formation of a solid bloc of opinion in the country against further revision of the Covenant—by amendment, by reservation, by anything. One of its recent bulletins had said:

> The opponents of the Covenant in the Senate probably will stake everything upon amendment. While amendments probably will defeat the plan just as effectively as absolute rejection, they offer a means to knife the Covenant without standing openly before the people as its assassins.

To many, many Americans, however, Taft was the symbol of the League to Enforce Peace. He was its President, and its outstanding spokesman. And here he was suggesting reservations!

Taft submitted his resignation, offering to get out if his stand was embarrassing. The executive committee held an excited, unhappy meeting.

The Washington representative send word that he thought the organization should accept Taft's resignation and remain steadfast for unconditional ratification of the treaty. He wrote: "To do less would weaken our position, would have a tendency to cause some of our supporters to vacillate between conflicting positions, would serve to postpone the getting together of all favorable forces. The country in general now understands that we favor the Covenant, *just as it is,* with any amendments to come through action by the League itself. My judgment is that we weaken our position if we agree to anything less."

The leaders of the League to Enforce Peace fumed and vacillated. Finally, led by A. Lawrence Lowell, a majority decided a break with Taft would do more harm than good. The fact was that Lowell had already decided some reservations were necessary—although he didn't like Taft's proposals.

And so the League to Enforce Peace retained Taft as President, but issued a strong statement against "any amendment or reservation."

This contradictory course left the countless friends and followers of the organization hopelessly muddled.

Should they favor reservations or should they fight reservations?

Taft was through as a powerful force for the League of Nations, and so was the League to Enforce Peace.

July 26, 1919. "I'm Not Interested in the Bill of Sale!"

Once, long after the League of Nations fight, when Calvin Coolidge heard that Senator Borah had been seen galloping through Rock Creek Park on horseback, he commented, "I'm surprised he was willing to go along with the horse."

For Bill Borah was not a man to play follow the leader. He was the perpetual dissenter. And now, just when Lodge's strategy seemed to be working out to perfection, Borah threatened to desert him.

A feeling of optimism was sweeping through the ranks of the irreconcilables, and Borah got the idea they were strong enough to win an open fight without Lodge's finesse and his strategy of simulation.

The break almost came when Senator Smith of Arizona said bitterly to the irreconcilables, a few hours after news of Taft's letter to Hays reached Washington:

"Why not quit trying to scare the people with these spectres and hobgoblins scurrying among the ruins of our once glorious Constitution? . . ."

Then Senator Pittman challenged the reservationists, crying, "If you are against the League of Nations, then say so and vote against it! Kill it openly and quickly, but do not give it slow poison that must result in its death."

This was an invitation to the sort of battle Borah had been longing for, and he leaped to his feet to declare:

"It is either fundamentally right to enter into this enterprise or it is fundamentally wrong, as I view it. If it is fundamentally right, I do not expect the President of the United States or any other man to perfect the instrument in the first instance; no one but the divine power Himself can, without experience, perfect a thing out of mind; and if it is fundamentally a correct proposition, I am not going to waste my time with reference to details in regard to it."

For several days, Borah had been saying things like that, and Lodge was horrified. He would draw Borah into the cloakroom, and patiently he would explain all over again that the Senate wanted the League of Nations, the press wanted the League of Nations, and the people wanted the League of Nations, and so it had to be defeated indirectly. And the way to defeat it indirectly was by demanding revision.

Borah would shake his big head, and pace up and down, declaring he could shout the thing down if he was given enough time. Lodge would smile, and persist. Finally Borah would agree to stay in line, but as he strode out on the Senate floor he would mutter grimly:

"If my country's going to be sold, I'm not interested in the bill of sale!"

July 27, 1919. "But, My Dear James..."

Taft had intended to make his reservations strong enough to satisfy men like Nelson and Kellogg who wanted mild reservations, yet mild enough to be acceptable to men like Hitchcock and Pittman, who wanted no reservations.

Lodge, meanwhile, was trying to draw up reservations strong enough to satisfy men like Borah and Sherman who wanted no League of Nations at all, yet mild enough to be acceptable to the mild reservationists like Nelson and Kellogg.

Taft was trying to bring together all the real supporters of the League of Nations; Lodge was trying to unite the supporters who wanted amendments with the outright opponents.

Obviously, the Lodge reservations were going to be a good deal stronger than the Taft reservations, but Senator Jim Watson got to worrying about them. He had been annoyed by Borah's threats to bolt, but suddenly it struck him that perhaps Borah had a point when he ridiculed the reservationists for their timidity and talked about making it an open fight. Watson wondered if maybe Lodge was overlooking one great danger involved in his plan of attack.

So he dropped in on Senator Lodge at his home one evening.

"Senator," he said, "suppose that the President accepts the Treaty with your reservations. Then we are in the League, and once in, our reservations become purely fiction."

Lodge sat back and smiled at Watson with supreme confidence: "But, my dear James, you do not take into consideration the hatred that Woodrow Wilson has for me personally. Never under any set of circumstances in this world could he be induced to accept a treaty with Lodge reservations appended to it."

"But," protested Watson, "that seems to be rather a slender thread on which to hang so great a cause."

"A slender thread!" cried Lodge. "Why, it is as strong as any cable with its strands wired and twisted together."

July 28, 1919. The Old Man from Mississippi

Word got around that Senator John Sharp Williams planned to speak in the afternoon, and most of the Senators drifted in to their seats soon after lunch.

The fiery old man from Mississippi was famed all over America for his eloquence and wit, and for the awesome strength of his convictions. Vice President Marshall, who sat in the presiding chair throughout the long League debate, said, "Of all men I have ever known, John Sharp Williams had the most intimate knowledge of world history and world politics."

Williams was an old school Jeffersonian Democrat, and he believed with all his heart and soul that Old Tom would have been for the League of Nations. He was a bit beyond his prime, but he was still a mighty orator when he got riled up—and he was getting madder every day over the way the Versailles Treaty was being kicked around in the Senate.

Early in the afternoon, Senator Williams strolled into the Senate: a scowling, rakish-looking character with scraggly white hair, bristling eyebrows, flashing eyes, a feathery white mustache. His old suit was rumpled and made no effort at all to fit him; a black string tie was carelessly looped around his neck and dangled down his front.

He stood in the middle aisle by his desk, winked at a passing little page, looked up at the Vice President and begged to be recognized. Then he swung about and glared at Senator Borah, who had been saying that human nature could not be changed and so wars were inevitable.

"You cannot change human nature!" he exploded, and he shook his head scornfully. "What a stupid, barbarous utterance that is! If human nature had not been changed from the day our ancestors were drinking mead and beer out of the skulls of their enemies, this world would . . . be in a much worse fix. . . . Oh, you cannot change human nature! What was Christ born for?"

The mighty Borah did not choose to attempt to answer that question, so Williams contemptuously turned his attention elsewhere. He stared around the Senate, singling out one by one the reservationists, the little men who had been picking little flaws in the Covenant. When he had completed his survey, he said slowly: ". . . a man could go through the Lord's Prayer and find fault with it here and there provided he put his own interpretation upon it."

To demonstrate he pretended he had a rather stupid friend who had been considering the prayer, and finally came rushing to him to say: "I do not like one thing in the Lord's Prayer; it says 'Lead us not into temptation,' whereas it ought to say, 'Teach us to resist temptation.' "

Senator Williams turned to the charge that members of the League of Nations might make mistakes, might render bad decisions.

"Of course they may," he said. "I have represented clients in ten or a dozen lawsuits where the court went wrong, in my opinion, but it was a great deal better for the court to decide the issue than it was for my client and the other lawyer's client to cut each other's throat.

"The chief good about municipal law and about international law for the preservation of peace is not that the decision shall always be right, but that there shall be a decision and an end of litigation."

The man from Mississippi lit into the sentiment that was leading some of his fellow-Senators to say: "I want my nation left free and untrammeled to do whatever it pleases. I do not want to enter into any entangling agreement with anybody to do anything, whether it is right or wrong. I want to be left free at the time to judge for myself."

"What would become of a municipal society composed of individuals founded upon that sort of basis?" demanded Williams. "Suppose the Senator from Utah, as a citizen of the State of Utah, went out and said: 'I decline to be trammeled; I decline to enter into an agreement to abide by the pistol-toting law, or by the homicide law, or by the thievery law, or by anything else. I will do right myself. I am my own sovereign, responsible to nobody but God, and at the right time I will do the right thing, and I want to be free to say when I shall do it and where I shall do it and how I shall do it.'

"Could you get civilization in a State out of citizens of that persuasion? Suppose each State in the Union said that to the other States of the Union? Could you get civilization in the American Union out of that? Why is it that thus far you have never gotten any civilization in the international world? Just simply because one nation after another, in blind chauvinism, has uttered that infernal, stupid selfishness."

July 29, 1919. A Man on Lodge's List

A bit before noon, Senator Lodge completed reading line by line, paragraph by paragraph to the end of the 87,000 words of the Versailles Treaty. The Washington correspondent of the *New York Tribune* described the finale of the two-weeks' performance:

"Chairman Lodge began reading aloud when the committee convened. One by one the Senators slipped out of the committee room, until finally Senator Lodge looked up to see that he was reading to Charles F. Redmond, clerk of the committee, and no one else. Without comment, Mr. Lodge continued.

"A little while later, his eyes again lifting from the pages, he noted that Mr. Redmond had slipped out to attend to some mail and he was reading alone. Continuing to read, Mr. Lodge completed the formal reading for the committee."

Lodge's filibuster had served its purpose. The situation regarding revision had changed drastically since July 15: Taft had come out for reservations, the League to Enforce Peace was collapsing, and all supporters of the Covenant were in utter confusion.

When the Senate met in the afternoon, Senator Knute Nelson of Minnesota gave a speech typifying the position of more and more people who wanted the League of Nations. The old man was for the Covenant heart and soul, and he said he didn't think much of the proposed revisions—but he was willing to support them so that passage of the treaty would be assured. He thought a reservation explaining our attitude toward Article 10 would probably be wise, since there was so much controversy about it; and he thought the Shantung settlement should be changed.

"I have not groped around to find objections to defeat the treaty," he carefully explained, "for I am imbued with the faith that fundamentally the general purpose of the League is sound and fully warranted. . . ."

Knute Nelson had a few words to say about the advice of George Washington. "It surely cannot be more dangerous to 'entangle' us in securing a permanent peace in Europe than to 'entangle' us in a war in Europe."

Senator Nelson sat down, tired out.

He would have been the last man in the Senate to advocate revision of the Covenant in order to destroy it. Vice President Marshall said of him: "Knute Nelson, of Minnesota, was one of God's great gifts to the world—an honest man, honest personally, officially and intellectually."

But Henry Cabot Lodge kept a little list of men whose Senate votes he counted upon to kill the League of Nations by trying to perfect it. One of the names on Lodge's list was that of Senator Knute Nelson.

July 30, 1919. Warren G. Harding in the White House

President Wilson was now holding conferences with some of the Republican Senators less friendly to the League of Nations.

Senator Warren G. Harding visited the White House. He told the President that if he would agree to accept reservations, the Senate would promptly approve the Versailles Treaty.

July 31, 1919. "Another War Far Greater Than This..."

Senator Joseph Randsdall of Louisiana, who had spent a long time making a careful study of the weapons of war, tried desperately to warn the Senate of his findings.

A bit self-conscious, feeling uncomfortably like a prophet of doom in the serene Senate, he took the floor early in the afternoon. He said he was convinced that World War II—if we permitted any World War II—would produce weapons worse than anything he could dream of, weapons that would kill men, women, and children and destroy property with dreadful efficiency.

He said that the Chief Statistician for the General Staff estimated that in the war just won, deaths from battle alone had been 7,500,000, and the direct monetary cost had been $186,000,000,000.

"Mr. President," he said, "our only safe criterion for the future is the past, and just as the present war exceeded in blood and treasure the great wars of the past, so will future wars exceed this one. If the art and means of killing progress in the same ratio as they have in the past, only divine interference can prevent the world from destroying itself, and we have reason to believe that the next twenty-five to fifty years will see greater efficiency in the agencies of destruction."

One of his predictions was that if we permitted any more wars, we would soon see airplanes "completely mastering the air and bringing opponents within a few hours of each other, though separated by thousands of miles." Fearful that his forebodings sounded far-fetched, Senator Randsdall sought to substantiate them by reading a passage from a book by Captain Thomas G. Chamberlain, U.S. Army, entitled *Why We Fought:*

> I was in Paris when "Big Bertha," the German long-range gun, opened fire on the city. At regular 15-minute intervals the bursts occurred, and each burst spelled destruction and death. There were only two guns—why should there not be 200, with bursts occurring at intervals of a few seconds or continuously?
>
> . . . within the last few months we have come to classify bombs by tons rather than by pounds as previously . . . To consider the possibilities of the developed engines of war—the developed aeroplane, tank, long-range guns, gas bomb . . . submarine, under the system of competitive armaments is to arrive at the inevitable conclusion that civilization must here and now end war or be ended by it.

Senator Randsdall put the book down on his desk, looked up, and said that the only way to end war, and the only way to protect the United States, was to create a world organization.

"The recent conflict has conclusively demonstrated the absolute dependence of nations on each other," he declared. "The time has passed when a war against an individual nation is merely an attack on that country. Unless the attempt is frustrated in the embryo, as provided by the League, every people of the world will finally become embroiled."

Seeking to move the Senate by shock, Randsdall tried to give a "faint idea" of the horrors of modern war to the men sitting in the safety of the Senate by reading a letter from a man who had been wounded in France:

> To The Editor of the *New York Times:*
>
> To those who oppose the proposed League of Nations, either because they are not in favor of the policies of our President (which would be very narrow minded of them), or because of some other reason, and who were unable to be in a battle, I address the following:
>
> You who have never seen the horrors of war, who have never seen a man disappear, literally blown to atoms, on being struck by a shell, who have never heard the shrieks of wounded human beings, who have never heard the hysterical laughter of a man as he gazes at the stump where his hand was a moment ago, who

have never heard the cries, the groans, the swearing, the praying of men with festering wounds, lying in a first aid station, waiting too long and in vain for ambulances and who have never witnessed the terror of those men when the station is gassed and there are no gas masks, who have never seen convalescents totally blind and with both hands amputated above the wrists, can you say that we should stop at anything in order to prevent this frightfulness, this savagery, this horror from occurring again?

Is there any other way than by a League of Nations and combination of power?

Will a simple treaty among the greater nations prevent a recurrence of such an attempt as Germany has made? Is not the League of Nations, as proposed, elastic enough and broad enough, whatever its defects, to insure world peace? Is it not a step, and the only possible step, in the right direction? I firmly believe so. If there is another way, speak it out. If not, for God's sake stop opposing this one remedy.

Wyman Richardson
(Wounded in Action)

Senator Randsdall paused for a moment to let the words sink in. Then he said earnestly:

"And yet, Mr. President, as terrible as this war was, if the League of Nations be not adopted and no concert of powers be entered into to preserve the peace, we have every reason to believe that within a few years—ten or twenty years at most—another war far greater than this will take place. . . . Something must be done, and that quickly, to prevent the coming of such a day."

August 1, 1919. "Never! Never!"

President Wilson saved Senator Jim Watson until the very last. Now, he, too, was invited to the White House.

Joe Tumulty showed him into the Red Room, and in a few moments Wilson walked in. Watson remarked later upon the real cordiality of Wilson's greeting.

"Senator," said the President as they sat down, "they tell me that you know how this fight in the Senate is going, and, furthermore, they tell me that you will tell me the truth about the situation."

Lodge's deputy replied that he felt twice flattered. He modestly protested that he didn't know the situation precisely, but he promised that anything he said would be the simple truth.

"Where am I in the Senate on this fight?" asked Wilson.

"Mr. President, you are licked."

"By what majority?"

"It depends on the vote on each reservation." Watson had with him his estimate of the vote on each reservation Lodge planned to demand, and he reached into his pocket. "Mr. President, I can show you these votes, if you desire to see them."

"I don't want to see the votes. I just want your résumé of the situation."

"Well, take the subject of mandates. You will receive twenty-four votes in the Senate in favor of that proposition."

Watson later told of the amazement that came to Wilson's face as he exclaimed, "You mean to tell me that twenty-four votes is all I can get in the Senate on that proposition?"

"Mr. President, that is the sum total."

The conversation drifted to other things, and a joke or two was told. Then Watson rose to take his leave. He walked to Wilson, took his hand, and said:

"Mr. President, there is just one way by which you can take the United States into the League of Nations by the ratification of this Treaty."

"What way is that?" demanded Wilson.

"Accept it with the Lodge reservations."

"Accept the Treaty with the *Lodge* reservations?" cried Wilson, and Watson afterward said there was scorn in his voice as he emphasized the name.

"Yes, with the Lodge reservations. . . . That is the only way in which this country will ever ally itself with the League of Nations."

"Never! Never!" declared Wilson, according to Watson. "I'll never consent to adopt any policy with which that impossible name is so prominently identified."

As Watson turned toward the door, he recalled his conversation with Lodge, who had told him of "a cable with its strands wired and twisted together" that would keep the United States out of the League of Nations.

"I'll appeal to the country," said Wilson.

"Mr. President," said Watson, swinging around, "it is too late. You are like a man in quicksand now, and every struggle you make will only sink you the deeper. . . ."

August 12, 1919.
"Cynicism That Invites the Scorn . . ."

Senator Lodge delivered his first prepared address since the Senate had received the Versailles Treaty. For the occasion the galleries were carefully packed with representatives of some small nationalist women's organizations, with certain war veterans, and with all available relatives, friends, and office employees of the Senators fighting the League of Nations.

"Mr. President, in the *Essays of Elia,* one of the most delightful is that entitled 'Popular Fallacies,'" said Senator Lodge by way of opening. "There is one very popular fallacy, however, which Lamb did not include in his list and that is the common saying that history repeats itself."

The Gentleman from Massachusetts then set out to prove that there was no threat of a World War II that necessitated a League of Nations. Said he: "We are told that we shall 'break the heart of the world' if we do not take this League just as it stands. I fear that the hearts of the vast majority of mankind would beat on strongly and steadily and without any quickening if the League were to perish altogether."

Reading from a manuscript, Lodge ranged over the Covenant, picking away at provision after provision. However, he was careful to leave the impression that if all these errors were righted, he would be willing to vote for it. He flatly declared that as it stood the League of Nations would order American boys to fight in any part of the world it chose, and he said he stood against such needless sacrifice of American life.

"You may call me selfish, if you will, conservative or reactionary, or use any other harsh adjective you see fit to apply, but an American I was born, an American I have remained all my life," he cried with passionate voice, his face red. "I can never be anything else but an American, and I must think of the United States first. . . .

"I have never loved but one flag and I cannot share that devotion and give affection to the mongrel banner invented for a league."

That was the signal for a wild demonstration in the galleries, led by a woman who worked for one of the irreconcilables. The people in the galleries, paying no attention to the pounding gavel of the Vice President, cheered and whistled and shouted for three minutes. When they were done, Lodge made a curious statement:

"Internationalism, illustrated by the Bolshevik and by the men to whom all countries are alike provided they can make money out of them, is to me repulsive."

When Lodge finally sat down, amidst thundering applause from the galleries, Senator John Sharp Williams was hopping up and down in the middle aisle, waving his arms and trying to catch Vice President Marshall's eye.

"Mr. President," he said, when the cheering died down. "I hesitate very much to undertake to reply extemporaneously and in a few minutes to the greatest possible prepared presentation of the selfishness of American policy ever made even by the Senator from Massachusetts. I would have to have more egotism than even I have, if I thought I could answer fully 'off the bat' the things the Senator from Massachusetts has been cogitating and laboriously studying to express for three weeks, more or less, with a view to capturing the Senate and the galleries, whose occupants have come by announcement to hear him today. It is not a new presentation of the personality of the Senator from Massachusetts. He has always attempted to make a show of himself."

Williams was interrupted by hisses and catcalls from the galleries.

"Just a moment—" ordered Vice President Marshall, rapping on the rostrum with his gavel.

"I hope the Chair will not interfere with the galleries," said Williams.

Vice President Marshall warned the hecklers that the Senate rules forbade them to express approval or disapproval. He said he would clear the galleries if there was another outburst.

"As I was about to say," Williams went on, "ties of commerce, literature, law, religion, ties of history, ties of future idealism as well as of past traditions bind us to the balance of the world; and the man who stands forward in the twentieth century and says that any country . . . can direct its own course to please itself, regardless of the balance of the world, has not sense enough to deserve to be a member of a town council. . . .

"It is easy . . . for the Senator from Massachusetts to scorn and cast obloquy upon the sentence of the President when the President said, 'If you defeat the League of Nations you will break the heart of the world.' Has the Senator had any sympathy with breaking the heart of the world? . . . With an absolute, cold, New England, Brahmin cynicism that invites the scorn of every honest, human-loving man he merely made fun of the phrase. . . .

"The Senator says, 'You are talking to us about internationalism, and I want to talk about nationalism.' Do you imagine, Mr. President, that I surrender my nationalism whenever I confess myself an inhabitant of the earth? . . .

"Are we, individual against individual, to fight our quarrels out? Are we, State against State, to fight our quarrels out? Are we, nation against nation, to fight our quarrels out, when we can of our own free will construct some machinery that will come to a fairer and more just conclusion of our quarrels? I imagine not; but that is the question presented to the American people today.

"It is not whether you would, if you could, amend Article 10, or Article 11, or Article 22, or Article 25 of this treaty; but the question is: 'Take it all in all, as a measure for the advancement of civilization and peace and humanity and justice, does it meet with your approval or does it not?' If as a whole it does not, cast it aside; but if as a whole it does, although in your opinion some things in it ought to be amended, then you are a narrow-minded selfish ass if you cast it aside—a narrow-minded barbarian, because you throw aside justice and humanity and civilization and peace for a clause, the crossing of a 't' or the dotting of an 'i.' . . .

"I listened very attentively to the Senator from Massachusetts, and . . . I boldly say that he never touched the question of the peace of the world. . . .

"There cannot be a war started in Thrace tomorrow, there cannot be a war started in Livonia tomorrow, there cannot be a war started in the Balkans tomorrow that will not sooner or later, under the present modern system of commerce and intercourse, bring the United States into it, in spite of the fact that we want to stay out of it. . . .

"So what are you going to do? Are you going to leave our necessary entanglement to accident or are you going to direct your part in it? . . . Are you going back to the conditions of 1914 and leave it to accident and incident and murder and midsea assassination to bring us in or are you going to say beforehand upon what grounds we are going in and upon what grounds we are going to stay out? . . .

"The Senator from Massachusetts speaks of 'the right of all the powers to call out American sailors and soldiers.' I want to appeal especially to the Senator from Idaho [Borah], because however mistaken he may be, however radical he may be, I pick on him as a man on the other side of the Senate who is honest; at any rate who has intellectual integrity—and I do not mean by that that there are on his side no others who have, of course. But the Senator from Massachusetts speaks of the right of all the powers to 'call out American soldiers and sailors.' I wish that the Senator from Idaho would tell me when he gets the floor—or now, if he chooses—where that treaty at any place gives any right to the League to 'call out American soldiers or sailors.' He cannot do it, because it is not in the treaty, and the Senator from Massachusetts knew it was not in it. He knew it as well as I do. Why did he say it? 'To tickle the ears of the groundlings' while he 'made the judicious to grieve.'"

August 13, 1919.
Senator Jim Reed Looses a New Weapon

Senator Jim Reed underwent an unpleasant and embarrassing experience while stumping through the Southland against the League of Nations. The American Legion boycotted the meeting he addressed in Montgomery, Alabama, and attracted a great deal of publicity in the process.

When Reed returned to Washington, he set out to mend his military fences, and now he loosed a new weapon against the Covenant. He put into the Congressional Record an article by Major Harry B. Hawes of Missouri suggesting that it was entirely due to the plans for setting up a League of Nations that 1,500,000 American soldiers remained in Europe after the Armistice.

Soldiers and their loved ones were given to understand that the League of Nations was keeping American boys away from their homes.

August 15, 1919.
"I Have Heard Them Say Again and Again . . ."

Senator John Sharp Williams did not permit Senator Reed's attack to go unchallenged. He counterattacked by placing in the Congressional Record an article by Frederick Palmer, one of America's best known war correspondents:

> We are making the League of Nations a partisan question when it is no more partisan than fresh air for school children. . . .
>
> It no more revolves around a single statesman's personality than the president of a railway is indispensable to the daily schedule of trains. Woodrow Wilson is one man, and 10,000,000 men have died on the Continent of Europe. He is 60 years old, with perhaps 20 years of life before him. The League of Nations concerns the life and livelihood of billions of human beings for generations to come and the whole structure of world civilization. . . .
>
> The soldiers who fought in Europe were fighting to preserve their children from another such war, as I have heard them say again and again. . . .

August 19, 1919. Inquisition at the White House

The Foreign Relations Committee went to the White House at ten o'clock in the morning for what the *New York Tribune* called the "most searching inquiry ever directed, for a public record, at any President of the United States, or for that matter any other head of a great power."

No reporters were present, but they were a few yards away in the White House basement with their typewriters and telephones. Every few minutes messengers rushed down to them with the word-by-word transcript of the cross-examination.

"Mr. Chairman . . ." said Woodrow Wilson to Henry Cabot Lodge, "I am absolutely glad that the committee should have responded in this way to my intimation that I would like to be of service to it. I welcome the opportunity for a frank and full interchange of views."

He read a prepared statement urging speedy approval of the Versailles Treaty so life and industry in the United States and the world could get back to peaceful ways. He reminded the committee that the Covenant had been amended to meet objections made at his meeting with them in February.

Wilson then suggested a compromise on reservations. "It has several times been suggested, in public debate and in private conference," he said, "that interpretations of the sense in which the United States accepts the engagements of the Covenant should be embodied in the instrument of ratification. There can be no reasonable objection to such interpretations accompanying the act of ratification provided they do not form a part of the formal ratification itself."

This compromise—proposing a way for America to interpret the treaty without requiring that the whole thing be submitted all over again to other nations—was not mentioned after the President completed his statement. Instead, the Senators started to fire questions at him on the provisions of the treaty.

"Who was the author of Article 10?" demanded Brandegee.

"I suppose I was as much as anybody," replied Wilson.

"And you recommended it to your fellow-American commissioners?"

"Yes."

At the beginning of the discussion of Article 10, Wilson stated with great emphasis that unless our representative in the Council of the League of Nations voted for military and other sanctions, there would be none, due to the unanimous vote provision. He pointed out that even after a unanimous vote for sanctions the League of Nations would only be empowered to *recommend* but not to *order* us to join the other members to stop an aggressor. He stressed that we would be under a "moral" obligation to carry out the unanimous recommendation of the League of Nations, but that we would be under no "legal" obligation.

Thereafter, no Senator made any attempt to get Wilson to confirm their charges that the League of Nations would be a "superstate" empowered to give orders to our army and navy. They resorted to the opposite tack. If the League could not *order* sanctions against an aggressor, how could it prevent war? Was it anything more than a debating society?

"Right there, Mr. President," said Senator Harding, "if there is nothing more than a moral obligation on the part of any member of the League, what avails Articles 10 and 11?"

Wilson lost his patience at Harding's suggestion that a mere moral obligation was meaningless.

"Why, Senator," he replied, "it is surprising that that question should be asked. If we undertake an obligation we are bound in the most solemn way to carry it out."

The opposition Senators then shifted their fire to the Shantung settlement. Hiram Johnson asked if Wilson had done all he could to protect China's interests.

"Oh, indeed, I did; very seriously."

"And the decision ultimately reached at the Peace Conference was a disappointment to you?"

"Yes, sir; I may frankly say that it was."

"You would have preferred, as I think most of us would, that there had been a different conclusion of the Shantung provision, or the Shantung difficulty or controversy, at the Paris Peace Conference?"

"Yes; I frankly intimated that."

"Did it require the unanimous consent of the members of the Peace Conference to reach a decision like the Shantung decision?"

"Every decision; yes, sir."

Senator Brandegee promptly interrupted to read a statement Secretary of State Robert Lansing had made a few days before at a Foreign Relations Committee hearing. Lansing had said that it had not been necessary to make the Shantung settlement in order to get Japan to sign the Versailles Treaty.

Wilson's white face turned crimson, and he said sharply, "Well, my conclusion is different from his, sir."

There followed a close examination concerning Japan's promises to return sovereignty in Shantung to China. Senator Knox shot an acute question:

"Mr. President, the economic privileges that they originally acquired in Korea, and subsequently in Inner and Outer Mongolia, and in northern and southern Manchuria, have almost developed into a complete sovereignty over those countries, have they not?"

"Yes, Senator; in the absence of a League of Nations they have," smiled Wilson.

"You think the League of Nations would have prevented that, do you?"

"I am confident it would."

Senator Pomerene developed this thought.

"Mr. President, if I may, I should like to ask a question or two along that same line," he said. "If this treaty should fail of ratification, then would not the opportunity be open to Japan to treat the Shantung question just as she has treated the Manchurian situation?"

"I think so; yes."

"So that if the treaty should fail of ratification, China, so far as Shantung is concerned, would be practically at the mercy of Japan;

whereas if the treaty is ratified, then at least she will have the benefit of the moral assistance of all the other signatory powers to the treaty to aid in the protection of Chinese rights?"

"Senator," replied Wilson, "I conceive one of the chief benefits of the whole arrangement that centers in the League of Nations to be just what you have indicated—that it brings to bear the opinion of the world and the controlling action of the world on all relationships of that hazardous sort, particularly those relationships which involve the rights of the weaker nations. After all, the wars that are likely to come are most likely to come by aggression against the weaker nations. Without the League of Nations they have no buttress or protection. With it, they have the united protection of the world; and inasmuch as it is the universal opinion that the great tragedy through which we have just passed never would have occurred if the Central Powers had dreamed that a number of nations would be combined against them, so I have the utmost confidence that the notice beforehand that the strong nations of the world will in every case be united will make war extremely unlikely."

Senator Borah brought up the secret treaties Great Britain and France had made with Japan about Shantung, and with Italy about expansion of her frontiers. He asked if Wilson had only found out about them after he reached Paris.

No one will ever know what went on in Wilson's mind at this moment. The treaties, made before the United States entered the World War, came to light early in the Russian Revolution. The Communists discovered copies in the Tsar's archives, and promptly published them.

The treaties had been featured in the *New York Post* and in several American newspapers in January 1918. Everyone in the American Government should have known about them, and the evidence is incontrovertible that in the course of his work Wilson did learn about at least some of them. Yet he said:

"Yes, the whole series of understandings were disclosed to me for the first time then."

Later Wilson was accused of deliberately lying to the Senators about his knowledge of the treaties. However, the Senators were unable to assail him too sharply on this point since they, too, had had ample opportunity to find out about them.

Wilson's friends felt that his earlier knowledge of the treaties simply slipped his mind. Some believed the episode showed that the strain of the struggle was beginning to tell on the President.

After exhaustive examination of the Covenant, Brandegee wanted to know why the United States couldn't make peace with Germany without signing the Versailles Treaty.

"Senator," said Wilson, "I would say that there is no way which we ought to be willing to adopt which separates us, in dealing with Germany, from those with whom we were associated during the war."

"Why?"

"Because I think that is a moral union which we are not at liberty to break," answered Wilson, too tired to repeat all over again what he had already said about the need for international co-operation to prevent future wars.

Brandegee asked why the Senate couldn't simply strike the League of Nations out of the treaty, and ratify only the terms of the peace with Germany:

"We could have peace and resume all our business in relation to copper mines and zinc mines, etc., and we could export to Germany, and re-establish the consular service, could we not?"

"We could, sir," Wilson responded, "but I hope the people of the United States will never consent to it."

At one thirty-five in the afternoon, Senator Lodge brought the critical, merciless prodding and probing to a halt:

"Mr. President, I do not wish to interfere in any way, but the conference has now lasted about three hours and a half, and it is half an hour after the lunch hour."

"Will not you gentlemen take luncheon with me?" asked President Wilson. "It will be very delightful."

August 20, 1919.
"The People Must Deal with the . . . Obstructionists"

"U.S. ARMS AT LEAGUE'S BECK, WILSON ADMITS"

That was the *Chicago Tribune* headline.

But the *New York Times* reported: "In his address and in his frank answers to innumerable questions it seems to us, and we are altogether confident it will seem to the country, that Mr. Wilson met and disposed of every reasonable objection that has been advanced against particular provisions of the treaty.

"If the President's interpretation of the letter and spirit of the treaty, of the purposes of its authors, and his straightforward replies to the questions of the Senators have not removed from their minds all reasonable doubts and misgivings, then evidently nothing can remove them, and the country will be forced to the conclusion that the grounds of their objection do not lie in the treaty or in the League Covenant, but somewhere outside.

"If that be true, then the people must deal with the Senatorial obstructionists, for the President has exhausted the resources of reasoning and exposition."

Washington correspondents had canvassed all the committee members as soon as they returned to their offices from the White House. They reported that not a vote had been changed.

Seeking to carry out the compromise proposed by Wilson, Senator Key Pittman introduced a separate resolution embodying reservations covering the main objections made to the Versailles Treaty. It was referred to the Foreign Relations Committee, to languish there.

Lodge, backed by the mild reservationists, planned to insist that the reservations be tied directly to the Versailles Treaty, so that they would have to be approved by other signatories.

August 21, 1919.
The Plans Laid at Senator Knox's Luncheon

The Foreign Relations Committee voted to hold a little Peace Conference of its own. It decided to grant hearings to American representatives of every racial and national group with any complaints concerning the Versailles Treaty.

Lodge had won the hearts of Italian-Americans on the Fiume issue, and now he would win the support of many other groups by providing them a sympathetic forum. Clamoring against the treaty were certain Hungarian-Americans unhappy over the fate of the Hapsburgs, certain Greek-Americans who frowned on the new Greek frontiers, and more than a dozen similar groups. Many of them had established headquarters in Washington. George Creel commented: "The forces of hyphenation were boldly called into being and no effort spared to revive and exaggerate the divisive prejudices of American life."

When the committee adjourned, Senator Knox entertained Senators Borah, Johnson, Brandegee, Fall, Moses, Poindexter, and Reed at a private luncheon.

There were rumors that Wilson was considering touring westward in an effort to drum up support for the League of Nations. Senator Knox proposed that the irreconcilables put on a high-powered campaign of their own in all parts of the United States. The friend of Messrs. Andrew Mellon and Henry Clay Frick talked in grandiose terms: huge mass meetings, parades, bands, posters, leaflets, full-page advertisements.

His guests eagerly agreed it was a great idea. Someone produced a canvas of the Senate showing sixteen Senators openly opposed to the treaty in any form, and nearly forty now favoring reservations. There were excited comments, and the men determined to shoot for outright rejection of the Versailles Treaty; they agreed, however, to keep on supporting all reservations and amendments under Lodge's leadership.

The *New York Tribune* correspondent telephoned his paper an intimate account of the plans laid at the luncheon: "It was decided that immediately after the Foreign Relations Committee reports the treaty to the Senate, Senator Johnson will go to the Pacific Coast, Senator Borah to start in Minneapolis and work west, and Senator Poindexter and Reed to follow routes so far undecided.

"The plan is to attempt the conversion of those states whose Senators are wavering between reservations and downright opposition to the League as a whole. . . .

"If a wave of opposition can be started east from the Pacific Coast and west from the Mississippi, they believe enough votes can be obtained in the Senate to make rejection of the Covenant certain."

August 23, 1919. Amendment No. 1

The Foreign Relations Committee started amending the Versailles Treaty at the morning meeting.

Senator Lodge moved to substitute "China" for "Japan" in the Shantung provision. The motion barely carried, nine to eight. Lodge's packed committee was running to form.

August 24, 1919. "I Am Suspicious of You All the Way Through"

The foes of the League of Nations hailed the Shantung amendment. They cried that at last *justice* was prevailing, championed by Henry Cabot Lodge.

Some of the friends of the League of Nations denounced the amendment, but there was a good deal of uncertainty among them. The Shantung settlement really *was* unfair. Even President Wilson said so. Therefore, how could you oppose Senator Lodge's effort to straighten it out?

The thinking of many liberals, and of a great many plain, everyday people all over America, was about like that of Senator George Norris on the Shantung business. Known as one of the most progressive men in the Senate, hard-working Norris was a native product of the corn and hog country of Nebraska, where the troubles of Europe and Asia seem far, far away. Norris had voted against our entry into the World War, but he was ready for the League of Nations, after the Armistice.

Yet, bit by bit, he drifted away, and revelation of the Shantung settlement put the black-browed, gray-haired Senator right in the middle of the irreconcilables. He detested Sherman and Reed and the rest for almost everything they stood for, yet he became a full-fledged member of their little band of wilful men. He announced he would never vote for the League of Nations if it meant he had to swallow the Shantung deal.

"I started this thing in good faith," he said one day in his frank, friendly way. "No man had more honest and beautiful intentions than I had when that Peace Conference met at Versailles. No man in all the world was more anxious to have a permanent peace than I. No man under any flag would sacrifice more, according to what he had to sacrifice, than I would to have brought about a league that was honest and honorable.

"I believed that our Allies were honest and honorable. I thought they were square; I thought they were fair; and when the League of Nations part of the treaty was first given to the world, while I disliked some of it very much, I was almost on the point of swallowing it. . . .

"Later it developed what they had done in making the treaty; but although it seemed to me there were a lot of sins even in the League as they had promulgated it, when the treaty came forth it made the League look like a banner of purity compared to the deceit, the wrong, and the sin that was bound up in that treaty.

"When I discovered that these men who had talked eloquently here to us had in their pockets secret treaties when they did it; when . . . I saw our own President lie down and give in and submit to the disgrace, the dishonor, the crime, and the sin of that treaty, then I said:

"'Great God! I don't believe I want to have any dealings with any of you people. I am suspicious of you all the way through.'"

The Shantung amendment proposed by Lodge did more than confuse a good many of the supporters of the League of Nations. It seemed more than a coincidence that the amendment followed so closely upon the announcement of the western invasion planned by Senator Knox and his friends, and the *New York Times* voiced a suspicion that the amendment was intended to cater to anti-Japanese sentiment on the Pacific Coast. It would serve to please Far Westerners now; and later, when the Senate defeated the amendment, displeased Far Westerners would feel like defeating the treaty. For the *Times* doubted that Senator Lodge "with all his carefully cultivated art of incandescent partisanship" expected the Senate as a whole to approve the work of his committee.

This, of course, was true. Lodge knew there was small hope that any amendments would get by the Senate, but he was certain that in the course of debate on amendments a good many Senators, in their efforts to defeat them, would be led to say:

"I will never vote for an amendment of this provision, but I am willing to vote for a reservation covering the same point."

The Gentleman from Massachusetts planned to get reservations by demanding amendments, and then to get rejection by demanding reservations.

August 26, 1919. "Yes, Midsummer Madness—"

Chairman Lodge's Foreign Relations Committee adopted fifty more amendments, all of them introduced by Senator Fall of New Mexico. They were devoted to striking out provisions for American participation in all of the commissions established to carry out the terms of the Versailles Treaty *except* the Reparations Commission designed to get money from Germany.

In the afternoon, Senator Porter McCumber, who had been horrified by the Shantung amendment and had been studying the subject since its adoption in the committee, rose in the Senate to indict it. An honest plodder who was usually easy-going, Senator McCumber was terribly angry, and his voice trembled:

"It is to create trouble between this country and Japan and thereby send the first dagger thrust into the body of this treaty."

The League of Nations was China's guarantee of justice, said McCumber, and the Shantung amendment was designed to kill the League of Nations.

"Is it an act of true friendship toward China or a mere political move to defeat the treaty?" he demanded. "If its sponsors now fail to come forward and openly pledge that if Japan is driven out of this treaty then the United States will proceed single-handed and alone to drive Japan out of China, will renew the World War and send our soldiers into the Orient to fight for her, then by this act they are betraying China with a false kiss."

The Shantung issue became the great territorial issue of the Versailles Treaty debate, overshadowing all others, overshadowing the League of Nations itself in many minds. The opponents of the treaty stuck by their guns, demanding justice, demanding that the treaty assign Shantung to China. Many one-time supporters of the League of Nations joined them. They all ignored the argument that Shantung would be at Japan's mercy unless the League of Nations existed to see that she kept her promise to observe the rights of China.

"If the treaty is rejected," argued Senator Walsh of Montana, "Shantung remains with Japan until she restores it to China of her own free will or until she is compelled to do so by force of arms. Are Senators prepared to make war upon Japan to compel the evacuation of Shantung?

"China loses no territory by the treaty; she simply does not get back what she lost to Germany twenty-one years ago . . . she does get, if she signs the treaty, the obligation of all the civilized nations of the earth, by virtue of Article 10, that never again need she fear the loss of a foot of territory by foreign aggression.

"The Shantung section of the treaty is not satisfactory, but the compensations are so great that it would be madness—yes, midsummer madness—in our country to reject it on that account."

The opponents suggested no practical way to return Shantung to China. They simply repeated and repeated, over and over, that the Shantung settlement was unjust, and they would never approve it. Most of the members of the Foreign Relations Committee who voted for the Shantung amendment were bored by the long debate, for even if the amendment was accepted by the Senate, they intended to vote against the whole Versailles Treaty, amendment and all, when it finally came to a vote.

Strangely, Lodge and Borah and the whole crew shouting so

about the protection of justice, and the protection of the United States, showed small interest in some other German possessions taken over by the Japanese—some islands in the Pacific. When the nations planned the peace at Paris, they had intended that these islands would be mandated to Japan, but that the whole world would really share the responsibility for them through the League of Nations—a strong League of Nations that would see to it that Japan did not fortify the Carolines and the Marshalls and the Marianas.

August 27, 1919. The Disgusted *New York Times*

The sedate *New York Times* was about as disgusted by the success of the Fall amendments as it had been by any previous performance in American history. It protested in a blazing editorial:

"Do these rabid men at Washington ever pause even for one instant to inquire what is the controversy in which they are engaged? In the lead are the Republican members, eight or nine of them, of the Senate Foreign Relations Committee, which ex-President Taft declared was packed against the League of Nations. It is charged that they are prompted chiefly by motives of partisanship—the desire to destroy Woodrow Wilson politically.

"The fact that some of them or most of them are aspirants for the Republican nomination next vear lends appreciable confirmation of the charge.

"By our plenipotentiaries, by the Chief Executive himself, who is the negotiating power, we have come to agreement with other nations in respect to the Treaty. This small body of Senators repudiates the work and the signatures of the plenipotentiaries, it maims and transforms the whole meaning of the Treaty by amendments—some fifty of them in a day, we might say in a bunch. If such things can be, what respect and consideration will be shown to plenipotentiaries of the United States in future serious negotiations? All the Powers are put on notice that our international engagements are to be held always subject to the strifes of our party politics. . .

"To insure the success of a party we are willing to shatter the new safeguard of peace, again to deliver the world over to war; at least we declare that we do not care whether peace is preserved and war abolished, we are concerned only with party plans and triumphs."

August 28, 1919. "I Must Go"

Woodrow Wilson, sitting in the White House, tired, graying, felt lonely, abandoned.

The League of Nations was slipping away, even though most of the people and most of the Senate still seemed to want it. Something had to be done, and he had to do it.

Those he had counted on for help were failing. They were shouting about Shantung, deciding that Germany was getting harsh treatment, and bickering about Article 10, the Monroe Doctrine, the votes controlled by the British Empire. Taft had gone his way, and the League to Enforce Peace was disintegrating.

The leadership in the Senate was as aimless as the leadership among the people. Senator Thomas Martin of Virginia, the Democratic leader, had broken his health working on war appropriations, and he had been seriously ill for many, many months. Senator Hitchcock was filling in, and while he was pleasant, engaging, honest, loyal, he was a bit bovine, not brilliant—and no match for Henry Cabot Lodge.

It seemed to Wilson that he had done everything there was to be done in Washington. He had talked to the Senators singly, in groups, and all at once. He had accomplished nothing. He had offered to compromise, and the offer had been ignored.

When Admiral Grayson came in this morning for his regular visit, Wilson told him he had made up his mind to carry the issue to the people. He would go on a tour to the West to seek support; he would fight it out with Senator Knox's team out in the grass roots.

Grayson was horrified. He protested, remonstrated, threatened. Wilson had never been too strong and he had returned exhausted from the trials of Paris. The fight at home, combined with the terrible heat of the Washington summer, had spent his strength. The doctor warned Wilson in the strongest possible terms that he should not undertake the trip.

The President walked to the window of his office, and gazed for a few moments from the White House toward the tall Washington Monument. He swung about. His face was grave. His voice was tense and tight.

He had seen the battlefields in France, and the long, endless rows of white crosses, and he said no personal consideration could stop him.

Admiral Grayson sent Mrs. Wilson in to plead with her husband.

"I promised our soldiers, when I asked them to take up arms, that it was a war to end wars," he told her, "and if I do not do all in my power to put the treaty into effect, I will be a slacker and never able to look those boys in the eye. I must go."

Up in the Senate in the afternoon, Senator Townsend of Michigan declared the League of Nations might cause American boys to be taken from their homes to fight in Europe and Asia for many years. "Something other than hazy dreams or untried theories should form the foundation for such a sacrifice," he roared.

August 29, 1919.
Wilson Determines to Accept Reservations

Woodrow Wilson decided he would have to accept some reservations to the Versailles Treaty.

While Tumulty, working with a map and a Congressional Directory, charted the course of the tour, Wilson sat down at his typewriter. He pecked out a list of reservations that would make the position of the United States clear on disputed provisions of the Covenant, without destroying the League of Nations.

He summoned Senator Hitchcock to the White House, handed him the list, and told him to use them in efforts to work out a compromise with the opposition. He warned Hitchcock to act as if they were his own, and to hide the fact that the President had written them.

Wilson had learned a bitter lesson at Paris. He was convinced it would be useless to accept any reservations until Lodge had accepted them. As Hitchcock explained later: "The popular impression was that the President was as opposed to reservations as to amendments. This is not the fact. . . . President Wilson, however, felt that if he began to assent to reservations, his enemies would make use of his yielding to demand more and more because they wanted not only to defeat the League but to discredit and overthrow him. He therefore concealed from the public his willingness to accept reservations and got the reputation of being more stubborn and unyielding than he was."

August 30, 1919.
William Randolph Hearst to the Taxpayers

William Randolph Hearst told the American people the real purpose of the League of Nations, as he saw it, in an editorial featured in the Hearst newspapers:

"The proposed League of Nations, which Mr. Wilson has not dared to refer to the judgment of the people of this country, is merely a license for Mr. Wilson to continue with authority the costly wars and dangerous entanglements with European intrigues which he is now carrying on without the sanction of Congress or the consent of the people."

Hearst addressed himself to the American taxpayer: "If it is the primary purpose of you taxpayers to support and finance the imperial plans of foreign nations; if you are willing to pay to destroy democracy not only abroad but at home; if you actually desire to reach the point of financial bankruptcy and economic demoralization which European nations have reached, then you should accept the League of Nations and re-elect Mr. Wilson to carry out its programme of perpetual war and interminable taxation.

"But if you, as patriotic American citizens, desire to adhere to the wise policies of the farseeing founders of this republic, policies which have made this nation the greatest, the richest and the happiest nation in the world, then you should reject this foreign League of Nations, continue the true and tried American policies of non-interference in foreign affairs. . . ."

The entire Hearst chain, publishing in big cities all over America, was fighting the League of Nations desperately. "MAKE AMERICA 'SAFE FOR DEMOCRACY' "—ran the slogan above the masthead every day in the *New York Journal.*

Almost every day the banner head and the lead story in the Hearst press in New York, Chicago, Boston, San Francisco, Los Angeles, and elsewhere was an attack, a denunciation, a startling "exposé" of some new horror found in the Versailles Treaty and the Covenant. Agile Hearst reporters turned them up in a never-ending stream.

Owner and founder of the Spanish-American War, Hearst had felt left out of the World War, and his attitude toward it until the spring of 1918 led many to call him pro-German. Now he violently opposed the plans to prevent another World War. Two of his biographers later explained: "He hated the League of Nations because to his mind it represented a union of the two most detestable things on earth, Woodrow Wilson and Great Britain."

Herbert S. Houston, one of the founders of the League to Enforce Peace, said: "Who is the real leader of the real opposition in New York to the League of Nations—indeed, the real leader in the whole country? It is William Randolph Hearst, who is using all the power of his newspapers from the Atlantic to the Pacific to keep America from entering the League of Nations."

September 4, 1919.
"I Am Trying to Tell the People . . ."

Wilson was on his way to the people. The train stopped at Columbus, Ohio. President Wilson walked through a cordon of war veterans to mount a platform in Memorial Hall. He said: "I felt that I could salute them because I had done the job in the way I promised them I would do it, and when this treaty is accepted, men in khaki will not have to cross the seas again."

He told of the Covenant, the things it would do and try to do, and looking at crippled men who had fought in France he said, "The League of Nations is the only thing that can prevent the recurrence of this dreadful catastrophe and redeem our promises."

Later in the day, his train paused at Richmond, Indiana, and Wilson stood on the rear platform and spoke again:

"I am trying to tell the people what is in the treaty. . . ."

September 5, 1919.
"In the Vengeful Providence of God . . ."

Woodrow Wilson passed through Illinois in silence. Nothing he could say would change the votes of Senators Medill McCormick and Lawrence Y. Sherman. The President had no prepared speeches with him when he left Washington, and he spent the traveling time trying to put ideas down on paper. He found it hard to do; headaches were bothering him badly.

To the people of St. Louis he said:

"I conceive it a privilege to discuss the matters that I have come away from Washington to discuss. I have come away from Washington to discuss them because apparently it is difficult to discuss them in Washington. The whole subject is surrounded with a mist which it is difficult to penetrate. I brought home with me from the other side of the water a great document, a great human document, but after you hear it talked about in Washington for a while you think that it has just about three or four clauses in it.

"You fancy it has a certain Article 10 in it, that it has something about the Monroe Doctrine in it, that it has something about quitting, withdrawing from the League, showing that you do not want to play the game. I do not hear about anything else in it. Why, my fellow-citizens, those are mere details and incidents of a great human enterprise, and I have sought the privilege of telling you what I conceive that human enterprise to be."

Wilson spoke of war and of peace, and of co-operation between nations as the way to have peace and not war. He spoke much of Article 10, and he said: "If it should ever in any important respect be impaired, I would feel like asking the Secretary of War to get the boys who went across the water to fight together on some field where I could go and see them, and I would stand up before them and say, 'Boys, I told you before you went across the seas that this was a war against wars, and I did my best to fulfill the promise, but I am obliged to come to you in mortification and shame and say I have not been able to fulfill the promise. You are betrayed. Yo fought for something that you did not get.'

"And the glory of the Armies and the Navies of the United States is gone like a dream in the night, and there ensues upon it, in the suitable darkness of the night, the nightmare of dread which lay upon the nations before the war came; and there will come sometime, in the vengeful Providence of God, another struggle in which, not a few hundred thousand fine men from America will have to die, but as many millions as are necessary to accomplish the final freedom of the peoples of the world."

September 8, 1919.
"The People . . . Want the Peace Treaty Ratified"

"There have been three outstanding developments in connection with President Wilson's tour to the Western coast, so far as it has progressed," reported the *New York Times* correspondent from the campaign train as it paused in Des Moines, Iowa.

"1. The people in the States which Mr. Wilson has passed (Ohio, Indiana, Missouri, and Iowa) want the Peace Treaty ratified, and are absolutely opposed to any efforts to make the treaty a 'football of politics' which may result in a moment's unnecessary delay.

"2. The people in these States are pretty well satisfied that the treaty of peace, with its League of Nations, is not an instrument of war and are about ready to accept Mr. Wilson's assurances that it will go far, instead, to assure world peace.

"3. Business and financial interests, or at least a comfortable majority of them, are convinced that the treaty of peace should be ratified without delay and the fact established, once and for all, whether the United States is to play a prominent part in the League of Nations or remain out of it. It is probable that the sentiment in financial circles at present is in favor of American participation, feeling that such a development would assure the safety of moneys which they are called upon to use in the rehabilitation of European countries."

September 10, 1919. "Impeach Him! Impeach Him!"

Wilson carried the crusade for the Covenant on across the land. He spoke at Omaha, Nebraska, and Sioux Falls. South Dakota; at Minneapolis and St. Paul, Minnesota.

The crowds grew larger and larger as he traveled westward; the enthusiasm became greater and greater. When his train stopped for water at Mandan, North Dakota, the natives gathered around his private car, and Wilson stood on the platform and said a few words. He spoke again of the men who fought in France:

"We may think that they finished that job, but they will tell you they did not, that unless we see to it that peace is made secure they will have the job to do over again, and we in the meantime will rest under a constant apprehension that we may have to sacrifice the flower of our youth again."

Wilson's foes were trailing him, haranguing huge crowds in his wake at meetings staged by the League for the Preservation of American Independence. The Senate spellbinders stirred passion and emotion, waving the Stars and Stripes and crying for America first.

Hiram Johnson and William Borah spoke together at a mass meeting in the Chicago Coliseum, Medill McCormick presiding. Tens of thousands cheered and shouted inside, and milled around outside. Some carried banners bearing the inscription:

"WELCOME TO THE MEN WHO ARE BRINGING OUR BOYS BACK FROM SIBERIA!"

Borah strode up and down the stage, his thumbs hooked in his armpits.

"It took George Washington seven years to gain independence from George III," he shouted, "and now they want to give it back to George V!"

He proclaimed that Wilson had betrayed the Fourteen Points, and demanded:

"Who quit?"

"Wilson!" roared the crowd. "Impeach him! Impeach him!"

When Hiram Johnson's turn came, he declared:

"He is asking us to hand American destiny over to the secret councils of Europe. It is the duty of the Senators of this nation to uphold the Constitution, to keep America American."

"VAST AUDIENCE CHEERS ATTACK ON THE LEAGUE," screamed the *Chicago Tribune*.

Senator Spencer of Missouri stood up in the Senate back in Washington and charged that Wilson had misrepresented the issue in his St. Louis speech. Spencer said the issue was not between the Covenant and no Covenant, but between a revised Covenant and no Covenant. In the little notebooks of the floor leaders, Spencer had been written down as a mild reservationist; now he was marked as a strong reservationist.

Word went around the corridors and the cloakrooms that Senator Kenyon of Iowa, who had refused to sign the round robin and who had never said a word in the Senate about the League of Nations, was preparing a speech demanding strong reservations.

Two or three Democrats were telling friends they were joining the reservationists. Senator Ashurst of Arizona, Democrat, gloomily predicted reservations were inevitable, and he seemed to know that meant defeat, for he said:

"The future is what President Wilson must look to for his vindication. We may be winning elections about 1940 on the strength of Woodrow Wilson's memory, but not in the near future."

September 11, 1919. The Committee Splits Four Ways

The reporting of the Versailles Treaty to the Senate by the Foreign Relations Committee was announced in the morning papers.

Senator Lodge had flatly refused to compromise when Senator Hitchcock proposed reservations based on the secret list Wilson had given him, and the majority report recommended drastic amendments and reservations, including one gutting Article 10. Seemingly foreseeing the fate of the world if the League of Nations was destroyed, the authors of the report nonetheless said:

"The other nations will take us on our own terms, for without us their League is a wreck and all their gains from a victorious peace imperiled."

The report did not recommend that the Senate approve the Versailles Treaty even if the amendments and reservations were adopted.

It was signed by only nine members of the committee—Chairman Lodge, and Borah, Brandegee, Fall, Knox, Harding, Johnson, New, and Moses.

The remainder of the committee was split three ways.

One minority report, signed by six Democrats—Hitchcock, Williams, Swanson, Pomerene, Pittman, and Smith of Arizona—said: "We deplore the long and unnecessary delay to which the treaty has been subjected while locked up in the committee, whose majority decisions and recommendations were from the start a foregone conclusion. They could have been made in July as in September and would have been the same. . . . This is government by obstruction as well as by a minority."

The amendments and reservations, said the minority report, would defeat the treaty if adopted: "In our opinion they have no merit, but whether they be good, bad or indifferent, their adoption by the Senate can have no possible effect except to defeat the participation of the United States in the treaty. . . .

"Those who oppose the League of Nations realize that it is inevitable on a square fight and they hope to destroy it by this indirection. . . .

"We renew our recommendation that the work of the Peace Conference be confirmed, the will of the people fulfilled, and the peace of the world advanced by the ratification of this treaty—'the best hope of the world'—even if, like all human instrumentalities, it be not divinely perfect in every detail."

Senator McCumber, the lone Republican on the committee who was friendly to the treaty, did not associate himself with the Democrats. He submitted his own minority report: "It is regrettable that the consideration of a matter so foreign to any kind of partisanship should be influenced in the country as well as on the floor of this Senate by hostility toward or subserviency to the President of the United States. No matter how just may be any antagonism against President Wilson, the aspiration and hopes of a wounded and bleeding world ought not to be denied because, under our Constitution, the treaty must be formulated by him."

Most of Senator McCumber's criticism was directed at the report of his fellow-Republicans. He commented: "Not one word is said, not a single allusion made, concerning either the great purpose of the League of Nations or the methods by which these purposes are to be accomplished."

He lauded the aims of the Covenant, analyzed and answered the attacks made in the majority report and the proposed revisions, and wound up by proposing six mild reservations of his own. He thought they would be enough to quiet the fears that had been aroused about the League of Nations without weakening our own position in it.

Senator Shields, Democrat of Tennessee, failed to join in any of the reports, nor did he submit one of his own.

September 12, 1919. "Bullitt's Breach of Confidence"

This was the day that Woodrow Wilson said at Coeur D'Alene in Idaho:

"America is absolutely necessary to the peace of the world. Germany realizes that; and I want to tell you now and here—I wish I could proclaim it in tones so loud that they would reach the world —Germany wants us to stay out of this treaty. . . .

"She wants to see America isolated. . . . She wants to see one great nation left out of this combination which she never would again dare face. Evidences are not lacking—nay, evidences are abounding—that the pro-German propaganda has started up in this country coincidently with the opposition to the adoption of this treaty."

This was the day that Wilson hurried along to Spokane, Washington, to tell the people there of the League of Nations: "I call it frankly a *chance* to insure the peace of the world."

This was the day of fascism's first aggression. A band of men in black shirts, led by Gabriel d'Annunzio and cheered on by Benito Mussolini who remained safely in Milan, marched across the Italian frontier and seized Fiume in defiance of the dying Versailles Treaty.

This was the day, too, that William C. Bullitt testified before the Foreign Relations Committee, Chairman Lodge presiding. The only other committee members present were Knox, Brandegee, Fall, New, and Harding. No one knows how it happened, but no members friendly to the League of Nations were present—so Bullitt was never subjected to cross-examination.

Bullitt had held a small post in the American Peace Commission, but the effect of his testimony was great—the most damaging delivered throughout the hearings. To Bullitt, a young chap who had honeymooned in Germany in 1916, where he and his bride traveled as guests of the German High Command, foreign affairs were (as Raymond Moley later put it) "full of lights and shadows, plots and counterplots, villains and a few heroes."

He testified that he had gone to work in the State Department under Joseph C. Grew when we entered the war. After the Armistice, he went to Paris as a member of the Peace Commission, and made a trip to Russia.

Lodge asked: "Did any member of our delegation, any member of the Council of Ten, express to you any opinions about the general character of this treaty?"

"Well, Mr. Lansing, Colonel House, General Bliss, and Mr. White had all expressed to me very vigorously their opinions on the subject," he replied, revealing he had written records of conversations with the four American delegates.

"Were they enthusiastically in favor of it?" queried Lodge with a sly smile.

"I regret to say, not," replied Bullitt.

At first Bullitt seemed a bit reluctant to divulge details of "personal conversations" with the American diplomats. Lodge pressed him, and finally, producing his memoranda, he cut loose. He said this of Lansing: "I do not think that Secretary Lansing is at all enthusiastic about the League of Nations as it stands at present. I have a note of a conversation with him on the subject.... This was a conversation with the Secretary of State at 2:30 on May 19. . . . This is a note which I immediately dictated after the conversation.... He said: 'I consider that the League of Nations at present is entirely useless.... I believe that if the Senate could only understand what the treaty means, and if the American people could only understand, it would unquestionably be defeated. . . .' "

Bullitt then read this from his notes: "He expressed the opinion that Mr. Knox would really understand the treaty and that Mr. Lodge would; but that Mr. Lodge's position would become purely political and therefore ineffective."

There were guffaws. Lodge snapped, "I do not mind."

The opponents of the League of Nations immediately made much of Bullitt's testimony, particularly of the statements about the views of Secretary of State Lansing and the other three American delegates.

Lansing promptly issued a statement flatly declaring he favored ratification of the entire treaty without amendment or reservation, and as soon as he heard of the affair, Henry White wrote to Lodge about William C. Bullitt:

"He was not one of the regular experts on the Delegation, but merely an attractive and rather brilliant personality, who had been taken on by the State Department for a while during the war, and got himself attached to the Commission. His chief duty while here, so far as I can make out, was to visit each Commissioner every morning and bring him a summary of the news of the previous twenty-four hours, as ascertained and boiled down—in an attractive form, certainly—by him.

"His trip to Russia, to which he refers, was in no sense as an official representative of our Delegation, although I am afraid he gave that impression to Lenin and Trotsky. He was merely sent by Lansing and Colonel House to ascertain conditions. . . .

"I am not prepared to say that I never expressed to Bullitt during his morning visits, to which I have referred, any dissatisfaction with the terms of the treaty; on the contrary, it is not impossible that I may have done so, as I certainly have in my letters to you; but I naturally assumed that I was talking to a man who could be trusted not to make public views expressed at random and not as the result of mature deliberation or in a formal way. No one whom I have yet come across connected with the treaty is satisfied with it in all respects, which is perhaps the best thing that can be said in its favor."

To this, Lodge replied, "He insisted on giving the report of his conversation with Lansing, which Lansing has not denied. I have no defense to make of Mr. Bullitt's breach of confidence. That is his affair."

White considered Lodge responsible for the whole affair, and the old man wrote to Representative Rogers, "Really, it requires some patience at times not to become indignant with him."

Clemenceau commented, "I got my bullet at the Conference, but Lansing got his afterward."

September 15, 1919. "Shall It All Go for Nothing?"

Senator Overman of North Carolina reminded his colleagues of the price of the peace we had won in the World War, the blood and the treasure spent, and he cried:

"Shall it all go for nothing?"

Hunger and strife were spreading as the world limped along, planless, almost hopeless. Little wars were breaking out all over the Balkans, and there were riots all across Europe. "Here I desire to read a statement by Mr. Venizelos, the great Premier of Greece, probably the greatest statesman of them all," said Senator Overman, and he read from a paper in his hand:

I permit myself to say that the outlook in Europe would be one of utter despair without the League of Nations. . . .

I allow myself to say that opposition in America arises in large measure, if not wholly, from a misinterpretation of the significance of the clauses of the Covenant and the lack of full understanding of the extent to which the treaty depends on the Covenant for the working out of the terms. . . .

Perhaps we have not been very happy in the wording of this [Monroe Doctrine] provision, but I am sure I speak for everyone. Nobody had any thought of interfering with the Monroe Doctrine.

I finish by saying I fear America has not yet an exact idea of the greatness of her position.

You have taken such a position in the world that you cannot ignore its responsibilities.

September 16, 1919. The Second Reading

The Secretary of the Senate began to read the Versailles Treaty—already read in full by Chairman Lodge to the empty room of the Foreign Relations Committee—to a deserted Senate chamber.

Lodge and his lieutenants would have two more weeks to line up the votes on the Foreign Relations Committee amendments and reservations.

September 17, 1919. "The Hope of Germany Has Revived . . ."

"The hope of Germany has revived," warned Wilson in San Francisco, "because in the debates now taking place in the United States she sees a hope of at last doing what her arms could not do—dividing the United States from the great nations with which it was associated in the war."

His face grave, his voice tense, he read a startling statement made in Germany by Ex-Minister von Scheller-Steinwartz. The German had said, "Senator Lodge is an extraordinary influential statesman, who, under five Presidents, has played a more important role in foreign affairs than the Secretaries of State who came and went. Lodge is no enemy of Germany. He hates all non-Americans equally. His basic principle is Washington's declaration against mixing in entangling European politics. He and a large number of other distinguished Senators, on more or less similar grounds, are fighting the treaty and League, which are linked. . . ."

The German predicted their course would lead the United States to sign a separate peace with Germany. "That course is thus to be hailed like the morning red of a new dawn," exulted von Scheller-Steinwartz.

President Wilson did not read the entire statement to the San Franciscans; he omitted Senator Lodge's name.

With solemnity born of his conviction that the choice between the people of the United States was between war and peace, Wilson went over the Covenant, article by article, striving to refute the claims made against it. And then he pled, almost wistfully: "I beg, my fellow-citizens, that you will carry this question home with you, not in little pieces, not with this, that, and the other detail at the front in your mind, but as a great picture including the whole of the Nation and the whole of humanity, and know that now is the golden hour when America can at last prove that all she has promised in the day of her birth was no dream but a thing which she saw in its concrete reality, the rights of men, the prosperity of nations, the majesty of justice, and the sacredness of peace."

Senator Charles Thomas of Colorado sent a message to the people of his state while Wilson spoke in San Francisco. He declared his opposition to the Versailles Treaty. It was too hard on the Germans!

Protested Thomas: ". . . this is a victor's treaty, a treaty of force, a treaty of punishment, a treaty of partition, a treaty burdened with conditions accepted by the vanquished only at the point of the sword."

He said he greatly admired President Wilson, and he knew he had tried hard at Paris and done about as well as anyone could have done. He said it was with real sorrow that he took up the cudgels against him.

More and more people, like doubting Thomas, were opposing the Versailles Treaty on liberal grounds. They were sympathetic to all the fine purposes of the League of Nations, but they were frightened by the concrete proposal.

Many seemed to assume that if the United States signed the Versailles Treaty, all the boundary settlements in it, all the colonial and territorial concessions, the bad with the good, would last forever. "Subject peoples under this Covenant would remain subject till the crack of doom," opined Hiram Johnson.

"It is a perfectly gratuitous assumption," stormed hard-headed, practical Senator Tom Walsh of Montana, "that the political map of the world can never undergo any change unless nations are permitted to wage aggressive warfare against each other."

Senator Cummins, the aging liberal, listened to Johnson, and he was not swayed by any arguments that only through world organization would peaceful processes of change and progress really be made possible. He feared the effort to plan the future.

"The statesmen gathered in Paris might with equal propriety have ventured to set the bounds to the Heavenly Kingdom or prescribe the activities of the Prince of Darkness," he protested. "How dare we attempt to determine what sovereignties the civilization of the next century will demand? How dare we attempt to give judgment upon the welfare of all the coming generations?"

The dreamers of dreams gazed in surprise at the realization, the Covenant. In disbelief they broke it into the little pieces Wilson spoke about in San Francisco, and—just as they expected!—they found imperfections.

Oswald Garrison Villard of *The Nation* was one of those who wound up fighting the Versailles Treaty and the League of Nations tooth and nail. He afterward said:

"It was hard for us to oppose the League, for all of us had dreamed of a parliament of man, and still harder to find ourselves fighting alongside of Boies Penrose and Henry Cabot Lodge and his satellites, but fight we did, and so gave aid and comfort to those whom we opposed at every other point, whose whole influence upon our public life and social and economic progress seemed to us about the most dangerous in our politics."

September 18, 1919. The Soldiers and Sailors of Grand Rapids

Strong reservations were even beginning to win the support of war veterans—in Grand Rapids, Michigan.

Senator Truman Newberry called to the attention of the Senate a poll taken among local war veterans by Arthur H. Vandenberg of the *Grand Rapids Herald*. The results:

For ratification unconditionally	21
For ratification with reservations	196
For complete rejection	13

Editor Vandenberg lumped the votes for ratification with reservations together with the votes for complete rejection.

He said in an article accompanying the poll: "By a vote of 209 to 21 . . . they are opposed to the program for which President Wilson contends in his transcontinental sweep—because all those favoring complete rejection must be joined with the reservationists in any such accounting."

He said in an editorial: "Here is a real mandate if the soldier will and the sailor wish are to be consulted. . . .

"The issue . . . is reservations. And the 'mandate' from ex-service men speaks up in thunders on their behalf. It is the view the *Herald* has preached for months. For the sake of its possible influence upon the world for good and peace, we must ratify the treaty with its Covenant; for the sake of avoiding the delays attendant upon reopened Versailles negotiations, we must not attempt textual amendments, if America can be adequately protected otherwise; but for the sake of perpetuated American constitutional independence, we must attach reservations to our signature so that American safety is left neither to chance nor to an unshared idealism."

September 23, 1919. "There Will Be Another War If . . ."

As Wilson swung eastward from California, a group of the leading men of the state, most of them Republicans, many of them Hiram Johnson's life-long political friends and supporters, were drafting a telegram to the Senator telling him he was not representing the sentiment of the state:

"WE APPEAL TO YOU TO WITHDRAW YOUR OPPOSITION."

Wilson felt he was winning. The enthusiasm of the people exceeded all his hopes. He resolved to carry the campaign right into the New England of Henry Cabot Lodge.

He was carefully setting his sights for every kind of American—those who live in the big and little cities where he gave his major addresses, and those in the small towns where his train stopped for coal and water. He was shooting for farmers, fishermen, storekeepers, bankers, workers, industrialists—everybody. He was convinced everybody had a general and a personal stake in world organization, and he believed he was getting them to see it.

When he was in the farm belt of the Middle West he talked of foreign trade in an era of peace, he spoke of the rich farmlands as the bread basket of a hungry world. When he took up Article 10, he asked the farmers how they would get along if their land titles were insecure. Wouldn't every farmer be busy sitting behind his fence with a shotgun, to drive off squatters and invaders? The Covenant of the League of Nations would give the same protection to nations that the law of the United States gave to American citizens.

When he spoke to workers, he stressed Article 23—establishing the International Labor Office—and of how it would raise wages and working and living standards all over the world, and therefore in the United States, too. To immigrants he spoke of the League of Nations as the protector of the old country. With Article 10, Poland, Czechoslovakia, Belgium, Yugoslavia, Greece—all these and more would live free and unafraid.

To businessmen and bankers, he said we could do more business with friendly traders than hostile traders, make more money by dealing with people who trusted us than people who feared us. The financial, industrial, commercial leadership of the world was ours for the asking.

When Wilson spoke of the Covenant in terms of business profit, of selfish advantage, a little note of apology crept into his voice. He was at his best, he was happiest, when he was proclaiming America's destiny in terms of freedom and security for all peoples.

"The greatest nationalist," he said once, "is the man who wants his nation to be the greatest nation, and the greatest nation is the nation which penetrates to the heart of its duty and mission among the nations of the world. With every flash of insight into the great politics of mankind, the nation that has that vision is elevated to a place of influence and power which it cannot get by arms, which it cannot get by commercial rivalry, which it can get by no other way than by that spiritual leadership which comes from a profound understanding of the problems of humanity."

Sometimes he spoke very, very simply. That was his aim, all the way across the nation, and the length of the West Coast and as he turned homeward.

"One cannot have an omelet without breaking eggs," he told one throng. "By joining the League of Nations, a nation loses, not its individual freedom, but its selfish isolation. The only freedom it loses is the freedom to do wrong. Robinson Crusoe was free to shoot in any direction on his island until Friday came. Then there was one direction in which he could not shoot. His freedom ended where Friday's rights began."

Again and again he said that a nation could not preserve its freedom except through concerted action with other nations. We surrender a bit of our freedom to save the rest of it, he said.

President Wilson felt on firmest ground when he warned of the alternative to the League of Nations. "I have it in my heart that if we do not do this great thing now, every woman ought to weep because of the child in her arms. If she has a boy at her breast, she may be sure that when he comes to manhood this terrible task will have to be done once more. Everywhere we go, the train when it stops is surrounded with little children, and I look at them almost with tears in my eyes, because I feel my mission is to save them. These glad youngsters with flags in their hands—I pray God that they may never have to carry that flag upon the battlefield!"

Once he calmly said:

"I can predict with absolute certainty that within another generation there will be another World War if the nations do not concert the method by which to prevent it."

Traveling day and night, talking day and night, standing in swaying cars in long parades, sitting in sweltering summer heat in crowded banquet halls and eating banquet meals, shaking thousands upon thousands of hands, meeting with the endless committees and delegations, the governors and the mayors and the party leaders—all this took its toll.

Once, in the midst of a wild, frantic throng trying to press his hand, to touch his sleeve, the President murmured to his wife, "They are killing me."

Correspondents covering the trip watched his face grow white and thin and drawn. They noticed Wilson would often press his temple with his hand, and close his eyes for long moments. They wondered among themselves if he would be able to finish the trip, and they even spoke of it to him. He managed to grin and to say that maybe his constitution was exhausted, but he would live on his by-laws for a while yet.

"He appeared to grow older by years with the passing of each day," recorded Admiral Grayson.

In the tear and strain, Wilson said some things better left unsaid. He challenged the foes of the League of Nations with bitterness and scorn.

"Put up or shut up!" he cried.

Once he said: "When at last in the annals of mankind they are gibbeted, they will regret that the gibbet is so high."

Wilson spoke without a manuscript, and Senator Lodge, carefully studying all he said, noticed that sometimes he said Article 10 was the heart of the Covenant, and sometimes he said Article 11 was the heart, and sometimes he said some other Article was the heart. Lodge pointed out the discrepancy to Capitol Hill reporters, remarking that in its Wilsonian wanderings the Covenant seemed to be developing an ambulatory heart.

The irreconcilables trailed Wilson relentlessly. Hiram Johnson went on from Chicago to speak in St. Louis, Indianapolis, Kansas City, Des Moines. So great was the support he was stirring that some of his very good friends in Washington began to fear he was running away with the next Republican Presidential nomination. After a meeting attended by Lodge, Brandegee, Borah, Knox, and Will Hays, Chairman of the Republican National Committee, word was sent to Johnson that he was needed in Washington to lead the fight for his amendment giving the United States as many votes as the British Empire in the League of Nations. Johnson came back wildly overflowing with optimism to plead:

"If we could just get sixty days before the final vote, the American people would make their desires known in such unmistakable terms that nothing would be left of this treaty."

September 25, 1919. "I Believe That Men Will See the Truth"

The last great speech of his life was delivered by Wilson at Pueblo, Colorado.

A few hours before it was time to speak, he seemed terribly tired, and his suit was soaked with perspiration. Dr. Grayson and Mrs. Wilson urged him to call the speech off, and take a few days' rest.

"No," he protested stubbornly. "I have caught the imagination of the people."

Just before he was introduced, he told Tumulty he had a blinding headache. He admitted he would have to cut his speech very short. Instead, he gave one of the longest, strongest, most touching addresses of his career. He told the people how he had brought a draft of the Covenant back to Washington in February:

"I asked the Foreign Relations Committees of both Houses to come to the White House and we spent a long evening in the frankest discussion of every portion that they wished to discuss.

They made certain specific suggestions as to what should be contained in this document when it was to be revised.

"I carried those suggestions to Paris, and every one of them was adopted. What more could I have done? What more could have been obtained?

"The very matters upon which these gentlemen were most concerned were, the right of withdrawal, which it now expressly states; the safeguarding of the Monroe Doctrine, which is now accomplished; the exclusion from action by the League of domestic questions, which is now accomplished. All along the line, every suggestion of the United States was adopted after the Covenant had been drawn up in its first form and had been published for the criticism of the world. There is a very true sense in which I can say this is a tested American document."

The Commander-in-Chief spoke of the men who had fought in France.

"There seems to stand between us and the rejection or qualification of this treaty the serried ranks of those dear ghosts that still deploy upon the fields of France," he said, as he brushed his hand across his throbbing head.

Wilson's last words were these: "Now that the mists of this great question have cleared away, I believe that men will see the truth, eye to eye and face to face. There is one thing that the American people always arise to and extend their hand to, and that is the truth of justice and of liberty and of peace. We have accepted that truth and we are going to be led by it, and it is going to lead us, and through us the world, out into pastures of quietness and peace such as the world never dreamed of before."

Meanwhile, Senator Harry New was saying in the Senate: "The President says he believes the League will prevent war . . . I have seen and known people who believed firmly that a potato carried in the pocket would prevent rheumatism; that a silk thread around the neck would prevent a sore throat."

September 26, 1919. Journey's End

Admiral Grayson rapped on the door of Tumulty's compartment at four in the morning, and told him the President was seriously ill.

Tumulty hurried after the physician to Wilson's car. On the way, Admiral Grayson said they would have to tell the President he must cancel the rest of his trip.

Tumulty entered Wilson's drawing room to find him fully dressed, and seated in his chair. His face was white, and one side sagged loosely. Tears were streaming down his cheeks. He looked at Tumulty and said in a voice that could scarcely articulate: "My dear boy, this has never happened to me before. I felt it coming on yesterday. I do not know what to do."

He begged Grayson and Tumulty, in a broken, strained voice, not to cancel the trip. "Don't you see that if you cancel this trip, Senator Lodge and his friends will say that I am a quitter and that the Western trip was a failure, and the Treaty will be lost?"

Tumulty bent down, and took Wilson's hands in his, and said, "What difference, my dear Governor, does it make what they say? Nobody in the world believes you are a quitter, but it is your life that we must now consider. We must cancel the trip, and I am sure that when the people learn of your condition there will be no misunderstanding."

Wilson tried to move closer to Tumulty, to press his pleas, but his left arm and his left leg refused to function. Tumulty realized for the first time that Wilson's whole left side was paralyzed. The President had suffered a stroke, not the massive kind that kills almost instantly, but the kind that paralyzes. He looked up at Tumulty, and said:

"I want to show them that I can still fight and that I am not afraid."

There was no choice. Admiral Grayson and Tumulty told correspondents the trip was off. With drawn blinds, and a pilot engine racing ahead, the train dashed through the darkness toward Washington.

October 4, 1919. "He Has Shot His Bolt . . ."

Woodrow Wilson had bravely struggled to his feet and walked from his train when it reached Washington. He had remained secluded in the White House ever since, wandering restlessly from room to room, driven by a terrible pain in his head.

On this day, he suffered a new, far more serious stroke. His wife found him lying semi-conscious on a bathroom floor in the White House.

Also on this day, Colonel George Harvey said in his magazine: "He has shot his bolt. . . . Now let the Senate act!"

October 5, 1919. France Approves the Versailles Treaty

The President of France was authorized to sign the Versailles Treaty by the Chamber of Deputies, by a vote of 372 to 53.

October 6, 1919. Senator Lodge's Strategy

The people were appalled by Woodrow Wilson's sudden collapse. A wave of sympathy for the man and the cause he was willing to die for swept the country.

The opponents of the treaty privately admitted that if the stroke had killed Wilson, the memory of his spirit would have carried the Covenant through the Senate. But Wilson lingered, lying helplessly in bed in the White House, and the bitter battle went on.

Henry Cabot Lodge, aware of the pitfalls in the new situation, executed a brilliant bit of strategy. Within a week of Wilson's stroke, he had the supporters of the League of Nations lulled into a sense of false security. He rushed the Fall amendments to a vote on October 2. They were defeated overwhelmingly—all fifty of them, as Lodge knew they would be. None of them won more than 31 votes, and there were as many as 58 votes cast against some of them by a coalition of Republicans and Democrats. The Senate voted them down so fast that the votes weren't even counted after the first few, and they were disposed of by simple voice votes.

Senator Hitchcock joyfully hailed the defeat of the amendments as "a signal victory for the forces favoring ratification of the treaty without deadly changes."

The *New York Times* editorial was typical of the comment in all newspapers except the powerful few fighting the League of Nations:

"The defeat of the Fall amendments to the Treaty is a rebuke to the Foreign Relations Committee of the Senate, a rebuff to the extreme obstructionists, a repudiation by Republicans of Mr. Lodge's leadership, and it assures the country that the Treaty is not to be . . . mishandled."

The friends of the League of Nations seemed to be in full command of the Senate. Citizens who favored the treaty lost the urge to gather together and carry on the crusade for the stricken leader. They relaxed. Senator Lodge did not relax.

October 8, 1919.
The Logic of Senator Medill McCormick

"We are . . . passing rapidly out of the zone momentarily created by the League of Nations circumstances at Paris," reported Frank Simonds, the noted foreign correspondent, from Europe.

England, France, Japan, and many smaller nations had ratified the Versailles Treaty, but it was suspended, and the League of Nations was delayed—pending action by the United States.

Europe could not stand still, and the idea of a concert of nations was dying while the United States Senate debated. Nationalism, the power of the sword, seemed destined to be the New Order—all over again.

The Italian fascists still held Fiume. The Rumanians had invaded Hungary. The Poles were laying plans for expansion. Most alarming of all, the German Junkers were astir. A German army of uncertain status, led by one General von der Goltz, had boldly seized Riga.

Simonds summed up the rising tide of nationalism and militarism in the *New York Tribune,* and said:

"Had the United States accepted the Treaty of Versailles without delay and by a unanimous, or approximately unanimous vote the European reaction would have been far different from what it now is. . . . But what happened in America since the President returned has been at once a surprise and a shock to the European Statesmen. . . .

"The Paris conference decisions were actually a compromise between the American ideas, as Mr. Wilson's views were invariably described abroad, and the European ideas. Now Italy and Rumania have repudiated any compromise and insisted upon settling their problems in a thoroughly European fashion, while the United States, so far as the Senate is concerned, has challenged the American idea. . . . Therefore it seems to me that France, Poland and the rest of the continental nations will . . . seek a continental solution conforming with Italian and Rumanian action."

This prediction that all Europe would turn to the fascist form of rampant nationalism tested by the fascists at Fiume, as a result of the failure of the Senate to approve the League of Nations, was put in the Congressional Record by Senator Medill McCormick.

To him, it was new evidence that the United States should defeat the League of Nations!

October 12, 1919. Home on a Stretcher

Colonel House had left France to see if he could be of aid in the fight in the United States, but his health, too, failed. He was carried ashore from a transport on a stretcher. He was so weak that his doctors refused to operate to remove the gall stones that had him in desperate pain.

"At a moment when energetic action is imperative, I am bedridden," moaned Colonel House, "and all we fought for is in grave danger."

October 14, 1919.
The Bars on the White House Windows

There were weird rumors in Washington and all over the nation about Wilson. Many people were convinced he was dying, some thought he was dead. A Senator was telling intimates his mind was affected. Since no one except Admiral Grayson, his consultants, and Mrs. Wilson had seen the President for days, no one knew.

Suddenly the story spread through Washington that workmen had just put bars on the White House windows. A whispering crowd gathered to see. The bars were there!

A madman was in the White House! Actually, the bars had been up since 1902, put there to keep TR's boys from breaking the windows when they played baseball on the White House lawn.

Grayson issued a statement that Woodrow Wilson's mind was "clear as a bell."

The Foreign Relations Committee developed a deep curiosity about the President's condition, and Senator Poindexter introduced a resolution demanding he give the committee certain papers concerning Shantung.

"I think it would not be in good taste to adopt this resolution owing to Mr. Wilson's condition," protested John Sharp Williams. "Why annoy the President at this time? Why not ask the Secretary of State for this information? When President McKinley was down on his sick-bed, the Senate did not bother him with requests for information."

"But at that time Mr. McKinley's condition was known to Congress," snapped Lodge. "There was no secret that he was dangerously wounded and incapable of handling the affairs of his office."

"It is a brain lesion from which the President has been suffering, I am reliably informed," said Senator Moses, who had written a public letter to a constituent containing a similar statement.

Senator Moses was reminded that Dr. Grayson had declared he was not an expert physician in his diagnosis of the President's ailment.

"Well," smiled the Senator, "I believe I am as expert a physician as he is a navigator."

October 16, 1919. "I Intend to Vote for a Reservation"

The Lodge amendment to reverse the Shantung provision of the Versailles Treaty was debated and defeated by the Senate, 35 to 55.

To the country, the defeat of Lodge's own amendment seemed even better proof than the defeat of the Fall amendments that Lodge was losing his fight.

To Lodge, the debate was more significant than the vote. In it he found proof that he was winning his fight. For as Senator after Senator—from states north, south, east, west—spoke up against his amendment, there cropped up again and again a pledge to vote for a reservation.

"I shall vote against the Shantung amendment. . . ." said Senator Hale of Maine. "I shall be satisfied at the present time with a reservation."

Said Senator Sterling of South Dakota: "I would not vote for an amendment that I believe would defeat the treaty if at the same time we can protect American rights and interests by reservations. I believe we can."

Senator Smith of Georgia: "I shall vote against the pending amendment. I shall do so because I consider a wiser way to handle the subject will be . . . by reservation. . . ."

Senator Smoot of Utah: "I intend to vote for a reservation."

October 20, 1919. Public Opinion Confounded

"I consider Wilson next to Christ," said a Bostonian.

"So was Judas Iscariot," replied his friend, in one of the jokes told by the followers of Lodge and Borah and Johnson.

And one of the jokes told by the followers of Wilson had it that this was really the prayer murmured every day by the Senate chaplain:

"God bless the Senate. God save the people."

The propagandists on both sides were hard at work. The League for the Preservation of American Independence had nationalists chanting a little jingle at their meetings:

Freedom to Defend a Right:
Freedom to Refuse to Fight:
Freedom to Mind our Business!

Colonel Harvey had coined a constitutional catchword: "Give Wilson the advice, but not the consent."

There was no doubting the fact that the elaborate, skilful, hard-hitting campaign put on by the irreconcilables was building up a strong bloc of opposition to the League of Nations, and somewhat as a by-product, to all forms of internationalism. A rabid nationalist sentiment was growing rapidly in Chicago and the Middle West. The omnipotent *Chicago Tribune* was convincing tens of thousands that the League of Nations would land us in a World War II. George Sylvester Viereck was leading a vigorous campaign designed to convince millions of German Americans that the League of Nations would betray both the United States and the *Vaterland*. Mobs attending the mass meetings staged by the League for the Preservation of American Independence behaved like Holy Rollers when Borah and Johnson performed.

The country was stirred to its roots by the struggle. Violence flared. Hecklers made nasty scenes at pro-League meetings. When Senator Reed went to Ardmore, Oklahoma, to deliver one of his anti-League diatribes a few days after the President was stricken, women who had lost sons in the war drove him off the platform with a barrage of rotten eggs.

There was ample evidence that the bulk of the country still supported the plan for peace, despite the costly campaign of the League of Nations foes.

On the Pacific Coast, the *Los Angeles Times* took a poll based on this question: "Do you favor the League of Nations as outlined and defended by President Wilson and opposed by Senator Johnson?" The results showed 10,941 for the League, 997 against it. These were the replies from some representative groups:

Board of Directors of Chamber of Commerce	17 to	0
Ministerial Union	156 to	0
Board of Education	7 to	0
District Attorney's staff	24 to	8
Superior Judges	15 to	10
Trinity Methodist Church	2000 to	0
Kiwanis Club, Long Beach	100 to	0
Bakersfield Labor Council	42 to	16
Lobby of Hotel Maryland, Pasadena	12 to	2
Street crowd in Pasadena	31 to	1
Van Nuys Presbyterian Church	1200 to	0
City of Porterville	250 to	25
City of Redlands	150 to	0
San Diego Sun poll	2268 to	399
Imperial High School	83 to	21

On the Atlantic Coast, the League to Enforce Peace sent a post-card questionnaire to war veterans in Fall River, Massachusetts, and got back 554 cards for the League, 12 opposed, 5 for reservations.

Every day, the press carried statements by industrial and financial leaders favoring it, among them Judge Gary, head of the United States Steel Corporation, Bernard Baruch, and Henry Ford. A pro-League petition was sent to the Senate by a list of two hundred and fifty leading Americans—governors, university presidents, bankers, lawyers, judges, bishops, publishers, labor leaders, men like Luther Burbank, Alexander Graham Bell, Thomas Edison.

Petitions for the Versailles Treaty, Covenant and all, were passed by the American Federation of Labor, the American Bankers Association, the Associated Advertising Clubs of the World, and other organizations as varied and as strong as these. The Massachusetts Republican State Convention defied Lodge by approving a motion in favor of the Covenant. The American Bar Association, well posted on the implications of amendments and reservations, met at Boston and voted for ratification without change.

However, there was no powerful pressure in the country for approval of the League without revision. Many groups, including the League to Enforce Peace, failed to take a crystal-clear stand on amendments and reservations, and so the widespread sympathy for the League of Nations had no real effect in the Senate. Due to Lodge's strategy, the issue in the Senate did not seem to be League or no League. It seemed to be revision or no revision.

October 23, 1919. "The Dead Body Will Be on Their Own Doorstep . . ."

Seeking to frighten supporters of the League of Nations into opposition to revision, Senator Hitchcock announced that the Democrats would vote against ratification if the far-reaching amendments or reservations proposed by Senator Lodge were adopted. He called for a compromise.

Senator Lodge flatly refused to consider any compromise. He told a *New York Times* reporter: "Whatever compromise there is will not come from the majority side of the Senate. We do not have to compromise, with a clear majority in our favor."

And then he made an effort to shift the blame from the Republicans to the Democrats in case the plan for peace was defeated. Referring to Senator Hitchcock's threat to vote against the Versailles Treaty if it was emasculated, Lodge declared:

"If the Democrats want to kill the treaty by any such move as that, the dead body will be on their own doorstep, and they will have to bury it."

October 24, 1919. "Come Out in the Open Like Men . . ."

Senator Hitchcock found his efforts to pull together a large enough group of Senators to force approval of only moderate revision frustrated at every turn.

Senator Lodge had obtained a pledge from the mild reservationist Republicans that they would consider no Democratic proposals for compromise unless they were made through him. This made it impossible to talk compromise with any Republicans.

The reservations Wilson had secretly given Hitchcock before his western trip had been turned down by Lodge, and Wilson was in no condition to provide Hitchcock with a new set or to take the lead in any compromise negotiations.

Senator Hitchcock's leadership of the Democrats in the Senate was on very unfirm ground. The real minority leader, Senator Martin, was reportedly dying, and there was a movement among many Senators to elect Senator Underwood to succeed him, instead of Hitchcock.

William Howard Taft visited the capital early in October to see if order couldn't somehow be brought out of the chaos. He found the situation hopeless. He reported to his friends that every Senator favored his own particular reservations, and disliked the reservations advanced by everybody else. No one agreed with anyone else as to what should, could, or would be done. The situation, in effect, was that although most Senators seemed to want *a* League of Nations, everybody was supporting his own particular kind of a League of Nations.

Taft had found Senator Kellogg in a state of "great nervousness," convinced that the League of Nations was doomed despite the widespread demand for it. Kellogg broke forth with a damning of the President and a damning of the Versailles Treaty. He declared he wished the treaty was in hell. Taft asked him if he wasn't for the treaty. He said he was.

Tempers were short, and the debate in the Senate took on an angry tone. The Senate seemed beyond listening to mere words.

"I am sure that no one can change a single vote on this floor by further analysis and dissection of the myriad provisions of the treaty," admitted Senator Smith of Maryland one day. ". . . I have never for an instant doubted the wisdom and duty of ratifying this treaty as submitted as promptly as possible and without amendments or reservations. I shall vote for no reservations unless convinced of the absolute necessity of doing so in order to save from failure the gigantic constructive principle involved."

When Wilson was stricken, John Sharp Williams took the Senate floor in a fury. His eyes glittering beneath his shaggy white eyebrows, his white hair bristling, he decried the personal attacks on the President of the United States.

". . . you cannot tear down this man," he said scornfully. "He is too big a man, too great a man, he is too much of an idealist—just the very thing that you curse him for being; the best thing in the world that a man can be; a thing bringing him nearer to the angels than any other human characteristic can bring him."

Williams looked around the chamber, letting his eyes rest upon certain members sitting at their desks, and upon others whispering in the doorways leading to the cloakrooms.

Only pity was in his heart, he said, for the little men who fought the greatest aspirations of all mankind. What were they fighting, really? Nothing but an attempt to perpetuate peace as well as poor, fallible humans could do it.

Then he hurled a challenge at the amenders, the reservationists, the men who posed as perfectionists: "If you want to beat the treaty and beat the League of Nations, come out in the open like men. . . . Do it like men, open and above board. Just say you will not have it, you do not believe in it."

The Senator admitted that the subtle use of reservations might cause the United States to fail to enter the League now and for many years to come. It might mean there would be no world organization, no permanent peace, for many years. But he quietly added:

". . . the time will come when there will be a League of Nations and when we will be members of it, substantially, if not identically according to the very provisions of this treaty."

October 27, 1919.
Johnson's Amendment to Increase Our Votes

The amendment that won the widest support was one by Hiram Johnson to give the United States as many votes as the six British nations.

Senator Lodge suddenly brought the amendment to a vote in the middle of the afternoon, without warning. Many Senators were absent, and there was a frantic rushing about the cloakrooms, and much telephoning.

The matter of votes had caused trouble enough in Paris. Actually, all the other nations believed the United States would control more votes than Great Britain or any other power, through the Caribbean and Latin-American nations—and they knew Canada would be as likely to vote with us as with England.

When the Senators started shouting that we would be outvoted, however, no American official could proclaim our influence over these votes.

The friends of the League of Nations pointed out that in the whole history of mankind, whenever any group of men have gathered together to form a representative body, there have been bitter arguments about how to assign the voting power, and that it is utterly impossible to satisfy everybody.

Senator McCumber had spent an entire afternoon proving that the charge that the British Empire could dominate the League of Nations was not based on fact.

"Why did France agree that Great Britain should have six votes and France only one?" he demanded. "France has been the most persistent stickler for her rights and her safety of all the nations which signed the compact. Is it not strange that Italy, a country with a population as great as Great Britain, and particularly surrounded by about as disorderly and eruptive a set of States as there are on the face of the earth, is it not strange that Spain and Portugal made no protest? If it had been true that this Covenant gave Great Britain six votes to one given each of the other members in disputes with her, or in fact in any dispute, the other members to this compact never would have signed it."

Senator McCumber flatly declared that Great Britain would be unable to control the votes of the self-governing dominions of Canada, Australia, New Zealand, and South Africa. He admitted she would probably control India's vote, but he pointed out that only one of the six British nations would hold a seat in the Council of the League of Nations, where authority would be concentrated.

But all sober statements of fact were overwhelmed by the wild shouts against the British Empire by Borah and Johnson and Reed and Sherman, by the *Chicago Tribune* and the Hearst Empire. The Hearst papers ran cartoons showing poker games with a prosperous John Bull holding six cards, and poor Uncle Sam only one; they ran cartoons showing a big John Bull herding five meek little boys labeled Canada, Australia, New Zealand, South Africa, and India into the Council of the League of Nations, saying, "Get your votes ready, boys." Said Hiram Johnson: "Great Britain proudly contemplates out of this peace a British world."

And the customary confusion was added by the accompanying protests that the small nations were not given sufficient voting power in the League of Nations. Colonel Harvey howled that the United States and the four great nations given five of the nine seats in the Council had *too much* voting strength. He wrote: "It would be a ghastly travesty to say that while the United States should have one delegate all her own, Argentina [and other Latin-American states] . . . should have only one among them all."

The Hiram Johnson amendment was rushed to a vote without any debate at all in the middle of the afternoon. Many Senators arrived too late to vote. "I was assured that there would be no vote during this hour," protested Senator Ashurst. The amendment was barely defeated, 38 to 40.

October 29, 1919. Scapegoat No. 6—A Godless League of Nations

Senator Lawrence Y. Sherman again sought to stir religious feeling against the League of Nations. Formerly he had asserted the Pope would run the League of Nations. This time he tried to turn Americans of all faiths against the Covenant.

"Mr. President," he said, "I now submit an amendment. . . ."

A clerk took a sheet of paper from the Senator, and carried it to the Vice President, who read:

"Amend, by inserting before the word 'agree' in the last line of the preamble or statement of the League's purposes, the following: 'invoke the considerate judgment of mankind and the glorious favor of Almighty God and.'"

The Vice President recognized Senator Sherman.

"I wish very briefly to state that the supreme worldly self-sufficiency of the Paris conference challenges the belief of mankind in an over-ruling Providence," said he. "I do not wish to discuss this matter save to say that the Declaration of Independence, the Articles of Confederation, the Emancipation Proclamation . . . all contain references to an over-ruling Providence. This document does not."

Senator Thomas of Colorado promptly rose to explain: "I think on several occasions in the past treaties which have been made between the United States and other Governments have been made in the name of Almighty God, or of the Holy Trinity, both, of course, representing the Deity in Christian conception. The vast number of our treaties, however, have made no reference whatever to that subject. Here, however, is a treaty which is designed to change the face of the world geographically, politically and morally, the constituents of which represent various forms of religious belief. That fact, in my judgment, justifies the absence of such a reference in this treaty; and I can easily understand how its insertion . . . might be the cause of serious disagreement with regard to the ultimate acceptance of the document. . . .

"I do not think I misstate the position of the Senator from Illinois when I say that it is not his purpose to vote for the ratification of this treaty whether his amendment is adopted or not."

Very few of the pro-League Senators wanted to speak on the amendment, let alone vote against it. They shuddered at the thought, visualizing their opponents in the next campaign shouting: "And this atheist voted against God!!!"

Senator Sherman watched them squirm, and saw several leave the chamber on urgent business elsewhere. The leaders gathered in a doorway to discuss the best tactic to adopt against the amendment.

"We can afford to adopt this amendment, but you gentlemen in this body cannot afford to defeat it," taunted Sherman. "Defeat it and take the consequences!"

Senator Walsh of Montana corrected Sherman on one point:

"I desire to call the attention of the Senate to the fact that the Senator from Illinois in the list of documents in which reference is made to the Deity, did not include the Constitution of the United States, and quite properly, because it contains no reference to the Deity. The Senator has now been a member of this body for something over five years, and if he has heretofore proposed an amendment to the Constitution . . . correcting that document in that respect, my attention has not been called to it. . . .

"We must therefore look for some other purpose in this amendment than a desire to perfect the document."

Sherman retorted: ". . . when this League of Nations treaty shall have been adopted, we can afford to dispense with the Constitution, whether it is sacrilegious or otherwise, because we will have no use for it hereafter. . . . I never prayed in my life. Born of Christian parents—"

Senator Robinson of Arkansas interrupted: "Does not the Senator think it is about time he was beginning to pray?"

"No, sir; not upon the appearance of any such antagonist as the Senator from Arkansas. I can take care of him by myself, if God will just leave us alone."

(Laughter in the galleries.)

"I do not care to discuss this problem," said Sherman. ". . . I offered the amendment in a deeply reverential sense. . . ."

"I cannot bring myself to what would be in me hypocrisy," said Senator Henry Cabot Lodge. "I do not ask, I am not ready to ask, the blessing of God on this document. I trust in His wisdom it may ultimately be turned to good purpose, but as it stands today I should personally think I were a hypocrite if I asked for the blessing of God upon it."

"My suggestion on that is, Mr. President," said Sherman, "that even thugs, before they strangle their victims, invoke the blessings of their god; even thieves before they steal, and the bloody warriors of an antique age before they went out to loot, to desolate, and to burn have invoked the blessings of their god."

"Mr. President, I only desire to make one observation," declared Senator Knox, rising to his feet. "It seems to me that the remarks made by the Senator from Massachusetts constitute the strongest argument for the adoption of the amendment, because the worse the treaty is the more it needs the supervision of the Almighty."

It was Senator David I. Walsh of Massachusetts, a devout Catholic, who finally suggested the way to defeat the amendment proposed by Senator Sherman.

"I do not believe Senators ought to be asked to go on record in opposition to this amendment," he said. "One cannot always explain the motive which actuates or prompts amendments of this kind, and one cannot always explain, without misunderstanding, his reasons for voting against amendments which ordinarily would be unanimously adopted."

Senator Robinson thankfully said: "I move to lay the amendment . . . on the table."

The motion carried, 57 to 27. Several Senators refrained from voting even on this harmless motion.

In the evening, after the Senate adjourned, Colonel Bonsal, assistant to Colonel House and President Wilson at Paris, paid a visit to Senator Lodge in his home on Massachusetts Avenue.

The white-haired Senator said: "You good people who were over there in Paris seem to have been entranced by the President's eloquence. You thought that his was the voice that breathed over Eden, proclaiming a new era, that the old Adam was dead. . . ."

"Not at all," replied Colonel Bonsal. "We knew he was not dead, but we did believe he had a wicked clutch on the throat of civilization, and that unless it was broken the world which men of good will loved was doomed to end."

Senator Lodge playfully ridiculed the grammar of the Covenant. "As an English production it does not rank high," he smiled. "It might get by at Princeton but certainly not at Harvard."

The Colonel diplomatically agreed, but he was not in a mood for play. Seriously, he pointed out the difficulties arising when treaties involving many nations are drawn:

"Every sentence had to be translated into several languages and then retranslated back a dozen times, and each time every word was subjected to the suspicious scrutiny of eyes which were looking for something other than grammatical mistakes or awkward phrases."

Colonel Bonsal told Senator Lodge that once Jan Christian Smuts had told the delegates at Paris when he presented a single, carefully worded provision concerning mandates: "I can see many places where there is room for improvement and clarification. But this agreement has been reached through long and weary nights of discussion within the Committee and I warn you that if even a word is changed or perhaps even a comma, the whole edifice will collapse. We would have to begin all over again."

Senator Lodge made it very plain to Colonel Bonsal that nothing could dissuade him from his determination to get reservations. The Colonel tried to get him to talk terms, and Senator Lodge finally got out a printed copy of the Covenant and penciled in notes. They consisted of slight modifications of the reservations he was demanding in the Senate.

Then the conversation went afield, and Colonel Bonsal impatiently looked for an opening to get away.

Once out of Lodge's home, he hurried to the post office near Union Station and mailed the copy of the Covenant—bearing Lodge's notations—to Colonel House, who was still sick in bed.

November 2, 1919. Colonel House to President Wilson

Colonel House sent to President Wilson the Covenant bearing Senator Lodge's markings, together with a long letter and a memorandum from Colonel Bonsal describing in detail his meeting with the Gentleman from Massachusetts.

In an accompanying letter, Colonel House urged Wilson to accept the reservations.

November 6, 1919. Senator Lodge's Delicate Task

While the debating and the voting on amendment after amendment—all of them destined for defeat—had been consuming every afternoon in the Senate, Chairman Lodge had been holding morning meetings with the Foreign Relations Committee to fashion new reservations.

Lodge later described in detail the situation he faced:

"We had in all forty-nine Republican Senators. There were fifteen Republican Senators who were ready to vote for reservations but would not vote for the treaty under any circumstances, whether reservations were adopted or not. They were known as the 'irreconcilables.' That left thirty-four Republican Senators who were ready to vote for the treaty with reservations, but there was a difference among the thirty-four as to the character of the reservations desired. There were eight or ten Republican Senators who were known as 'mild reservationists,' but they differed among themselves as to the degree of mildness which they were ready to accept. This situation introduced an element of difficulty and uncertainty in the problem with which I had to deal because I was Chairman of the Foreign Relations Committee as well as leader of the Republican majority. The fifteen irreconcilables could be counted upon to support all reservations; the stronger the reservations were the better they liked them. There were about eighteen Republican Senators who, like myself, were determined to have effective reservations; and then, lastly, there were eight or ten, some of whom were ready to accept the mildest kind of reservations and others who agreed generally with those who might be called the 'middle group.' It was essential of course from my point of view to secure, if possible, the vote of every Republican Senator for the reservations, and I need not say that under the conditions which I have tried to explain this required some compromises in language and form and a great deal of effort and discussion among ourselves. If I could secure a united Republican vote for reservations, there were three Democratic irreconcilables who could be depended upon to vote for all reservations and one more who generally voted with them. This was sufficient to make the reservations safe if we could secure, as I have said, a united Republican vote. *There was another object which I had very much at heart, and that was that if we were successful in putting on reservations we should create a situation where, if the acceptance of the treaty was defeated, the Democratic party, and especially Mr. Wilson's friends, should be responsible for its defeat, and not the opponents of the treaty who were trying to pass it in a form safe for the United States.*" [Italics: A. C.]

Thus, while intending to saddle Wilson with the blame in the end, Lodge had to produce reservations that would be supported in the Senate by men who thought the reservations would kill the League of Nations, and by men who thought they would save it. The reservations had to be mild enough to satisfy the eight or ten Republicans who wanted the League with slight revision, and yet strong enough to persuade Wilson to veto the Versailles Treaty. That Lodge fully intended to send Wilson a treaty he would veto was made clear in several of his private conversations, including those with Jim Watson.

Said Lodge in a letter to Elihu Root: "What I should like best is to have him [Wilson] refuse to make the treaty and then come before the people next year as a candidate for the presidency. He would be the worst beaten man that ever lived. . . ."

Lodge had studied Wilson carefully, sized him up constantly, estimated just how far he would have to go in his reservations in order to make them unacceptable to Wilson. He later described his careful study of the President:

"As the final vote drew near, however, I felt convinced that it was quite possible that the treaty with the reservations would be adopted by the Senate because it was obvious to me that on this final and crucial test a majority of the Democrats would be unwilling to vote against ratification. But I also felt convinced that President Wilson would prevent the acceptance of the treaty with reservations if he possibly could. I based this opinion on the knowledge which I had acquired as to Mr. Wilson's temperament, intentions and purposes. I had learned from a careful study of the President's acts and utterances during those trying days—and it was as important for me to understand him as it was for his closest friends—that the key to all he did was that he thought of everything in terms of Wilson."

Lodge added this: "The conviction held by me as to the governing quality of Mr. Wilson's mind and character was reached very slowly and only finally arrived at when I found myself confronted with a situation, the gravity of which in its public importance could not be exaggerated, and when a correct analysis of Mr. Wilson's probable attitude was an element of vital moment to me in trying to solve the intricate problem which I and those with whom I acted were compelled to face."

There was only one possible purpose behind all this careful study of Wilson. It was to guide Lodge in the creation of reservations Wilson would refuse to accept.

Wilson had said again and again that it would be ruinous if reservations had to be submitted to other nations; this was clearly his chief objection to reservations. A preamble was written by Lodge's committee stating that the Versailles Treaty would not go into effect, even if ratified by the United States, until all reservations adopted by the Senate had been "accepted by an exchange of notes" by at least three of the four principal Allies, Great Britain, France, Italy, and Japan.

Wilson had always emphasized that Article 10 was the most important provision in the Covenant. A reservation was written cutting away at it.

Fourteen strong reservations were written in all—lending a dramatic touch to the struggle:

It was Woodrow Wilson's "Fourteen Points" versus Henry Cabot Lodge's "Fourteen Reservations."

November 7, 1919. The Vote on the Preamble

Senator Lodge brought the preamble to a vote in the Senate, as the first test of strength on reservations. The feeling was tense in the chamber, and the galleries were packed. Many members of the

House of Representatives were watching, sitting in the leather sofas that line the walls.

Early in the debate, a gallery spectator jumped to his feet waving an American flag.

"Gentlemen of the Senate," he yelled, "I want to make a speech—"

Guards seized him, and he was dragged away, protesting that God had sent him a message to come to the Senate and make a speech on the League of Nations.

Senator Hitchcock stood up to reveal that he had just visited President Wilson's bedside. There was a sudden hush in the Senate, and all eyes were on the acting Democratic leader. He said that Wilson had declared he would accept any reservations which friends of the treaty thought necessary, so long as the terms of the treaty were not endangered. He said the President had given the party leaders in the Senate full discretion in accepting reservations.

Wilson considered the preamble and the Lodge reservations destructive, he declared.

Following Senator Hitchcock's statement, several supporters of the League of Nations urged defeat of the preamble, not only because adoption of reservations requiring approval by other powers would delay and endanger the peace, but because the wording of the preamble was an insult to the twenty-eight small nations who had attended the Paris Conference. The preamble provided that the Versailles Treaty would go into effect, so far as we were concerned, without their approval. Yet all precedents in international law indicated that every signatory power had a full right to consider any reservations attached to a treaty before the treaty would be considered in effect. The Democrats urged that reservations be considered in a separate resolution, to avoid the necessity of submitting them to any other nations.

When the vote came, the mild reservationists, with the exception of Senator McCumber of North Dakota, voted with Senator Lodge. He was also supported by three Democrats—blind Senator Gore of Oklahoma, David I. Walsh of Massachusetts, and, of course, Reed. The preamble was adopted, 48 to 40.

When Hitchcock, gloomy, head down, walked out into the corridors, he was surrounded by reporters who wanted to know how Wilson looked. He told them he was alert, and intensely interested in the developments in the Senate:

"He was in bed; an overturned chair and pillows behind him supporting his back. He was almost sitting up. He said he was glad the amendments had been defeated, and that our plans for the future were good."

The correspondents asked if the President approved Hitchcock's plan to bring about a deadlock by voting against severe reservations.

"Yes," was the reply. "The President said he was willing to leave the matter of compromise to the friends of the treaty here, but told me that any time a serious doubt arose in our minds about any procedure he would be glad to have the suggestions submitted to him.

"He said he would accept any compromise the friends of the treaty thought necessary to save the treaty, so long as it did not destroy the terms of the pact itself."

November 8, 1919. The Vote on Reservation No. 1

The first of the fourteen reservations concerned withdrawal. The Covenant provided in Article 1 that a nation could withdraw from the League of Nations if it had fulfilled all its international obligations up to the time of its withdrawal.

Senator Lodge proposed this reservation:

> The United States so understands and construes Article 1 that in case of notice of withdrawal from the League of Nations, as provided in said article, the United States shall be the sole judge as to whether all its international obligations and all its obligations under the said Covenant have been fulfilled, and notice of withdrawal by the United States may be given by a concurrent resolution of the Congress of the United States.

The opponents of the reservations pointed out that this was worse than the preamble, for it would be obnoxious to *all* other nations, large and small. They condemned it as a selfish demand by the United States for special privilege not given to any other nation. Was it in the spirit of a concert of nations for the United States to start off by saying it would be the sole judge of its own acts?

They also declared that, after all the talk by the opponents of the League about the Constitution, the reservation subverted a fundamental principle of the Constitution. It would give Congress unprecedented powers in foreign affairs. For a "concurrent resolution" is a bill passed through Congress in a form not requiring the signature of the President of the United States. The reservation would make it possible for Congress to remove the United States from the League of Nations at any moment, without even consulting the executive branch of the government.

Senator Knute Nelson, a mild reservationist, could not swallow this one. He told the Senate it was an attempt to cast a slur on Wilson.

". . . the President is now lying on a sick bed, and we are asked here in the Senate to put a slight upon him by putting in this provision in regard to a concurrent resolution in order to cut him off, as it is viewed here in the Senate. That goes against my grain, Mr. President. I am a Republican and have been all my days—but I do not approve of the intense partisanship that at this moment would put a slight upon the President of the United States, and would say to him, 'We do not trust you to have anything to do with denouncing this treaty.'"

Lodge had a clever reply. He said it was far more apt to be applying to Republican Presidents in the future.

There were snickers, and the Senate voted for the reservation, 48 to 40.

November 11, 1919.
"I Feel Humiliated and Outraged . . ."

To the Senate on the first anniversary of the Armistice, Senator Owen of Oklahoma solemnly read the last of the Fourteen Points:

"A general association of nations must be formed under specific covenants for the purpose of affording mutual guarantees of political independence and territorial integrity to great and small states alike."

Senator Owen declared that we had entered, fought, and won the World War with that as our professed aim. He recounted the negotiations with the Allies and with the enemy culminating in Germany's surrender on November 11, 1918, on the basis of the Fourteen Points.

He said the Senate consented by its "persistent" silence. Yet, a year later, there was no peace. There was mounting militarism. And he said we were to blame, for we were breaking a contract with all the world.

A big barrel of a man got to his feet. "The President of the United States has no more authority to bind the United States than I have," bellowed Senator Boies Penrose, Philadelphia boss, "and far be it from me to convey the impression that I concur in every proposition advanced in the Senate against which I do not rise and protest. . . . As an American I feel humiliated and outraged at the conduct of the Executive of the United States in this instance—"

"That is denunciation, not argument," interrupted Senator Owen.

"—going to Paris without authority, obsessed with an egotistical idea about a peace covenant which no one wanted or cared about."

"That is denunciation, not argument," repeated Senator Owen.

"It is both," snapped Penrose.

"It is valid as neither."

Down the hill at the White House, Woodrow Wilson observed Armistice Day by leaving his sick bed for a wheel chair.

November 12, 1919. Death of Senator Martin

Senator Thomas S. Martin of Virginia, Democratic leader in the Senate, died.

November 13, 1919. The Reservation on Article 10

Senator Lodge called the second reservation to a vote. Concerned with Article 10, it said:

> The United States assumes no obligations to preserve the territorial integrity or political independence of any other country or to interfere in controversies between nations—whether members of the League or not—under the provisions of Article 10, or to employ the military or naval forces of the United States under any article of the treaty for any purpose, unless in any particular case the Congress, which, under the Constitution, has the sole power to declare war or authorize the employment of the military or naval forces of the United States, shall by act or joint resolution so provide.

The irreconcilables attacked the reservation as way too weak, but Lodge and Root agreed it nullified Article 10.

The unqualified supporters of the League of Nations held it was contrary to the entire spirit of international co-operation against aggressors. It would mean the world did not guarantee as a matter of incontestable right the political independence and integrity of members of the League of Nations. It would indicate that the United States did not oppose aggression unless it threatened the United States. It would mean serious delay in action against aggressors. Wilson later said: "If we were to reject Article 10, or so to weaken it as to take its full force out of it, it would mark us as desiring to return to the old world of jealous rivalry and misunderstandings from which our gallant soldiers have rescued us and would leave us without any vision or new conception of justice and peace. We would have learned no lesson from the war, but gained only the regret that it had involved us in its maelstrom of suffering. If America has awakened, as the rest of the world has, to the vision of a new day in which the mistakes of the past are to be corrected, it will welcome the opportunity to share the responsibilities of Article 10."

All through the debate on the fourteen Lodge reservations, the Democrats offered compromise reservations. However, the pledge the mild reservationist Republicans had given to Lodge prevented advance discussion of the compromise proposals, and when they came to a vote, Lodge refused to accept them. One by one, all of them (including some suggested by Senator McCumber, too) were voted down.

The friends of the League of Nations kept right on trying. Before the vote on the Lodge reservation on Article 10, Senator Kenneth McKellar, Democrat of Tennessee, offered a compromise reservation. It was defeated, 46 to 18. Senator Hitchcock offered a compromise reservation. It was defeated, 44 to 19. Hitchcock charged that many of the negative votes were cast due to pledges more than to preferences.

The Senate then passed the Lodge reservation, 46 to 33.

November 15, 1919. Senator Lodge Invokes Cloture

Once the preamble and the reservations concerning withdrawal and Article 10 were approved, there was no doubt in anyone's mind that the other reservations would be adopted by the Senate.

Senator Lodge was not interested in playing for further time, and to cut down debate he proposed that cloture be invoked. It would limit debate on the entire Versailles Treaty to one hour for each Senator. Requiring support of a two-thirds majority, cloture is almost never invoked; it makes filibustering impossible, and the irreconcilables opposed the motion. Most Senators were tired of talk, however, and the motion was approved, 78 to 16.

Then, with virtually no debate, ten more reservations were rushed through. Some of them were not debated at all. The votes ranged around 53 to 40.

Among the ten were reservations providing that no mandate would be accepted by the United States without the consent of Congress; that the United States would be sole judge of what questions were domestic and none of the League's business; that the United States would decide what questions came under the Monroe Doctrine and were none of the League's business; that the United States would not be bound by the Shantung settlement; that the

United States could disregard disarmament plans of the League; and that the appointment and activity of American delegates to the League or any of its agencies would be controlled by Congress.

While the United States Senate was adopting these reservations in wholesale fashion, a meeting was being held in Berlin.

Vice Chancellor of the Reich Mathias Erzberger and others came to the meeting to speak for the League of Nations and for international co-operation between all nations. A gang suddenly swooped down and broke up the meeting. The ruffians then marched to the Wilhelmplatz and stood before the American Embassy.

"Down with Wilson!" they shouted. "Down with America!"

November 17, 1919. "Like Hell You Are . . ."

For the first time since his return to Washington, President Wilson went outside the White House. He was rolled in a wheel chair to the lawn near the south portico, and for more than an hour he sat in the fresh air and sunshine.

Senator Hitchcock visited the President for an hour, and afterward told reporters he found him greatly improved, bright, cheerful, and fully acquainted with the treaty events as they had developed in the Senate since his visit of two weeks before.

"The President told me he has read and considered the Lodge reservations," said Hitchcock. "He characterized them, as a whole, as a nullification of the treaty and utterly impossible of acceptance. He has not changed his mind as to their effect upon the treaty.

"President Wilson will pocket the treaty if the Lodge program of reservations is carried out in the ratifying resolution. The President did not say, however, that all the Lodge reservations were not acceptable."

Senator Hitchcock stated the President was particularly opposed to the preamble, and it was believed that he also considered the reservation concerning Article 10 absolutely unacceptable.

Meanwhile, the Senate approved the last two Lodge reservations. One of them declared the United States would not be bound by any decision of the League of Nations in which the British Dominions voted. The time for the vote on the Versailles Treaty was at hand.

The attention of the entire country was focused on Washington, but the fight for and against the League of Nations was still raging in the grass roots, and it was ever more bitter and sharp. The *New York Times* received dispatches from two Minnesota towns:

> Ortonville, Minn., Nov. 17—"I am going to speak on the League of Nations" remarked ex-Congressman Ernest Lundeen of the Fifth Minnesota District, as he entered the opera house here, where he was scheduled to speak tonight against the League.
>
> "Like hell you are," replied a member of the American Legion, and a few moments later Lundeen was taken bodily from the stage by members of the local post of the ex-soldiers organization and escorted to the railway station.
>
> About fifty former service men succeeded in placing him in a refrigerator car and fastened the door. . . .
>
> Appleton, Minn., Nov. 17—Ernest Lundeen who was locked in a refrigerator car at Ortonville, about twenty miles from here, tonight, arrived at Appleton just before 11 p.m. Members of the train crew heard his shouts, released him from the car, and permitted him to ride in the caboose to this city. . . .

November 18, 1919. The Senate on the Eve

The vote on the Versailles Treaty was expected to come in the Senate on November 19.

On the eve of the decision, there was appalling confusion among the supporters of the League of Nations.

Should they support the treaty, reservations and all?

Should they support some reservations, and oppose others? And if so, which ones?

Should they oppose the treaty as long as the reservations were included?

The advice was conflicting. From all sides came all advice.

For months, some top officials of the League to Enforce Peace had been working for reservations, and some against them. Members had been getting advice to put pressure on their Senators for and against reservations. Those working for reservations were working for varying sets of reservations.

The Executive Committee of the League to Enforce Peace held a long, angry, last-minute meeting on November 15, and now they issued a baffling statement. It admitted that some of the reservations were "harmful" but urged acceptance of the treaty with the reservations. Then, it demanded elimination of the preamble.

Many of the Executive Committee members opposed the statement. Herbert Hoover, a new member, declared that if "we attempt now to revise the treaty we shall tread a road through European chaos." Alton B. Parker charged the reservations were the weapons of Senators who were out to "scuttle" the League of Nations. Some were shifting their positions overnight. George W. Wickersham, one-time Attorney General, said on November 13 that the League to Enforce Peace should oppose reservations. On November 17 he decided they should be supported.

The Washington office of the League to Enforce Peace kept right on working against reservations despite the declaration of the Executive Committee.

It was rumored that President Wilson was preparing a letter to the Democrats telling them to vote for the treaty even with the reservations. It was rumored that President Wilson was preparing a letter to the Democrats telling them to vote against the treaty with the reservations.

Colonel House had received no word from Wilson concerning Lodge's compromise suggestions, and thought possibly they had never reached him. Mrs. Wilson was deciding what matters should or should not be brought to her husband's attention. House was somewhat disappointed at first, but he concluded that Lodge's good faith in the private suggestions made to Colonel Bonsal was to be held in doubt. For, at the time Lodge suggested one set of reservations to Bonsal, he was concocting a different set in his committee, and meanwhile he was demanding amendments on the Senate floor. It was said, too, that Lodge was assuring his intimates that if Wilson ever agreed to anything, he would find an excuse to make some new demands. Colonel House liked to quote a fellow-Texan on the subject of the Gentleman from Massachusetts:

"To have followed the track of Lodge in that Treaty battle would have broken the back of the most supple rattlesnake."

Colonel Bonsal went on this last day to see well-meaning Senator Hitchcock, whose temporary party leadership in the Senate was being challenged by Senator Underwood.

"I confess the Massachusetts Senator is an enigma to me," said Hitchcock. He declared that for a while he had thought Lodge just wanted to get "some of his great thoughts" into the Covenant so it would not be a Democratic document.

"I admit that in some of my unofficial cloakroom talks with Lodge he expressed views which even to me seem reasonable," said Hitchcock, "but when I ask him to get down to cases and state what changes he would suggest, his attitude stiffens and his face hardens."

Colonel Bonsal pointed out that the Covenant was actually in good part a Republican document, due to the hard-won amendments made by Wilson in accordance with the criticisms and suggestions of Lodge, Taft, Root, and others.

Senator Hitchcock laughed bitterly.

"I made the same remark to Lodge—not once but at least twice. His only answer was a blank stare."

November 19, 1919. The Day of Destiny

Shortly before the Senate assembled to vote on the Versailles Treaty, the Democratic Senators held a conference. Senator Hitchcock read this letter from the White House:

My Dear Senator:

You were good enough to bring me word that the Democratic Senators supporting the treaty expected to hold a conference before the final vote on the Lodge resolution of ratification and that they would be glad to receive a word of counsel from me.

I should hesitate to offer it in any detail, but I assume that the Senators only desire my judgment on the all-important question of the final vote on the resolution containing the many reservations of Senator Lodge. On that I cannot hesitate, for, in my opinion, the resolution in that form does not provide for ratification, but rather for nullification of the treaty. I sincerely hope that the friends and supporters of the treaty will vote against the Lodge resolution of ratification.

I understand that the door will then probably be open for a genuine resolution of ratification.

I trust that all true friends of the treaty will refuse to support the Lodge resolution.

Cordially and sincerely yours,
Woodrow Wilson

When the Senate assembled at noon, the galleries were overflowing, and the corridors of the Capitol were filled with people who hoped to get in before the day was done.

The Senate Chaplain, the Rev. Forrest J. Prettyman, D.D., offered a prayer:

"Almighty God, we come before Thee as we face the tremendous responsibilities of this hour. The welfare of millions is dependent upon the action of the Senate. We would seek the guidance of the God of our fathers in the performance of our duty. We pray for Thy spirit, the spirit of wisdom and counsel, the spirit of a sound mind, that we may do our duty in God's sight, and so well perform it that it may have Thy approval. We ask for Jesus' sake. Amen."

Vice President Thomas R. Marshall said: "The Chair lays before the Senate the treaty of peace with Germany."

Majority Leader Henry Cabot Lodge then took over the proceeding on the Senate floor, and he ruled with an iron hand for the rest of the day.

"I suggest the absence of a quorum," he said.

"The clerk will call the roll," said the Vice President.

Everyone was present except Senator Fall, who was away in New Mexico.

Next, Lodge submitted to the Senate his resolution of ratification of the Versailles Treaty, containing the preamble and the fourteen reservations. Instead of suggesting an immediate vote on it, however, Majority Leader Lodge offered Acting Minority Leader Hitchcock an opportunity to propose any compromise resolution he might have in mind: "Now is the time for any resolution the minority leader wishes to put in."

"I thank the Senator from Massachusetts for the suggestion," replied Senator Hitchcock, "but it is the consensus of opinion over here that inasmuch as the Senate has already taken up these reservations and has committed itself to the reservations prepared by the Senator from Massachusetts, it would not be timely to propose now, while Senators are bound by pledge, a resolution of unqualified ratification. If the Senator will permit us to secure unanimous consent for such a resolution immediately following the vote upon his resolution we shall be very glad to avail ourselves of it."

"If the Senator from Nebraska thinks that the majority of the Senate will not keep their pledge to support the majority reservations after the majority resolution is defeated, he is mistaken," snapped Lodge. Actually, he had no intention of putting the Republican mild reservationists to any such test. He intended to permit no vote on any compromise resolution containing milder reservations, if his own resolution was defeated.

The speeches began.

"Mr. President," said Senator Sherman, "I turn for solace and for guidance to Holy Writ and quote from the book of Job. 'Shall not the multitude of words be answered? And shall a man full of talk be justified?' . . . The future of this measure is shrouded in uncertainty. Perchance it sleepeth only and waits for our all-wise Executive to rouse it from its torpor and again threaten us with its pristine beauty and excellence. It may be pleasingly arrayed in alliterative phrase and sonorous periods cunningly placed to obscure the selfish, boiling hell of the original text. Every ambush to the military man who is caught thereby looks mild until it starts into action. Beware of future reservations that do not reserve. . . .

"If, happily, the reservations adopted prove the death of this treaty, let this be my funeral oration over the defunct remains.

"It is the potent, insidious sneak thief of Europe, designed in the cloakroom of international philanthropy."

Senator Brandegee bluntly reminded the signers of the round

robin of their pledge. He asserted he was going to keep his vow to vote against the League of Nations:

"I would consider myself a candidate for a madhouse if I were to vote for any such thing."

"Mr. President," interposed Senator Hitchcock, "how can Senators view this great attempt to organize the world for peace as a matter of jest and gibe and joke? . . . How can they when we are only fresh from the terrible experiences of war, look upon a great world-wide attempt to prevent it in the future as a matter for gibe and jest?"

He reminded the Senate once more that one of our professed war aims had been the creation of a world organization. Then he quoted a resolution Senator Lodge had once introduced:

"That in the opinion of the Senate an independent Polish State should be erected . . . whose political and economic independence and territorial integrity should be guaranteed by international covenant."

He then quoted from Senator Lodge's reservation concerning Article 10: "The United States assumes no obligation to preserve the territorial integrity or political independence of any other country . . . or to interfere in controversies between nations. . . ."

And then he demanded: "Is that not repudiation? How can the Poles look at it as anything else than repudiation? . . . How can the governments associated with us in the war, who have honestly assumed the obligation in ratifying the treaty, look at our action as anything else than repudiation and abandonment of them in the enterprise in which we started with them?

"We are charged with defeating this treaty because we cannot accept those reservations, because we claim they nullify the treaty that they are assumed to clarify. How can we think otherwise? Who made these reservations? Did we have any voice in them, we who were expected to furnish the bulk of the votes for the ratification of the treaty? No? The Senator from Connecticut [Brandegee] who has declared that he will never vote for the treaty in any form, was influential in making those reservations. So was the Senator from California [Johnson] and the Senator from Pennsylvania [Knox] and others, inside and outside of the Foreign Relations Committee who propose never to vote for the treaty . . . we cannot view as made in good faith reservations which are dictated by Senators who do not . . . believe in the treaty. . . .

"They have not drafted them for the purpose of helping the treaty. We have had no opportunity, as yet, on this side to get together with the thirty or more Senators on the other side of the aisle who would like to see this treaty ratified in some form. You of the other side have drafted these reservations just as a caucus drafts a platform, and you say to us, . . . 'Take it or leave it; that or nothing!' "

Senator Hitchcock then took up the reservations one by one, analyzing them and showing how compromise would be possible. Then: "I have not much more to say. I have said what I have, because I feel deeply that the time has come when . . . men in the Senate who want a league of nations in some form, who want to ratify the treaty in some form, should get together and do it . . . Is the world to be organized for peace or war?"

There was applause in the galleries when Hitchcock sat down.

Senator Borah delivered a long speech in a loud voice. "We are told this treaty means peace," he shouted. "Even so, I would not pay the price. Would you purchase peace at the cost of every part of our independence?"

Senator Owen reminded Lodge that in 1916 he had supported the idea of a league. Said Owen: "Nothing has happened since that time that justifies the change of opinion on the part of the Senator from Massachusetts who stands today . . . opposed to the League of Nations and determined to kill it by a parliamentary maneuver. . . .

"I believe that a majority of this Chamber desire to have a covenant which will secure the peace and happiness of mankind and the protection of this country. I feel perfectly assured that there will be found in this body two-thirds of its members who will be able to agree upon the ratification and that . . . reservations can be agreed upon . . . satisfactory to them. With that faith and that hope, I shall vote against the pending resolution."

At 5:30 p.m., after five and a half hours of debate and as Senator

McCumber was sitting down after a plea for the League of Nations, Senators all over the chamber set up the cry:

"Vote!"

"Vote!" "Vote!"

No other Senator rose to speak. Vice President Marshall ruled:

"The clerk will call the roll."

The clerk stood up and called:

"Ashurst?"

And the reply:

"No."

"Ball?"

"Aye."

"Bankhead?"

"No."

"Beckham?"

"No."

"Borah?"

"No."

"Calder?"

"Aye."

And so on through to:

"Wolcott?"

"No."

The Versailles Treaty was defeated, 39 voting for it, 55 voting against it.

In the galleries, tense through the vote, there was only a faint murmur as the vote was announced.

Senators conferred in clusters all over the floor of the chamber.

The fifty-five who had voted against the Versailles Treaty were the Democrats who had fought for it always, and the Republican irreconcilables, joined by Reed, Democrat, who had fought against it always.

The thirty-nine who had voted for it were the mild reservationist Republicans, and the strict reservationist Republicans. Senator Lodge was among them, thus going down in the records of the Senate as voting for the Versailles Treaty and the League of Nations.

Senator Hitchcock gained Vice President Marshall's recognition, and moved that the Senate adjourn. Now that the Lodge resolution had been defeated, he wanted time to work out a compromise overnight. Lodge had given Hitchcock to understand that he would allow a brief recess to provide an opportunity for working out an agreement.

Senator Lodge had other plans now. He intended to have the Senate adjourn until December in order to prevent all opportunity for hasty compromise.

The Hitchcock motion to adjourn was defeated, 51 to 42.

Vice President Marshall then ruled that the treaty was open to any amendment, reservation, or substitute resolution of ratification that might be offered—thus offering Hitchcock an opportunity to offer a compromise resolution of ratification containing reservations mild enough to satisfy the mild reservationist Republicans.

Lodge immediately raised a point of order. He stated that his ratifying resolution was before the Senate, and that the Versailles Treaty itself was not. Therefore any new resolution of ratification was out of order.

"The Chair overrules the point of order of the Senator from Massachusetts," said the Vice President.

"On that I appeal," declared Lodge.

Several Senators leaped to their feet and addressed the Chair.

"Unfortunately, these questions are not debatable," said the Vice President. "The Chair cannot give his reasons and the Senator from Massachusetts cannot give his."

When there is a dispute over a ruling made by the presiding officer of the Senate, however, the Senate can overrule him. There is no higher court. The Senate decides by vote whether it wishes to accept the Vice President's interpretation of the Senate rules or to make its own interpretation to suit the purposes of the moment.

Senator Lodge forced a vote, and the Senate overruled the Vice President, 51 to 42. Lodge controlled the same 51 votes that defeated Hitchcock's motion to adjourn.

"It appears that the Chair did not know the law," observed Vice President Marshall.

Senator Hitchcock's next move was to offer a substitute resolution of ratification without reservations of any sort. The operation of the cloture was bearing hard on the leaders of both sides; their time was running out. And so it was Senator Poindexter, acting for Lodge, who raised the point of order this time. He held once more that Hitchcock's resolution of ratification was out of order, since another resolution of ratification was before the Senate.

The Vice President overruled Poindexter, and the Senate promptly overruled the Vice President, 50 to 43.

Senator McCumber rose on the Republican side of the aisle and sought to achieve a compromise by offering an amendment to remove from the preamble to Lodge's resolution the provision that the reservations would have to be approved by three of the major Allies.

Senator Poindexter again raised a point of order, Vice President Marshall again overruled him, and the Senate again overruled the Vice President, 50 to 42.

Senator McCumber tried again. He moved to reconsider the vote by which the Senate had adopted the preamble in the first place. Senator Boies Penrose was on his feet like a shot, shouting to be recognized. He had a new point of order, declaring that Senator McCumber had voted against the preamble and therefore, under Senate rules, was ineligible to call for a reconsideration.

Senator McCumber subsided in his seat hopelessly, in the midst of what the *New York Sun* correspondent called "the most amazing parliamentary tangle that anyone could remember." The supporters of the League of Nations were nonplused. Senator Lodge's strategy was blocking every effort to compromise.

The Democrats, who had confidently expected to be granted full opportunity to work out a compromise once the Lodge resolution had been defeated, conferred frantically in gesticulating groups. Some met in the cloakroom to try to think of a way to stop the Lodge steamroller.

The mild reservationist Republicans, apparently still bound to Senator Lodge to make no compromise except through him, were contributing to the success of his strategy by voting with him to overrule the Vice President.

Senator Joe Robinson of Arkansas angrily took the Senate floor to sum up the situation: "The Senate is now proceeding in violation of all the precedents with which I am familiar.... The effect of the erroneous decision imposed upon this body by a majority of the Senate a few months ago is to deprive the Senate of the power to reach a decision. . . . Here we have the amazing spectacle of what we sometimes call the greatest deliberative body in the world consuming month after month in the consideration of a treaty. A resolution of ratification incorporating reservations is proposed. It does not even command a majority of the Senate . . . and yet the Senate is powerless to vote on any question save that same old question which . . . has been determined."

Senator Harding put all the blame on the Democrats. He said they had refused to compromise, and now it was too late. In a blunt admission of the drastic nature of the Lodge reservations, he said they left a "skeleton" of a League.

Senator Underwood, who had carefully nursed his time, took over from Senator Hitchcock, who had used up almost all of his sixty minutes. He assailed the Republican leadership for saying: "You shall ratify as we present or not at all."

Bitterly, he cried: "That is the issue. I am prepared to meet it and the American people will know who aims to ratify this treaty, and who to destroy it.... I say that if the majority party of this Chamber seeks to adjourn the Senate after it is defeated by the majority of the Senate in its proposal, without staying here and making further attempts to write a treaty of peace, it and it alone is responsible for the condition in which the country finds itself."

At this point Senator Lodge broke in: "There will be no adjournment . . . if I can help it, until we vote upon the treaty again."

Mr. Underwood: "I am delighted to hear that news. It relieves my spirit, because I do think we should write a treaty of peace."

Mr. Lodge: "I said until we had voted on it again."

Mr. Underwood: "Oh well—"

Mr. Lodge: "When we vote on it again—be under no misapprehension—it is final. You cannot make another motion to reconsider."

The Alabaman refused to discuss the parliamentary tactics further. He referred to Harding's speech: "My good friend from Ohio a while ago described so accurately what has been done with the treaty and the League of Nations . . . I want to emphasize it to the Senate. He stated that they had adopted . . . reservations . . . that they had improved the treaty, and then he said, 'But they left a skeleton of a League of Nations. . . .' A skeleton of the League of Nations. A skeleton is a dead man. They left a dead League of Nations for the world to function under."

Senator Pittman then demolished the contention that the pro-Leaguers wouldn't compromise. He placed in the record a compilation of the compromise reservations offered and voted down. The list was long and impressive. Said he:

"That is not all. All the way through, from the very beginning to the end, there were offered on the other side by the Senator from North Dakota [McCumber] or . . . on this side by the Senator from Nebraska [Hitchcock] . . . or other Democratic Senators, substitute reservations for practically every reservation offered by the majority, and in nearly every case those reservations which were offered as substitutes were . . . prepared by the so-called 'mild reservationists' on the Republican side, and yet the Democrats are said not to have offered any opportunity for compromise.

"I contend now, and the Record will disclose, that every reservation contained in the . . . resolution of ratification was dictated and framed by the identical men who voted tonight to kill the treaty. . . ."

Senator Fletcher, Democrat of Florida, begged the Republicans not to block efforts to reach agreement.

Senator Lenroot, Republican of Wisconsin, his face flushed, angrily replied, "There will be no compromise. If the President wants this treaty, he must take the reservations substantially as adopted today."

The vote was analyzed by Senator Owen, Democrat of Oklahoma: "There were 55 votes against the resolution of ratification. Of that number 13 Republicans voted against it because they were hostile to the treaty on any basis whatever; two others, whose position I am not absolutely clear about, supported that position, leaving 40 who voted against that form of resolution who really are in favor of the treaty, and I think all of them without exception are willing to agree to . . . reservations of an interpretative character, and some . . . may go further than that. On the other side there were 39 . . . who voted for the somewhat extreme reservations of the Lodge resolution. Those 39 Senators added to the 40 Senators make 79 Senators who, so far as this vote is concerned, are in favor of the treaty with reservations of some kind. This body can be controlled by a majority and that 79 far transcends a majority. If they will, those who have voted for the reservations can co-operate with those who are not willing to accept reservations going so far, and it is a question merely of the adjustment of differences of opinion. It seems to me that the 39 Senators who voted for the resolution with its reservations can hardly be regarded as earnest friends of the treaty . . . if they refuse to permit a parliamentary method by which the differences may be . . . adjusted."

Senator Pomerene of Ohio, one of the most faithful of the League's supporters, said: "Mistake not, Senators, the American people, who spent nearly $20,000,000,000, who raised an army of 4,000,000 of soldiers, and left 50,000 of their best sons on the battlefields of France and Flanders, are not going to be deceived by parliamentary tactics." Then he adopted a conciliatory attitude in a plea for compromise.

"If there has been any undue exhibition of temper on this side of the Chamber, I am sorry for it. I think there has been some on both sides of the Chamber. I think a good many things have been said in the Senate that ought not to have been said—"

Medill McCormick interrupted: "I was going to ask the Senator in the best of good humor if it was only in the Senate of the United States that things have been said which it would have been better to have left unsaid, and by persons more distinguished than the Senators. . . ."

Senator Pomerene said he knew there was one man in history whose very name irritated McCormick. He added: "I am quite willing to assume, for the sake of argument, that he [McCormick] is the repository of all virtue and that the other gentleman is the repository of all vice, if it will soothe him.

"But . . . that is not the question before us. It is simply another exhibition of the fact that it is not the treaty that is being considered so much by some Senators as perhaps it is one of the draftsmen of that treaty."

Pomerene then moved that the President of the Senate appoint a Committee of Conciliation—to be headed by Senator Lodge, and with Senator Hitchcock a member—to devise a resolution of ratification that not less than two-thirds of the Senate would support.

Senator Lodge opposed the motion, raising a point of order against it. Vice President Marshall overruled him, but Senator La Follette moved to lay the Pomerene motion for conciliation on the table. This was done, 48 to 42.

Senator Hitchcock then tried a new tactic. He presented a list of several compromise reservations, but instead of presenting them in the form of a resolution of ratification, he merely moved that the reservations be considered by the Senate. Lodge permitted a vote and the motion to consider the reservations was defeated, 41 to 50.

Senator David I. Walsh, Democrat of Massachusetts, made a long plea for ratification with the Lodge reservations. This was the first hint of a break in the Democratic ranks.

Senator Lodge permitted a second vote on his resolution of ratification, for he would have preferred to have the Versailles Treaty with his reservations killed in the White House rather than on the Senate floor. A veto would make it seem that Woodrow Wilson was the killer of the treaty.

But most of the Democrats held fast, and Lodge's resolution was defeated again, 41 to 51.

Senator Lodge immediately sought to prevent all further action. He quoted a rule stating that after one reconsideration, no further reconsideration is possible if the original vote is confirmed. Said he:

"The Senate has therefore taken final action."

Senator Underwood protested that the Senate had not yet disposed of the Versailles Treaty. It had simply disposed of the Lodge resolution. And then he said: "I send to the Secretary's desk and move the adoption of an unconditional ratification of the treaty of peace."

Senator Lodge had blocked every effort of the supporters of the League of Nations to compromise, but he was perfectly willing to allow a vote on the resolution proposed by Underwood. It involved no compromise by the Democrats, and Lodge was certain the mild reservationist Republicans would vote against it. He abruptly abandoned his claim that the Versailles Treaty was not before the Senate. "I make no point of order if we can take the vote at once," he said.

So Senator Underwood's resolution was read, voted on, and defeated, 53 nays, 38 yeas, and 4 not voting. Seven Democrats voted against it: Reed, Gore, Shields, Smith of Georgia, Thomas of Colorado, Trammell of Florida, and Walsh of Massachusetts. One Republican voted for it: McCumber.

A total of 76 Senators had now voted for the Versailles Treaty in one form or another. First, 39 voted for the Lodge resolution of ratification. Now, 38 voted for the Underwood resolution of ratification. Senator McCumber was the only man to vote for both resolutions.

The galleries were deathly still, the people watching every move intently. Many of them had come expecting to see the United States vote to enter the League of Nations. They understood that only 15 Senators had said flatly that they were against the United States entering the League of Nations, and they had been confident some compromise would be reached. Yet, down there on the Senate floor, the League of Nations was dying.

Senator Swanson rushed to Senator Lodge and gasped, "For God's sake, can't something be done to save the treaty?"

"Senator, the door is closed," was the cold reply. "You have done it yourselves."

Senator Key Pittman tried to keep the door open for compromise by offering another resolution of ratification. Lodge raised a point of order against him.

Vice President Marshall grimly declared he had been overruled enough in sustaining the minority, and now he would rule with the majority. He declared the Pittman motion out of order.

Senator Lodge then prepared to draw the affair to a close. He moved that the vote on the Underwood unconditional ratification resolution be reconsidered, and also moved that the motion to reconsider be laid upon the table. That was a parliamentary move designed to end debate. No one could oppose it successfully, and it was done. Lodge's control was absolute.

Senator Fletcher: "I make the point of order that the business next in order would be to communicate to the President the various resolutions and action thereon relative to the treaty."

Senator Lodge: "That order is not necessary. It was so held by the Senate in the case of the Chamberlain-Bayard Treaty, which was rejected as this has been."

Fletcher: "I observe that nearly all the precedents are to the contrary."

Lodge: "It has been done many times, but it was held in the case of that treaty that it was not necessary, and it is not necessary. I am sure the President will take official notice of the action of the Senate."

Fletcher: "I should like a ruling of the Chair on the point of order as made anyway."

The Vice President: "Well, the Chair overrules the point of order."

Thus, on the basis of one precedent, Henry Cabot Lodge did not deign even to send Woodrow Wilson the customary official notice of the Senate decision.

Senator Lodge was ready with something more: he introduced a resolution calling for a separate peace with Germany. It was referred to his Foreign Relations Committee for future consideration.

Then the Senate adjourned at 11:10 p.m. It would not convene again until December 1.

Just after the *New York Times* received a flash on the Senate defeat of the League of Nations, a message came over the wires from South Africa. It was from Jan Christian Smuts.

"I trust my appeal will not be resented," he said. "I appeal to America not to blast the hopes of the world. . . . The machinery of the League is wanted to save civilization from dissolving into fragments, from falling into decay. It alone can save tottering Europe."

ERVATION OF AMERICAN NATIONALISM WHEN IT WAS ASSAILED BY THE SINISTER AND DANGEROUS DOCTRINES OF INTERNATIONALISM."

November 30, 1919.
The Indictment of Senator Truman Newberry

This was the headline in the *New York Times:*

"NEWBERRY AND 133 OTHERS INDICTED FOR ELECTION PLOT."

"Prominent Detroit Men Accused of Wholesale Bribery to Beat Henry Ford."

The story began:

"Grand Rapids, Mich., Nov. 29—Truman H. Newberry, Republican, United States Senator from Michigan, was indicted by a Federal Grand Jury late today for corruption, fraud, and conspiracy in connection with the election by which he obtained his seat in the Senate, defeating Henry Ford, his Democratic opponent. . . ."

The victory of Newberry over Ford—by less than 5000 votes—had given the Republicans their one vote Senate majority. It had enabled Henry Cabot Lodge to become Majority Leader and Chairman of the Foreign Relations Committee.

December 6, 1919.
"We Have All Been Praying for You"

The people of the United States were not ready to accept defeat of the League of Nations.

Day by day the demand grew that the Senate take up the Versailles Treaty once more and find a way to approve it. Its supporters refused to believe that ratification was impossible as long as only fifteen Senators were in announced opposition.

"There is simply no acceptable alternative to a peace based on the principles of the Covenant. Necessity will force the Administration and the Republican friends of the Covenant to reach an agreement," declared the *Chicago Daily News* in an editorial typifying the view of many hundreds of papers and many millions of people.

Senator Lodge later described the situation he found when the new session of Congress convened: "I went to Massachusetts for a few days and while there and after I reached Washington at the opening of the regular session I found that a situation had developed, both in the Senate and in the country, which was caused by the continued assertion of the friends of the League that the reservations had been added and the defeat of the treaty had been brought about by disputes between the two parties on what were merely verbal differences.

"The statement was false, but I thought its falsity should be publicly exhibited. It seemed to me very clear, after considering the new conditions thus presented that, in order to make it perfectly plain to the world that the differences between those who supported the treaty and those who opposed it were not verbal but vital and essential, it was most desirable to make an effort, at least, to come to some agreement between the two sides. . . ."

And so Henry Cabot Lodge began to lay plans to prove that the differences over the reservations were deeper than they seemed.

First of all, he wanted to know more than he did about the condition of Woodrow Wilson. There were still all kinds of rumors circulating in Washington, and the controlling members of the Foreign Relations Committee were a bit skeptical about Admiral Grayson's bulletins and the reports of Senator Hitchcock.

On the pretext that the committee had to consult the President concerning Mexican affairs, Chairman Lodge sent Senator Fall of New Mexico—destined to be the first United States Cabinet member to go to prison—to look over Woodrow Wilson. Senator Hitchcock accompanied him.

They were met in the White House by Mrs. Wilson, who was holding a pen and a pad of paper to give her an excuse to avoid shaking hands with Senator Fall. She escorted the visitors to the sick room, and remained to take notes in order to be able to refute the Gentleman from New Mexico if he misquoted her husband.

They found a thin, spent Wilson sitting up in bed. Senator Fall said:

"Well, Mr. President, we have all been praying for you."

"Which way, Senator?" asked Wilson with a chuckle.

When they went back to Capitol Hill, Senator Fall agreed with Hitchcock that Woodrow Wilson might be sick of body, but not of mind.

December 9, 1919. "All Europe . . . Resentful . . . Fearful, Gloomily Watched . . ."

General Tasker Bliss and Henry White, who had remained in Paris to help carry out the terms of the Versailles Treaty, sailed for home. Allen Nevins, biographer of White, wrote:

"All Europe, half-resentful, half-fearful, gloomily watched the United States detach itself from her concerns."

December 17, 1919. "Mutilated and Paralyzed"

Like the people of America, the people of the rest of the world refused to believe it was all over.

The French were upset the most. The Senate had never deigned to consider the treaty Wilson had signed guaranteeing France against German aggression, and that had been bad enough; but most of the people of France had assumed we would eventually join the League of Nations, anyway. *Le Temps,* a Parisian newspaper, pleaded:

"We who sincerely wish for peace, so necessary to our wounded country, so necessary in the social crisis which runs through humanity, we speak to that sentiment at once idealistic and practical, which is a striking trait of the American character.

"We ask the United States not to conceive that it can remain clear of European questions and exclude itself from the peace for which they came to fight, the peace which must be the deliverance of the entire world.

"If America ratifies the treaty, if she intervenes with her perfect independence and with her immense resources to aid in putting the peace in force, if she gives life to the League of Nations, which is mutilated and paralyzed so long as the United States is not sitting in it, then there will be great chances for a new spirit to develop in international relations destroying these forces of the past, which spring from the soil in the Germany of today."

December 18, 1919.
The League to Enforce Peace Works for Lodge

The American supporters of the League of Nations were beginning to raise their voices.

The *New York Times* reported that both the Chicago Board of Trade and the Cleveland Chamber of Commerce had passed resolutions urging ratification. Newspapers were full of editorials, statements, letters demanding action.

But the pro-Leaguers remained leaderless and lost. Woodrow Wilson lay helpless in the White House, Senators Hitchcock and Underwood fought for party leadership in the Senate, and the League to Enforce Peace was working for Henry Cabot Lodge.

"We are advocating ratification on the basis of the Lodge resolution with the change only of the preamble," wrote William Harrison Short, Secretary of the League to Enforce Peace.

Meanwhile, the League for the Preservation of American Independence was still going strong, and so were all the foes of world organization. Ex-Senator Beveridge felt this was the critical hour of the whole fight, and he was peppering his friends in Washington with letters urging them to stand fast. He told Senator Brandegee he hoped "our men are strong enough not to be stampeded or seduced."

December 20, 1919. Senator Lodge Blocks Conciliation

Senator Lodge was not yet ready even for the pretense of carrying on compromise negotiations.

He blocked Senate consideration of a resolution by Senator Underwood calling for appointment of a Conciliation Committee of ten Senators.

December 27, 1919. An Ultimatum to Senator Lodge

There was talk of compromise all over Washington, and there were many meetings attended by various groups of Senators.

The *New York Times* reported that a dozen mild reservationist Republicans, provoked by Senator Lodge's killing of the Underwood conciliation resolution, had agreed to hand an ultimatum to the Gentleman from Massachusetts. Unless he made efforts to reach a compromise, they would ignore him and deal directly with the Democrats, who had asked them to propose compromise reservations.

1920

January 5, 1920.
Senator Lodge Plays the Same Old Game

The *New York Tribune* reported that the Republicans were now waiting for the Democrats to make "a special proposal for a compromise" before taking any steps themselves.

Senator Lodge was playing the same old game. He would avoid committing himself on any terms of compromise until he found out the precise position of the supporters of the League of Nations.

January 8, 1920. The Call for a Solemn Referendum

President Wilson sent a message to the Jackson Day dinner of the Democratic Party. He proposed that if the Senate would not approve of the League of Nations, the decision be left in the hands of the people:

> Personally, I do not accept the action of the Senate of the United States as the decision of the nation. I have asserted from the first that the overwhelming majority of the people of this country desire the ratification of the treaty. . . .
>
> I have endeavored to make it plain that if the Senate wishes to say what the undoubted meaning of the League is, I shall have no objection. There can be no reasonable objection to interpretations accompanying the act of ratification itself. But when the treaty is acted upon, I must know whether it means that we have ratified or rejected it. We cannot rewrite this treaty. We must take it without changes which alter its meaning, or leave it, and then, after the rest of the world has signed it, we must face the un-

thinkable task of making another and separate kind of treaty with Germany. . . .

If there is any doubt as to what the people of the country think on this vital matter, the clear and single way out is to submit it for determination at the next election to the voters of the nation, to give the next election the form of a great and solemn referendum, a referendum as to the part the United States is to play in completing the settlements of the war and in the prevention in the future of such outrages as Germany attempted to perpetrate. . . .

Our fidelity to our associates in the war is in question, and the whole future of mankind.

January 9, 1920. "We Should Get Together"

"The effect of the President's letter has been good," commented Senator Lenroot of Wisconsin, a mild reservationist Republican, according to the *New York Times*. "Never before have the Democrats been so ready to talk compromise and never has their talking been so definite."

Several Democratic Senators called on Senator Lodge early in the day to urge him to do all he could to foster the spirit of reconciliation.

"We should get together," they told him.

"I thought you did your getting together last night," he replied.

January 13, 1920. 20,000,000 Voters for the League

The League to Enforce Peace, in a new effort to push the Versailles Treaty through the Senate, joined with the American Federation of Labor to sponsor a huge conference in Washington.

It was attended by representatives of thirty-three organizations whose combined membership totaled 20,000,000 voters, according to the *Washington Post*. Among the groups represented were:

International Federation of Rotary Clubs
Federal Council of Churches of Christ
Church Peace Union

United Society of Christian Endeavor
World Peace Foundation
American Rights League
Associated Advertising Clubs
National Grange
Dairymen's League
Order of Railway Conductors
Brotherhood of Locomotive Firemen and Enginemen
Association of Collegiate Alumnae
National Education Association
National Conference of Social Workers
Women's Christian Temperance Union
General Federation of Women's Clubs
National Council of Women
Council of Jewish Women

The conference approved a resolution demanding that the treaty should be ratified immediately "on a basis that will not require renegotiation" and "with such reservations as may secure in the Senate the necessary two-thirds vote."

A committee was appointed to leave a copy of the resolution at the White House, and also to take copies of the resolution to Senator Lodge and to Senator Hitchcock.

Lodge did not give the committee much encouragement. "The reservations now before the Senate are in themselves a compromise between the two extreme views in the Senate, and they represented, as they do now, the views of the majority," he declared. "I shall be glad to consider any modifications that may be proposed by the minority, but they will have to get sixty-four votes."

Actually, of course, the Lodge reservations did not represent a compromise between the two extreme views in the Senate.

There had been no compromise with the whole-hearted Democratic supporters of the League of Nations. Actually, the reservations had been carefully designed to draw a veto from Woodrow Wilson if they ever reached the White House.

There had been a compromise only between the reservationist Republicans and the irreconcilable Republicans. The Lodge reservations were just mild enough to win the support of the reservationists like Lenroot, Nelson, Colt, and McNary, and just strong enough to win the support of the irreconcilables like Borah, Johnson, Sherman, and Brandegee. And even here, the compromise was not complete, for the irreconcilables would support the reservations only in votes attaching them to the Covenant. On November 19, the irreconcilables voted against the reservations when to support them would have meant voting for the League of Nations.

January 15, 1920. The Bi-Partisan Conference

A conference of Democratic and Republican Senators met in Senator Lodge's office to talk compromise.

The origins of the conference had been bright and hopeful, but by the time the conference convened, Senator Lodge had dimmed the prospects for success.

It all began one day after the Senate adjourned, when Senator Kenneth McKellar, Democrat of Tennessee, who was a fervent supporter of the League of Nations, was strolling back to the Senate Office Building with Senator Le Baron Colt of Rhode Island, the mild reservationist who had been kept off the Foreign Relations Committee because he would not promise to vote against the League of Nations. Their offices were on the same floor of the Senate Office Building, and they were good friends.

Senator Colt drew his arm through Senator McKellar's, and said:

"You and I could get together and adjust the differences about reservations and we could confirm this treaty, including the League."

Senator McKellar, a practical politician with a square face and a wave of black, curly hair tumbling over his forehead, was eager to try anything that might save the Covenant.

They walked arm-in-arm to Colt's office, closed the door, sat down, and thrashed the whole thing out. Carefully, painstakingly, they considered all the points at issue, one by one. They did not discuss what McKellar wanted and what Colt wanted. They discussed what they thought two-thirds of the Senate wanted.

They finally reached full agreement between themselves on what would satisfy enough Democrats and enough Republicans to pass the Senate.

Then Senator Colt proposed that they start calling in other Senators. He called in a fellow-Republican, Senator Kenyon of Iowa, and McKellar called in a fellow-Democrat, Senator Kendrick of Wyoming.

The four Senators reached an agreement.

Then Colt called in Senator Lenroot of Wisconsin, and McKellar called in Senator Simmons of North Carolina.

The six Senators reached an agreement.

Then Colt called in Senator Kellogg of Minnesota, and McKellar called in Senator Walsh of Montana.

The eight Senators reached an agreement.

And then they took the big, dangerous, yet inevitable step. Colt called in Senator Lodge, while McKellar called in Hitchcock.

The two leaders agreed that good results might come from the bi-partisan conference.

But Lodge, who promptly took charge of the proceedings, had never gotten along very well with Colt, who had been too sympathetic to the League. And it seemed to McKellar that Lodge also was displeased to find Kenyon among the Republicans present.

Lodge proposed that the group hold its next meeting in his office. It was agreed.

And now, when the group met to try to work out a real agreement, some changes had been made. To Senator McKellar's "very great surprise," Lodge had eliminated Colt and Kenyon, and substituted Harry New of Indiana, a reservationist so strong that some classified him as an irreconcilable. The prospects for compromise were lessened considerably.

The *New York Times* reported that Lodge's attitude, as he opened the conference, was "that of tolerance and amusement about the whole matter." Each of the Lodge reservations was discussed, and the Democrats proposed certain modifications. They did not submit them in final form, but merely as a basis for discussion. They informed Lodge that any agreement they could reach would receive the support of most of the Democrats in the Senate.

Senator Lodge, without committing himself to anything, agreed to take up the proposals with his Republican colleagues, and it was arranged to hold another meeting in two days.

"This is the first real attempt to get together on an agreement," Lodge told reporters afterward. "We have taken the first step."

Meanwhile, Democratic Senators held a caucus to elect their Senate leader. The vote ended in a deadlock, 19 for Hitchcock, 19 for Underwood, when Senator Hoke Smith of Georgia refused to vote for either candidate. The meeting adjourned without setting a date for another vote, and with the Democratic leadership left in a state of suspension despite the crucial compromise negotiations now under way.

January 16, 1920. The League of Nations Convenes

The Council of the League of Nations convened in Paris for its first session. It had been agreed during the Peace Conference that the President of the United States would call the meeting when enough countries had ratified the Versailles Treaty to put it into effect. In the summons issued from his sick bed for the meeting the United States would not attend, Wilson said:

"It will mark the beginning of a new era in international cooperation and the first great step toward the ideal concert of nations."

January 22, 1920. "Senate Near Compromise on Article 10"

The Bi-Partisan Conference had been meeting daily in secret session in Lodge's office, and according to reports that leaked out, substantial progress was being made. Full agreement was reached on modification of several of the less important reservations.

Then the reservation on Article 10 was reached. The negotiations stalled. Now the news was good once more, and the *New York Tribune* announced:

"SENATE NEAR COMPROMISE ON ARTICLE 10."

January 23, 1920. Senator Sherman: "I'll Bolt . . ."

The Bi-Partisan Conference reportedly was on the verge of reaching a compromise that would be quite certain to meet the approval of a majority of the Senate.

Senators McCormick and Brandegee were "greatly disturbed," according to the *New York Times*. Senators Borah and Johnson circulated among their friends all morning "energetically" trying to build up opposition to the compromise move.

They got results. Threats began to be heard concerning Lodge's leadership. Senator Frelinghuysen of New Jersey issued a statement that he would not be bound by any compromise agreement. Senator Sutherland of West Virginia, who had been considered a reservationist, announced he was really an irreconcilable at heart.

No one seemed to know what Lodge was up to. The irreconcilables feared that he was worried by the widespread public demand for ratification, and that he was planning to modify his reservations just enough to get them through the Senate. They thought Lodge wanted to throw the final decision in Wilson's lap, and thus relieve the Senate of the responsibility of killing the League of Nations.

The Bi-Partisan Conference was scheduled to meet at two o'clock in the afternoon. As Lodge was entering the door of his office to call the meeting to order, he was intercepted by a summons to Hiram Johnson's office. He excused himself temporarily, and vanished, taking Harry New with him.

The Bi-Partisan Conference waited for an hour. No Lodge. The group adjourned.

Lodge did not emerge from Johnson's office until five o'clock. He paused long enough to tell a *New York Times* reporter:

"We have been hearing some gentlemen who wish to protest against any change in the reservations. They represent a large number of Senators who are opposed to any such change. We represent nobody but ourselves, of course, and must hear both sides."

"Have the Bi-Partisan Conferences been called off?" asked the reporter.

"Oh, no; we shall meet again tomorrow at ten-thirty."

The irreconcilables were more willing to talk. They said they had informed Lodge they would desert him if he worked out any compromise. They did not produce a poll, but they declared they had thirty-eight Senators who would vote against any modification of the original Lodge reservations.

The irreconcilables made it clear they would stand for no retreat. Sherman said: ". . . if there is the slightest yielding on the Lodge reservations, I am through with the party. Let there be no misunderstanding as to my position. I will not support the organization in the Senate or in the country if it compromises on the Lodge reservations. In plain language, I'll bolt even to the point of supporting a third ticket."

Senator Johnson said that the "irreducible minimum" had been reached in the Lodge reservations.

Senator Borah announced he would withhold what he had to say for forty-eight hours. He gave the impression that if Lodge did not stop all talk of compromise by that time, he would break away from his leadership.

The Democrats were gloomy, but Senator Hitchcock said he still hoped an agreement would be possible when the Bi-Partisan Conference met again in the morning.

January 24, 1920.
Senator Lodge Reassures the Irreconcilables

There were countless conferences all morning, all afternoon, all evening.

The only important meeting was another between Senator Lodge and the irreconcilables. He tried to persuade them to promise to vote for the resolution of ratification containing his original reservations. If they did, he believed enough Democrats would join them to pass the Versailles Treaty. That would send it to Wilson; Wilson would surely veto it; and that would be that.

The irreconcilables were not so certain Wilson would veto the Lodge reservations. They turned down the suggestion.

They repeated their threats to desert Lodge if he compromised. He assured them there was not the slightest possibility that he and Senator New would concede anything that was essential or that was anything more than "a change in wording."

January 27, 1920. A New Objection to Article 10!

When the Bi-Partisan Conference met once more in Lodge's office, the Gentleman from Massachusetts announced firmly that there would be "no compromise of principle" concerning Article 10 and the Monroe Doctrine.

And then his group suddenly raised a new objection to Article 10. No one had ever before considered the possibility that we might have to help pay for policing operations undertaken by the League of Nations against aggressors, even if we refused to take part in the operations ourselves. The Republicans declared that financial obligations incurred under Article 10 "would be likely to prove as much of a burden to the United States as any military obligation. . . ."

In apparent horror at this new wickedness uncovered in the Covenant, they got up and marched out of the room, led by Lodge. They held a caucus to consider this new threat to America.

The situation in the Senate was once more deadlocked. And it was once more utterly confused, for charges and counter-charges flew concerning who had ruined the compromise negotiations.

The leading Republican newspaper in the country, the *New York Tribune,* reported: "Some of the irreconcilables were trying tonight to make the mild reservationists look at the situation as they view it. They feel that it is not merely a question of changing the wording of the reservations, but changing with the words the political party which would get credit for those reservations. So long as the reservations bore Lodge's name, the country, these Senators feel, would remember them as Republican reservations, but the minute they changed they probably would become known as the Hitchcock reservations, and the country might eventually come to believe that they were the result of Democratic effort."

The irreconcilables also pointed out that if the Republicans stood pat against all compromise, the Democratic Party would be likely to split wide open. Some Democrats would capitulate and accept the Lodge reservations, and some would refuse to accept them. According to the *New York Tribune,* the irreconcilables pointed out that there would then be a "rift in the Democratic Party which would be entirely favorable to Republican chances in the forthcoming campaign."

Meanwhile, one of the mild reservationists, Senator Le Baron Colt, blew up, crying: "Senator Hitchcock doesn't want a compromise. He wants to throw the blame for beating the treaty on the Republicans."

January 30, 1920. "I Had Made Up My Mind"

Lodge brought his Republicans back to another meeting of the Bi-Partisan Conference.

Hitchcock offered to accept a strict reservation on Article 10 proposed by Ex-President Taft. It only slightly modified the original Lodge reservation.

Senator Lodge said no modification of the reservation was to be accepted.

To the contrary, the almost neglected threat that the United States might have to finance military operations under Article 10 would make it necessary to make the reservation stronger, not weaker!

That, of course, put an end to the Bi-Partisan Conference.

The Democrats got to their feet and walked out in disgust.

A good while later, Senator Lodge admitted: "I had made up my mind at the beginning that if the conference was to break up it should be on Article 10, which was the crucial point throughout the contest over the Covenant of the League of Nations."

February 1, 1920. A Letter from London

A letter to the London *Times* was reprinted in the *New York Times,* and it brought new strength to Senator Lodge.

It was from Viscount Grey, British Ambassador to the United States, who had been sent to Washington in the fall when it became obvious that the League of Nations was in danger. Grey had been unable to see Wilson, due to his illness, but he had spent much time conferring with various Senators, particularly Lodge.

He had returned to London in January, convinced that reservations were inevitable and should be accepted. He wrote his letter to the London *Times* after conferring with his government. It indicated that England would sign the Versailles Treaty even if the Lodge reservations were attached to it by the Senate.

The letter, nominally to the people of England but actually to Woodrow Wilson and the Democrats in the United States Senate, declared that disappointment and regret over the deadlock in Washington was equally keen in England and the United States.

Viscount Grey said of the reservations: "I do not deny that some of them are material qualifications of the League of Nations as drawn up at Paris or that they must be disappointing to those who are with that Covenant as it stands and are even proud of it, but those who have had the longest experience of political affairs and especially of treaties know best how often it happens that difficulties which seem most formidable in anticipation and on paper never arise in practice.

"I think this is likely to be particularly true in the working of the League of Nations. The difficulties and dangers which the Americans foresee in it will probably never arise or be felt by them when they are once in the League. And in the same way the weakening and injury to the League which some of its best friends apprehend from the American reservations would not be felt in practice.

"If the outcome of the long controversy in the Senate is to offer co-operation in the League of Nations it would be the greatest mistake to refuse that co-operation because conditions are attached to it, and when that co-operation is accepted let it not be accepted in a spirit of pessimism."

The British press, and the French press, too, were virtually unanimous in their endorsement of Viscount Grey's letter.

Although the letter did not represent an official statement by the British Government, it ended all possibility of compromise by Lodge.

It was now up to the Democrats to capitulate, to accept the Lodge reservations *in toto*, if the League of Nations was to be approved by the Senate.

February 10, 1920. The Lodge Reservations Again

The Foreign Relations Committee reported the Versailles Treaty back to the Senate for consideration—again with the fourteen Lodge reservations.

February 23, 1920. "Who the Devil Cares What *Has* Been Said?"

The debate over the League of Nations grew dull and desultory; a good part of the time only about a dozen Senators were on the floor.

The friends and foes of the Covenant proposed various weaker and stronger substitutes for the Lodge reservations, and, one by one, most of them were voted down. No one was able to think of anything very new to say about the Covenant, and its supporters took to reading selections from Lodge's 1916 League to Enforce Peace address, and also this statement from a speech he delivered at Union College in 1915:

"There is no escape from the proposition that the peace of the world can only be maintained as the peace and order of a single community are maintained, and as the peace of a single nation is maintained, by the force which united nations are willing to put behind the peace and order of the world."

Vice President Marshall, who sat in the chair day after day presiding over the dreary debate, finally took a personal vow to leave the chamber every time anybody started to quote the Gentleman from Massachusetts. He would grimly get up, signal to a Senator to take over for him, and stalk off to the cloakrooms. There he would plop down in one of the overstuffed chairs, light a cigar, and tell the nearest Senator a story about the Indiana judge who got very, very tired of lawyers who tried to tell him about the law. One day one of them rose in his court, threw his head back like John C. Calhoun, and declaimed:

"May it please the court, it has been said—"

The judge cracked his bench with his fist, and bellowed: "Who the devil cares what *has* been said. What have *you* got to say?"

February 24, 1920. "A Fire Had Been Lighted . . ."

Senator Arthur Capper of Kansas, consistent reservationist Republican, presented to the Senate memorials of sundry citizens of Kansas remonstrating vigorously against compulsory military training.

Meanwhile, at seven-fifteen o'clock in the evening, the first great mass meeting of the Nazi Party was held in the Hofbrauhaus in Munich, Germany.

When the slight man with the odd mustache and the black shock of hair started to speak, there were shouts, and fighting broke out all over the beer hall. Men in brown shirts set upon the disturbers, and threw them out.

Then Adolf Hitler started to speak again, and he spoke for hour after hour, setting forth for the first time the twenty-five point program of his Nazi Party. There was wild applause for each point, and wilder applause at the end for the whole program and for the whole speech. Recounted Hitler in *Mein Kampf:*

"When after almost four hours the hall began to empty and the crowd, shoulder to shoulder, like a slow stream, began to push, to scramble, and to pour toward the exit, then I knew that now the principles of a movement which never could be forgotten walked out into the German people.

"A fire had been lighted, and out of its flames there was bound to come some day the sword which was to regain the freedom of the German Siegfried and the life of the German nation."

March 11, 1920.
Henry White Visits Henry Cabot Lodge

Henry White was in Washington to see if anything could possibly be done to save the peace plan he had helped construct. He had a talk in the morning with his friend Henry Cabot Lodge.

Senator Lodge predicted the Versailles Treaty would be defeated again in a few days. White asked him what would happen then.

"Probably an attempt to pass the Knox resolution," replied Lodge, referring to a resolution introduced by the Pennsylvanian calling for a separate peace with Germany.

"But will not the President veto that?" demanded White.

"Undoubtedly."

"Then what?"

Senator Lodge had no reply, except to say that President Wilson would get the blame for defeating the Versailles Treaty.

March 12, 1920. "Is That the Talk of Honest Men? . . ."

The Senate debated for many days on reservations and variations of reservations to Article 10.

By now, the debate seldom touched upon whether the United States should or should not enter the League of Nations. It was incessantly concerned with the form of reservations, with the implications of a word, a comma, a phrase, a clause.

This afternoon was spent in the investigation of a variation, proposed by Senator Frelinghuysen of New Jersey, of the original Lodge reservation. Main participants were Senator Lenroot of Wisconsin, mild reservationist Republican; Senator Brandegee of Connecticut, irreconcilable Republican; and Senator McKellar of Tennessee, firm supporter of the League of Nations and firm opponent of drastic reservations.

The aimless nature of the closing stage of the Great Debate was revealed when all three—representing the three most important groups of conflicting Senate opinion—agreed that the Frelinghuysen variation was really no different from the Lodge original, and that both left nothing at all of Article 10.

Senator Brandegee finally denounced the whole business:

"It is a pitiable exhibition. . . . What would anybody think of taking a square declaration such as is contained in Article 10 . . . in which we solemnly agree to preserve the territorial integrity and political independence of all our associated partners in this great international concern, and hitching onto it a set of words leaving that declaration standing and then saying, 'But in the preservation of your territorial integrity and your political independence, we shall not use troops, we shall not use economic pressure, we shall not use trade discrimination, we shall not intervene in the controversies of any nation?' After assuming the obligation, we intentionally deny any means by which it may possibly be executed!

"Is that the talk of honest men? . . . What would you think of the Senator from Pennsylvania [Mr. Knox] if he should take my note for $100 down to the Riggs Bank and write on the back of it:

" 'I guarantee payment of this note, but in doing so I want it distinctly understood that I am not to pay in gold certificates, or silver certificates, or silver dollars, or any obligations of the United States, or in any legal-tender currency; and, reserving full liberty of action for myself under all circumstances of each particular and specific case as it may arise in the future, I hereby and with this reservation cheerfully, heartily, cordially and sincerely indorse this note.' "

The Senate shook with laughter. When it subsided, Brandegee declared:

"I am sick of this tiptoeing around. I do not see why we have not the courage either to ratify this treaty or to decline to ratify it. . . ."

March 15, 1920.
Senator Lodge Takes Out Some Insurance

The Senate rejected the Frelinghuysen variation of the Lodge reservation on Article 10. Senator Kirby of Arkansas then proposed another variation—the reservation that the Bi-Partisan Conference had been on the verge of accepting in January. There followed some long, involved debate, concerned not with the merits of the reservation, but with whether or not the Bi-Partisan Conference had agreed on it in any way, shape, or manner before it broke up. It was finally defeated, 31 to 45.

Senator Kirby, a Democrat, promptly introduced another reservation. This one had been framed by Ex-President Taft, Republican. This time debate centered on whether future Congresses would understand it.

Said Senator Lenroot: "Does the Senator believe that any Congress would be less intelligent? . . ."

Said Senator Kirby: "I do not know what future Congresses will develop, but I hope they will be fully as intelligent as the present one."

The reservation was defeated, 30 to 46.

Senator Lodge called up a new reservation of his own on Article 10. It was *stronger* than his original reservation. A few days before, President Wilson had said in a public letter to Senator Hitchcock: "Any reservation which seeks to deprive the League of Nations of the force of Article 10 cuts at the very heart and life of the Covenant itself. Any League of Nations which does not guarantee as a matter of incontestable right the political independence and integrity of its members might be hardly more than a futile scrap of paper, as ineffective in operation as the agreement between Belgium and Germany which the Germans violated in 1914."

The new reservation proposed by Lodge made doubly certain

that it deprived the League of Nations of the force of Article 10. Part of it, based on the point that broke up the Bi-Partisan Conference, was designed to guard against any possibility of the United States having to pay for policing operations undertaken against aggressors. The reservation also contained new clauses emphasizing our hesitancy to participate in economic sanctions against aggressors, and affirming our unwillingness to participate in League action in the event that aggression threatened the territorial integrity or political independence of other nations.

This strengthened reservation was further insurance taken out by Senator Lodge that President Wilson would veto the Versailles Treaty, if it ever reached the White House.

It was approved, 56 to 26, with several Democrats voting for it. They had concluded that opposition to Lodge was hopeless, and they were willing to put the final decision up to the President.

Senator Lodge: "Mr. President, that completes the reservations reported from the Committee on Foreign Relations."

The Senate adjourned, amid expectations that the Versailles Treaty would come to a vote once more in a day or so.

March 18, 1920. Ireland, Korea, and the Civil War

A good part of the last afternoon before the final vote on the Versailles Treaty—supposed to wind up World War I and to prevent World War II—was spent in a debate concerning self-determination for the South and the Civil War.

The rest of the afternoon was devoted to a discussion of Irish and Korean independence.

Senator Peter Gerry, Democrat of Rhode Island, started it all by introducing a reservation expressing our adherence to the principle of self-determination, our sympathy for Irish aspirations for independence, and our hope that Ireland would soon enter the League of Nations.

The proposal completely shattered party lines.

Senator Hitchcock and Senator Borah joined in support of it.

Senator Lodge and Senator Williams joined in opposition to it. Senator Borah supported it because it would make it probable England would refuse to accept our reservations, and Senator Williams opposed it for the same reason.

Senator Hitchcock apparently supported it in the hope it would win Irish-American support of the Versailles Treaty. Senator Lodge risked the ire of the Boston Irish to save the symbolic symmetry of his fourteen reservations. He expressed his sympathy for Irish independence, but stated that he opposed the blanket endorsement of the principle of self-determination.

The debate went back to the Civil War when Lodge, following an address by Senator Phelan of California, said:

"I wish he would explain to us on what doctrine of self-determination we fought the South for four years."

When the debate finally got back to Ireland, Senator Reed brought out his old Anglophobe line with this protest: "Now we have a reservation that when Ireland secures the right from Great Britain to govern herself she then is to be cordially invited to become a member of a League of Nations which Great Britain will completely dominate."

Senator Thomas of Colorado, who was really against the Irish reservation, tried to defeat it by proposing an amendment expressing our sympathy for Korean efforts to gain independence. This failed to halt the flowery orations for Ireland. Senator Townsend of Michigan observed, "We do not have very many Koreans in this country and I do not imagine they cast very many votes."

Late in the afternoon, the Korean amendment to the reservation was defeated, 34 to 46.

The Irish reservation was approved, 38 to 36.

March 19, 1920. The Senate Votes Again

The people of the United States had looked on with mingled feelings of bewilderment and helplessness, rage and delight, while the stage was set in the Senate for the final vote on the League of Nations.

A majority still seemed to agree that the Senate should ratify the Versailles Treaty, but who could say on what terms? Every active supporter seemed to have his own ideas about the proper reservations, and to disagree heatedly with every other suggestion.

Some began to look beyond the Senate to the fall, and to place their hopes on the "solemn referendum" Woodrow Wilson had suggested.

When the Senate met at noon for the decision, Senator Lodge did not at once seek to bring the treaty to a vote.

The opponents of the League of Nations were worried about Lord Grey's letter and its widespread support in the British and French press. The new reservation on Article 10 seemed to insure that President Wilson would veto the Versailles Treaty if the Senate happened to pass it. But suppose he surprised everybody and accepted the "skeleton" if it reached him? Then, the British might accept our reservations despite the addition of the plea for Irish independence. If the British did accept them, the French probably would, too, and the Italians—and we'd be in the League of Nations.

The reservations would have failed in their purpose!

And so, some more insurance was taken out.

Senator Lodge proposed a surprise change in the preamble to the reservations. He had formerly opposed all change in it, but now he proposed abandonment of the provision requiring written acceptance of our reservations by three of the four major powers.

He proposed, instead, that our ratification of the Versailles Treaty should not take effect until the reservations had been accepted by *all* the other signatory nations. Canada had announced on February 16 that it opposed the reservation concerning votes of the British Dominions. Lodge told the Senate:

"I can state very briefly the purpose of my amendment. I was never satisfied with the clause which was adopted. . . . It did not seem to me to be the best way to confine the assent to three of the principal Allied and associated powers."

The irreconcilables eagerly endorsed the amendment of the preamble. Senator Brandegee, in a frank admission of the purpose of reservations as far as he was concerned, made it clear he doubted that all the other nations would be willing to accept our reservations. Said he:

"If I have any conception of the English language, a casual perusal of the reservations which we have already adopted might tend to induce a sensitive and over suspicious partner to think that we are not actuated by an uncontrollable enthusiasm for his company. . . ."

The amendment was accepted without a roll call. The friends of the Covenant decided not to oppose it, evidently feeling that it was not too important in view of the extremity of the reservation on Article 10.

The whole attitude on the Senate floor was listless, sluggish. There was none of the excitement of November 19. It seemed a foregone conclusion that the Versailles Treaty would be voted down once more.

A good many Senators spoke for the record, explaining why they were going to vote for or against the treaty. They repeated the arguments that had been heard over and over again for more than a year.

Senator Lenroot condemned the Democrats for refusing to accept the Lodge reservations. He said: "The Senator from Idaho [Borah] and the Senator from Missouri [Reed] have made a great fight to defeat the treaty, but President Wilson is the man who defeats it if it is defeated today."

He took up the reservations one by one, and when he reached the new one concerning Ireland, there was another long argument about self-determination and the Civil War.

Quite a few Democrats revealed they were going to desert the Hitchcock leadership for the first time and vote for the Versailles Treaty. Many of them thought Wilson would veto it, or else other nations would refuse to accept the reservations. But they believed the affair in the Senate was hopelessly deadlocked, and they thought they might as well try to pass the treaty and then see what would happen.

One Democrat who announced he would vote for the Lodge resolution of ratification was Senator Tom Walsh of Montana. He explained that he hated to vote for it, since he believed the reservations would make it impossible for the League of Nations to avert war.

"I shall vote for it because, after every reasonable effort . . . it is the best that can be secured . . ." he said grimly.

"I voted against the resolution of ratification embracing the Lodge reservations on November 19 in the belief, at least in the hope, that a sorely disappointed public would force opinionated and refractory Senators into some kind of a compromise. The sad story of the failure of every effort in that direction need not be retold. . . . No one not conversant with the situation can help but be impressed with the view that such influences as public opinion exerted after the rejection of the treaty in November operated to incline Democratic members to accept, if necessary, the Lodge reservations rather than to induce Republican members to yield in any degree. . . ."

Finally, the Chair put the question, Senator McKellar called for the yeas and nays, and the Versailles Treaty was defeated once more, 49 voting for it, 35 voting against it.

Twenty-one Democrats voted for ratification, fourteen more than did so on November 19. The other affirmative votes were again cast by the reservationist Republicans, led by Lodge.

The negative votes were cast by the irreconcilables, and by the Democrats, most of them Southerners, who were convinced the Lodge reservations killed the Covenant.

Senator Hitchcock again attempted to arrange a delay for a day in the hope of arranging a compromise vote, and Senator Lodge again blocked the way to conciliation. Said he: "I should think that after a year of debate we might ask for an end of this sort of thing To keep this thing here just to fool with it for a day or two is not to be thought of."

Senator Joe Robinson of Arkansas tried to get the treaty before the Senate again, and Lodge stopped him with a point of order

Many members got up and walked out of the Senate while Hitchcock and his aides struggled futilely with Lodge.

The Senate adjourned at 7:35 p.m. It was through with the Versailles Treaty, through with the League of Nations.

March 20, 1920. The People Could Decide!

There were three banner headlines on the front page of the *New York Times:*

"SENATE DEFEATS TREATY, VOTES 49 TO 35;

"ORDERS IT RETURNED TO THE PRESIDENT;

"GERMAN DISORDERS GROW, HUNDREDS SLAIN."

There were several stories on strife in Germany. One heading said:

"Anti-Semitic Wave Accompanies Revolt."

A report from Paris said the word from Washington was greeted in "sad silence."

The story on the action in Washington said: "The Senate spent a listless day." And the press and the people again hurled accusations in all directions.

"The President preferred to strangle his own child rather than have its crooked limbs straightened," said the *Pittsburgh Gazette Times.*

"The blood of the Treaty stains the floor of the Republican wigwam," charged the *Louisville Times.*

"The victors in the fighting over the Treaty are the Senate irreconcilables," said the *Baltimore Sun.*

The *New York World* said the dead had been betrayed, declaring, "Outside the little band of irreconcilables who have gone completely daft on the subject of the League there is not a Senator, Democratic or Republican, who does not realize that what the American people desired was ratification."

The papers contained many bitter, disgusted statements by supporters of the League of Nations. Dr. Lemuel H. Murlin, President of Boston University, said, "America and the Allies won the war, but it looks as if the devil was winning the peace."

Many Americans, like Woodrow Wilson, turned their eyes from the Senate, and looked forward to the fall elections. The people could decide! William Jennings Bryan, now a warm supporter of the Covenant, declared: "I think the world needs us, and that if we refuse to do our duty and enter the League of Nations, and if we are foolish enough to permit conditions in Europe to continue there will be a new war. I believe the people are greater than the United States Senate, and I will not believe in the impossibility of resurrection while the people have their faces toward the front and their hearts in the right place."

But the *New York Post* warned:

"To throw the Treaty into the campaign would bring about, not a 'great and solemn referendum' but a great and solemn muddle."

The *New York Journal* banner headline read:

"SENATOR NEWBERRY CONVICTED."

April 1, 1920. All Fools' Day

A resolution for a separate peace with Germany would soon come up for a vote, announced the *New York Tribune*.

April 27, 1920. Senator Hitchcock Loses His Leadership

Senator Underwood was unanimously elected Democratic leader in the Senate, after Senator Hitchcock withdrew from the contest.

May 27, 1920. "An Ineffaceable Stain . . ."

The resolution calling for a separate peace with Germany, steered through the Senate by Lodge, 43 to 38, approved by the House, 228 to 139, was vetoed by President Wilson. He sent it back to Congress with a stirring veto message:

"I have not felt at liberty to sign this joint resolution because I cannot bring myself to become party to an action which would place an ineffaceable stain upon the gallantry and honor of the United States."

The veto was sustained. We remained in a state of war with Germany.

June 10, 1920. Lodge versus Lodge

A little while before the Republican National Convention met in Chicago, Senator Lodge sent to Colonel Harvey a draft of the keynote speech he planned to deliver, inviting suggestions. Lodge told Harvey: "In regard to the League, no one knows better than you what a narrow channel I have to navigate in, with rocks on both sides. I want to condemn Wilson and all his works. That is comparatively easy, and I think I have done it. I also want to get the Convention to give a full approval of all that the Republican Senators did, drawing no distinctions between their differing opinions as to the final result. That is, I seek to make my speech, and I hope the platform, so broad that those of us who have fought the treaty for a year in the Senate can all stand upon it without any difficulty, and that we can use every argument, from Borah's down to McCumber's.

"I think the bulk of the Convention and the mass of the people at the present moment are in favor of the treaty with the reservations which bear my name. But I do not want to make any pledge as to the future."

When the convention met, Senator Lodge, who was elected Permanent Chairman, had a masterful speech ready. He gave blanket praise to the Republican Senators for protecting the United States against the League of Nations as Wilson brought it back from Paris.

"It became clearer to them every day that the Alliance called a League of Nations, instead of being a guarantee for the world's peace, was a breeder of war and an enemy of peace," he asserted.

But it was easier to deliver an oration ranging from Borah to McCumber than it was to write a plank acceptable to both, even after Jim Watson was made Chairman of the Resolutions Committee. There was a bitter battle. Senators McCumber, Kellogg, Lenroot, and others fought for a plank calling for United States membership in the League of Nations. Senators Borah and Johnson, as usual, threatened to bolt if any such plank was written. Senator Brandegee wept, and said he would bolt, too.

Someone finally suggested a plank pledging United States membership on the basis of the Lodge reservations.

But Senator Lodge took a violent stand against the Lodge reservations!

He served notice that he would leave the chair and fight from the floor against any attempt to put over a plank calling for membership on the basis of the reservations he had spent so long perfecting. This despite his admission to Colonel Harvey that the bulk of the Convention and the mass of the people favored his reservations. The League of Nations was dead, as far as Henry Cabot Lodge was concerned, and the Republican Party had no business talking about resurrecting it. The reservations had served their purpose. Now let them die, too!

Finally, a compromise plank was adopted. And, once again, it was not the irreconcilables who compromised. The plank assailed the League of Nations, and said: "The Republican Party stands for agreement among the nations to preserve the peace of the world. We believe that such an international association must be based upon justice and must provide methods which shall maintain the rule of public right by development of law and the decision of impartial courts, and which shall secure instant and general conference whenever peace shall be threatened by political action, so that the nations pledged to do and insist upon what is just and fair may exercise their influence and power for the prevention of war."

"My victory!" said Hiram Johnson.

June 11, 1920. Room 404, Blackstone Hotel, Chicago

Colonel George Harvey, who was not an official delegate to the Convention, invited Senator Lodge, Senator Brandegee, and Senator Curtis of Kansas to dine with him in his room in the Blackstone Hotel. Waiters brought up some food, and while they ate they talked over the deadlock in the fight out on the Convention floor.

The race for the Republican nomination for the presidency was in a hopeless tangle between General Leonard Wood and former

Governor Frank O. Lowden of Illinois, with Hiram Johnson running a bit behind them. Colonel Harvey proposed that all three be forgotten and a new candidate selected. The Senators agreed, and they began to talk over the possibilities.

They called in some of their friends—Senators Watson, McCormick, Wadsworth, Calder, and more—and tried to hit upon the logical candidate. They considered Charles Evans Hughes, Senator Knox, Will Hays, and even Henry Cabot Lodge, right in his presence. Lodge had just celebrated his seventieth birthday; he was too old.

Finally, at the proper moment, Colonel Harvey mentioned Senator Warren G. Harding. The others were a bit dubious, but Harding was from a strong state, Ohio. He had been receiving some votes on every ballot. He was regular. He had been OK in the League of Nations fight. Why not? Nobody got enthusiastic, but Senator Curtis went out to sound out some of the leaders of the key state delegations.

He came back after a while to report that several big states were willing to switch to Harding. The men finally agreed to support him. Colonel Harvey said: "One moment, gentlemen, let us first speak with Senator Harding himself."

It was after two o'clock in the morning when the silver-haired Senator walked into the room, heavy-eyed, suit rumpled. Colonel Harvey peered at him through his horn-rimmed glasses, assuming his most solemn air.

"We think," he said, "you may be nominated tomorrow. But first, Senator Harding, I wish you to assure these gentlemen and myself, upon your sacred honor and before your God, that you know of no reason, arising out of anything in your past life, why you should not stand with confidence before the American people as a candidate for the highest office within their gift."

Harding, somewhat stunned, was silent for a moment. "Gentlemen," he said, "I should like to be alone for a little while, if you please."

Colonel Harvey led him to an adjoining room. Harding stepped inside, and closed the door. Fifteen minutes later, he returned to

Colonel Harvey's smoke-filled room. He stated: "Gentlemen, there is no such reason."

June 12, 1920.
The Nomination of Harding and Coolidge

Chairman Henry Cabot Lodge presided over the Convention when it met to settle the nomination. "For a while he would watch the show idly, letting it get more and more passionate, vociferous, and preposterous," wrote H. L. Mencken. "Then, as if suddenly awakened, he would stalk into it with his club and knock it into decorum in half a minute."

Everything proceeded according to plan, and Warren G. Harding was nominated on the tenth ballot. There was no popular explosion for him. As Colonel Harvey put it: "He was nominated because there was nothing against him, and because the delegates wanted to go home."

There remained the task of choosing Harding's running mate. One delegation approached Lodge. He declined. Perhaps, unlike some men present at the Convention, he knew nothing about the condition of Harding's heart. Another man from Massachusetts, Governor Calvin Coolidge, was nominated on the first ballot, and the Convention adjourned.

July 2, 1920.
"We Advocate the Immediate Ratification . . ."

The League of Nations plank caused as bitter a battle at the Democratic National Convention in San Francisco as in Chicago.

The Resolutions Committee met at seven-thirty o'clock in the evening, and was going strong at midnight, behind closed doors, when correspondents for the New York newspapers had to file their stories. They were able to report only that angry shouts and howls of rage had been emitting from the committee room for four hours.

The meeting finally broke up at three-thirty in the morning, and some of the weary Senators were willing to talk a little before they staggered off to bed.

It seemed that Senator Carter Glass of Virginia, who had been appointed to the seat of the late Senator Martin, was acting as spokesman for President Wilson. He and Senator McKellar were trying to put over a fervent pro-League plank.

The democratic Senators who had voted for the Lodge reservations on March 19, however, were insisting on a plank they could stand on without repudiating their votes. Senator David I. Walsh of Massachusetts, acting as spokesman for a group including Senator Pomerene, Senator Walsh of Montana, and William Jennings Bryan, announced they would refuse to take the stump for the Democratic ticket unless a satisfactory compromise was reached.

Early in the morning, after the committee members had caught a few hours' sleep, they resumed the struggle. Finally, a compromise plank was adopted. It praised the League of Nations, and said: "We advocate the immediate ratification of the treaty without reservations which would impair its essential integrity, but do not oppose the acceptance of reservations making clearer or more specific the obligations of the United States to the League Associates."

July 6, 1920. The Nomination of James M. Cox

The contest for the Democratic nomination for the presidency was hopelessly deadlocked for many, many ballots between Secretary of the Treasury William Gibbs McAdoo, Governor James M. Cox of Ohio, and Attorney General A. Mitchell Palmer, with Governor Alfred E. Smith of New York running a bit behind.

No compromise candidate came forward. Smith fell out early, Palmer released his delegates on the thirty-eighth ballot, and Cox was nominated on the forty-fourth ballot.

July 7, 1920. The Nomination of Franklin D. Roosevelt

Assistant Secretary of the Navy Franklin D. Roosevelt was nominated for Vice President by acclamation, and the Democratic National Convention adjourned.

July 18, 1920. "We'll Make the Fight on the League!"

Governor Cox and Franklin D. Roosevelt had a long conference in Ohio on campaign strategy, after they left San Francisco.

They decided to play down the League of Nations in their campaign. They were both staunch supporters of world organization, but they and their most reliable advisers agreed it would be "calamitous" to carry on the fight until the election was over. They were afraid the people were so disgusted with the whole business that they were becoming hostile to internationalism and to whoever talked about it.

Cox had never met Woodrow Wilson, and so he and Roosevelt went to Washington to see him before they launched their campaign. They found Wilson sitting gaunt, cadaverous, broken, with a gray shawl wrapped around his shoulders. Cox's throat choked up when he tried to speak, but after a moment he managed:

"Mr. President, I have been a great admirer of your fight for the League."

Wilson gazed at him silently for a moment, and then a gleam of fire seemed to light his sunken eyes. He leaned forward and plucked Cox by the sleeve.

"Mr. Cox," he said in a low voice, "the fight can still be won."

The candidate for the presidency had tears in his eyes when he emerged from the White House, and his throat was choking all over again. He stood on the White House steps for a moment, brushing awkwardly at his wetted glasses. He turned on his running mate and struck him savagely across his husky, broad shoulders.

"Roosevelt!" cried Cox. "We'll make the fight on the League!"

July 23, 1920. "Our Sympathy for Europe . . ."

The town of Marion, Ohio, population 30,000, was overwhelmed by more than 30,000 visitors come to see Senator Warren G. Harding notified of his nomination.

Lunch stands, barbecues, and tents sprouted all over lawns and empty lots and street corners. Bands paraded up and down. Thousands of men roamed the streets with cards in their hatbands bearing Harding's portrait with the slogan:

"WARREN G. HARDING, A MAN OF THE PEOPLE."

For part of the day, Harding stood on his small front porch waving at the cheering throngs as they marched by with bands and banners. Then he went to the Chautauqua Auditorium in Garfield Park, where the men and women greeted him by standing on their seats and yelling and waving Harding pennants for two minutes.

Half a dozen bands played outside the auditorium and the crowd heard very little of the notification speech delivered by a harassed Henry Cabot Lodge. Harding heard him say:

"All who are familiar with your character and career and most especially those who have taken part with you in public service know beyond a peradventure that you are a patriotic American, imbued with the spirit of the great leaders of the past, of Washington, Lincoln and Roosevelt, whose services to the American people have become forever memorable in our history. You will always, and instinctively, in meeting the difficult questions and weighty responsibilities which confront you, think with complete unselfishness of your country and your country's interests first, a high qualification for an exalted office, not too familiar to us of late and, therefore, peculiarly necessary at this moment."

This led the way to an attack on the League of Nations: ". . . Mr. Wilson undertook to make us members of an alliance with foreign powers indefinite in extent and containing provisions which threatened the independence, the sovereignty and the safety of the United States. This effort on the part of the President was arrested by the action of the Republicans of the Senate, who proposed protecting reservations which he defeated together with the treaty itself. In that work, you, sir, took a conspicuous part and we know that you were in full accord with the belief of your Republican colleagues that the League of Nations as proposed by Mr. Wilson and upon which he and his party still insist ought never to be accepted by the American people."

Senator Lodge urged that the United States stay out of the League of Nations in order to save the lives of the country's young men:

"If the world needs us as they needed us in 1917 we shall not fail in our duty, but we can help other nations far better if we are free and untrammeled and do not permit our strength and our resources to be wasted and worn away and the lives of our young men to be sacrificed in endless hostilities with which we have no concern."

The people applauded politely for Lodge, even though they hadn't heard much of what he had said. They leaped on their seats again and stamped and shouted when Harding came forward to address them.

Harding failed to mention Wilson at all during his address, and he only mentioned the Democratic Party once or twice. But when he emphasized words like "autocracy" and "obstinacy" the crowd thought it knew what he meant, and there were delighted cries: "Give it to 'em!" "Go after 'em!"

Colonel Harvey had visited Harding, and he had helped him write his speech, which said this about the world:

"With a Senate advising as the Constitution contemplates, I would hopefully approach the nations of Europe and of the earth, proposing that understanding which makes us a willing participant in the consecration of the nations to a new leadership. . . . If men call for more specific details I remind them that moral committals are broad and all inclusive, and we are contemplating peoples in concord of humanity's advancement. From our point of view the program is specifically American, and we mean to be American first of all to the world. . . .

"If the supreme blunder has left European relationships inextricably interwoven in the League compact, our sympathy for Europe only magnifies our own good fortune in resisting involvement.

It is better to be the free and disinterested agent of international justice and advancing civilization, with the covenant of conscience, than be shackled by a written compact which surrenders our freedom of action and gives to a military alliance the right to proclaim America's duty to the world. No surrender of rights to a world council or its military alliance, no assumed mandatory however appealing, ever shall summon the sons of this Republic to war. Their supreme sacrifice shall only be asked for America and its call of honor. There is a sanctity in that right we will not delegate."

August 7, 1920. "The Supreme Issue of the Century Is Before Us. . . ."

Candidate Cox delivered his acceptance speech before a throng of 50,000 in Dayton, Ohio. He made his position on the League of Nations very clear.

"As the Democratic candidate, I favor going in," he declared.

There was a great outburst of cheering, and people shouted:

"That's the way to talk!"

Cox repeated the Democratic platform concerning the League of Nations, and made it clear he was willing to accept reasonable reservations: "Our platform clearly lays no bar against any additions that will be helpful, but it speaks in a firm resolution to stand against anything that disturbs the vital principle."

Stressing the importance he placed upon the need for world organization, he declared: "The house of civilization is to be put in order. The supreme issue of the century is before us, and the nation that halts and delays is playing with fire."

August 9, 1920. "To This Future I Dedicate Myself . . ."

At Hyde Park, Franklin D. Roosevelt stood on what newspapermen described as the largest front porch in the campaign. His neighbors, most of whom were Republicans, joined the crowd of

5000 scattered across the lawn to hear Roosevelt accept the Democratic nomination for Vice President.

He came out firmly for immediate ratification of the Versailles Treaty: "The League of Nations is a practical solution of a practical situation. It is no more perfect than our original Constitution, which has been amended eighteen times and will soon, we hope, be amended the nineteenth, was perfect. It is not anti-national; it is anti-war. No super-nation, binding us to the decisions of its tribunals, is suggested, but the method and machinery by which the opinion of civilization may become effective against those who seek war is at last within the reach of humanity. Through it we may with nearly every other duly constituted Government in the whole world throw our moral force and our potential power into the scale of peace."

Once during his address an airplane became visible over the treetops, and the audience stopped listening to gape at it. Roosevelt stopped talking, too, and stared up at the sky.

At one point, he interpolated on the spur of the moment a word that set his audience to laughing for several moments. Many seconds passed before the crowd recovered its composure. What he said was:

"Some people—some little people—have been saying of late: 'We are tired of progress, we want to get back to where we were before, to go about our own business to restore normal conditions'—I mean conditions of *normalcy*."

When the last giggle died down, he went back to talking about the League of Nations.

These were the closing passages of Franklin D. Roosevelt's speech:

"The coming years are laden with significance, and much will depend upon the immediate decision of America. This is the time when men and women must determine for themselves wherein our future lies. I look to it for progress: in the establishment of goodwill and mutual help among nations, in the ending of wars and the miseries that war brings, in the extension of honorable commerce, in the international settlement, which will make it unnecessary to send again 2,000,000 of our men across the sea. I look to our future for progress: in better citizenship, in less waste, in fairer remuneration for our labor, in more efficient governing, in higher standards of living.

"To this future, I dedicate myself, willing, whatever may be the choice of the people, to continue to help as best I am able. It is the faith which is in me that makes me very certain that America will choose the path of progress, and set aside the doctrines of despair, the whisperings of cowardice, the narrow road to yesterday. May the guiding spirit of our land keep our feet on the broad road that leads to a better tomorrow and give us strength to carry on."

November 1, 1920. The Solemn Referendum

The campaign of 1920 saw two presidential candidates from the same state for the first time since Lincoln and Douglas ran against each other. But there was no "great debate" between Harding and Cox.

Candidate Cox fought all through the summer and fall for the League of Nations. Said he: "We promise you this, that after March 4, 1921, with the least amount of conversation possible, we will enter the League of Nations."

Candidate Roosevelt, too, talked for the League of Nations incessantly, campaigning in all forty-eight states, delivering eight hundred speeches and setting an all-time long-distance campaign record. Said he: "The election of Cox means that the United States in particular with the other civilized nations of the world, will, through the League of Nations, solve international difficulties and prevent a recurrence of the holocaust of 1914–18."

Candidates Harding and Coolidge avoided the challenge. They preferred to talk of other things; Harding's happy pledge to lead America back to "normalcy" became the keynote. Coolidge, who didn't say a great deal, seemed to lean toward the League of Nations. He called Wilson "uncompromising" but he defended the Covenant from time to time. Said he: "I myself did not believe—do not believe—that the Covenant intended to create a supergovernment." He also said: "In our foreign policy our aims should be to use the power of this mighty nation to minimize the chances of war and to insure, so far as possible, a durable peace. If rejecting what is bad and adopting what is good of the present Covenant will bring about such a result the Republican Party can be relied upon to follow such a course."

Candidate Harding, helped a great deal on his speeches by Colonel Harvey, and advised by others including Editor Arthur H. Vandenberg of the *Grand Rapids Herald,* never made his position clear. Sometimes he seemed to propose fixing up the League of Nations and joining it: ". . . it can be amended or revised so that we may still have a remnant of world aspirations in 1918 builded into the world's highest conception of helpful co-operation in the ultimate realization." But sometimes he seemed positive the League was beyond redemption, declaring it had "undoubtedly passed beyond the powers of restoration."

Once he promised to consult the "best minds" in the country "to the end that we shall have an association of nations for the promotion of international peace." Said he: "Let it be an association, a society, or a league, or what not, our concern is solely with the substance, not the form thereof." Also: "It is folly to speak about a specific program."

Chester Rowell, editor of the *San Francisco Chronicle* and onetime Republican National Committeeman, described Harding's campaign speeches this way: "One half of the speeches were for the League of Nations if you read them hastily, but if you read them with care every word of them could have been read critically as against the League of Nations. The other half were violent speeches against the League of Nations if you read them carefully, but if you read them critically every one of them could be interpreted as in favor of the League of Nations."

Often some Republican papers interpreted a Harding speech as for the League, while others interpreted the same speech as against it. Anti-League Republicans, like Hiram Johnson, advised the nation to elect Harding as the best way to keep the United States out of the League, while a handful of anti-League Democrats, like Reed, said the same thing about Cox. Pro-League Republicans, like William Howard Taft, advised the nation to elect Harding as the best way to get the United States into the League of Nations.

Thirty-one prominent Republicans signed a highly important statement written by the faithful Elihu Root. It assailed Wilson and the Democratic plank as uncompromising, quoted Harding's best international statements, and said: "The question accordingly is not between a League and no League, but is whether certain provisions in the proposed League agreement shall be accepted unchanged or shall be changed." It concluded: "We therefore believe that we can most effectively advance the cause of international co-operation to promote peace by supporting Mr. Harding for election to the Presidency." Some of the signers of the statement hoped it would commit Harding to the League. Some felt that only a Republican President would ever get the Covenant through the Senate. Among the thirty-one who signed it were Charles Evans Hughes, Herbert Hoover, William Allen White, Henry L. Stimson, Nicholas Murray Butler, A. Lawrence Lowell, and four other members of the Executive Committee of the League to Enforce Peace.

Officially, the League to Enforce Peace took a "non-partisan" position, and had no effect upon the course of the campaign. It announced that it had been founded to secure "an association of nations" and that "both parties have confirmed the necessity and given assurance of the foundation of such an association."

The fight for the League of Nations in the "solemn referendum" wound up fully as confused, clouded, uncertain as the struggle in the Senate.

November 2, 1920.
"Not a Landslide . . . an Earthquake!"

The people went to the polls and Harding and Coolidge handed Cox and Roosevelt the most smashing defeat in the history of the Republic, 16,152,220 to 9,147,553. Nearly a million votes were cast for Eugene V. Debs, Socialist candidate, who was in prison for opposing the World War.

"It was not a landslide; it was an earthquake!" commented Joe Tumulty, dourly.

President-elect Warren G. Harding at long last made his position very clear on the League of Nations when cheering fellow-townsmen gathered on his lawn in Marion. He came out on his front porch and said:

"You just didn't want a surrender of the United States of America; you wanted America to go on under American ideals. That's why you didn't care for the League which is now deceased."

November 3, 1920. "The People *Can* Learn . . ."

Only Harding and the irreconcilables and their closest associates seemed to feel that the election had revealed the will of the people toward the League of Nations.

Calvin Coolidge, after a bit of thought, bluntly contradicted Harding's conclusions. He told some Boston businessmen: "I doubt if any particular mandate was given in the last election on the question of the League of Nations and if it was the preponderant issue."

The attitudes that moved the American people on election day were summarized by the *New York World:* "The American people wanted a change, and they have voted for a change. They did not know what kind of a change they wanted, and they do not know today what kind of change they have voted for."

A while later, Walter Lippmann wrote: "The Republican majority was composed of men and women who thought a Republican victory would kill the League, plus those who thought it was the most practical way to procure the League, plus those who thought it was the surest way offered to obtain an amended League. All these voters were inextricably entangled with their own desire or the desire of the other voters to improve business, or put labor in its place, or to punish the Democrats for going to war, or to punish them for not having gone sooner, or to get rid of Mr. Burleson

[Postmaster General], or to stop Mr. Daniels [Secretary of the Navy] from outbuilding the world, or to help Mr. Harding do the same thing."

Only one thing was clear now. The President-elect of the United States was against the League of Nations, and the new Senate would more than ever be controlled by men against it.

When Tumulty came to Wilson and told him of the verdict, Wilson said quietly: "The people will have to learn by bitter experience just what they have lost."

Then, in a halting, choked voice, Wilson read Tumulty a letter he had just received, a letter that helped him more than anything else on that day:

> Dear Mr. President:
>
> God didn't create the world in one act. I have never expected that we would win in the United States the first battle in the campaign for a League of Nations to keep the peace of the world. . . . We must now begin the war in earnest. We will win it. Never fear, the stars in their courses are fighting with us. . . .
>
> God still reigns. The people *can* learn, though not quickly.
>
> With regards,
>
> John Sharp Williams

1921

May 19, 1921. "Betrayal of Its Creators and Masters"

The new United States Ambassador to England, Colonel George Harvey, delivered a notable address in London at a dinner of welcome given by The Pilgrims.

"There still seems to linger in the minds of many here, as, indeed, of a few at home, the impression that in some way or other, by hook or crook, unwittingly and surely unwillingly, the United States may be beguiled into the League of Nations," he said. "Now let me show you how utterly absurd any such notion is . . . the question of American participation in the League came before the people, and the people decided against it by a majority of 7,000,000 out of a total vote of 25,000,000. Prior to that election there had been much discussion of the real meaning of the word mandate. There has been little since a single example provided the definition. A majority of 7,000,000 clearly conveyed a mandate that could neither be misunderstood nor disregarded.

"Anybody could see that it follows then inevitably and irresistibly that our present government could not without betrayal of its creators and masters, and will not, I can assure you, have anything whatsoever to do with the League or with any commission or committee appointed by it or responsible to it; directly or indirectly, openly or furtively."

The United States set out to observe to the letter the policy announced by Ambassador Harvey. The nations meeting at Geneva found it virtually impossible to deal with the vast political, economic, and social problems facing the world without our help, and they sent various notes to the State Department seeking our advice and co-operation. The notes were filed in Washington without acknowledgment for six months. When answers were finally sent, they were not addressed directly to the League of Nations, they were written in the third person, and they were unsigned.

We refused to co-operate with the League when it tackled the control of armaments. We even snubbed it in its efforts to curb the terrible epidemics that spread over the world in the wake of war. We not only rebuffed its efforts to enlist our help in putting down international traffic in women, children, and opium, but we tried to prevent the League from dealing with the problem. We scorned the World Court because it was linked to the League.

More and more isolated while some fifty nations tried to solve the problems of war and peace without us, we finally were compelled to send some observers to Geneva so we at least would know what was afoot. The observers were instructed to listen carefully but to take no official part in any League of Nations affairs. Clemenceau remarked that the United States was represented in the world "by an ear but not by a mouth."

October 18, 1921. Separate Peace with Germany

The United States Senate, led by Lodge, approved a separate Treaty of Peace with Germany.

1922

February 6, 1922. Japan Signs Some Treaties

The people of the United States were worried by signs of growing militarism in Japan. "Is Japan preparing for a war with America . . . ?" asked *Current History*. Two best selling books were called *The Menace of Japan* and *Must We Fight Japan?*

President Harding had to do something. He invited all the Pacific Powers except Russia, whose Soviet government the United States refused to recognize, to a conference in Washington. He made Senator Lodge one of the United States delegates.

Japan promised to observe the independence and territorial integrity of China, and signed the Nine Power Treaty.

Japan pledged to limit her navy, and signed the Five Power Naval Treaty. In accordance with the treaty, we set about scrapping battleships, limiting the size and caliber of guns on our cruisers, and tearing up plans for more aircraft carriers.

There was great approval throughout the United States, relief, and relaxation. The Senate was delighted, and there seemed no doubt it would ratify the treaties. What Henry Cabot Lodge did in the Senate was later described by Charles P. Howland, Director of Research of the Council on Foreign Relations, in his book *Survey of American Foreign Relations:*

"In fact, it would have been easily possible to secure an almost unanimous vote, but, according to Senator Lodge, this was not good strategy. Senator Lodge wished the conference to stand as a Republican success in the sharpest possible contrast to the Democratic failure under Wilson; he needed a few Democratic votes to make up the necessary two-thirds majority, but he wished to prevent the party from uniting in support of the treaties. It was the kind of parliamentary maneuvering at which Lodge was a past master; whenever there was a menace that too many votes might come from the Democratic side, he was able to let fly a barbed arrow that drove the unwelcome support back to the opposition. With an experienced astuteness Senator Lodge finally secured the ratification of the Washington treaties by the narrow margin he desired; public approval of the results of the conference was much more general than the Senate vote would indicate."

October 30, 1922. The March on Rome

Black-shirted Fascists marched on Rome to overthrow the Italian government. King Victor Emmanuel III capitulated, and appointed Benito Mussolini Prime Minister of Italy.

1923

November 8, 1923. The Beer Hall Putsch

Brown-shirted Nazis failed to overthrow the German government in a beer hall revolt in Munich led by Adolf Hitler, Hermann Goering, and General von Ludendorff.

November 11, 1923. "I Have Seen Fools Resist Providence . . ."

It was after church on this Sunday, after the Armistice Day prayers for peace, that a little throng of people—among them some war veterans—gathered before a home on S Street in Washington.

Woodrow Wilson limped out on the front porch, and Senator Carter Glass of Virginia spoke a few words of greeting. He said only a "conspiracy" had defeated the plan for peace. A band hired by Joe Tumulty played "How Firm a Foundation."

The former President of the United States haltingly said a very few words, and the very last were these:

"I have seen fools resist Providence before and I have seen their destruction, and it will come upon these again, utter destruction and contempt; that we shall prevail is as sure as that God reigns."

APPENDIX

BIBLIOGRAPHY

INDEX

APPENDIX

THE VOTES ON THE TREATY

November 19, 1919:
Vote on the treaty with 14 reservations:

FOR RATIFICATION

Democrats, 4: Thomas P. Gore, Oklahoma; John K. Shields, Tennessee; Hoke Smith, Georgia; David I. Walsh, Massachusetts.

Republicans, 35: L. Heisler Ball, Delaware; William M. Calder, New York; Arthur Capper, Kansas; LeBaron B. Colt, Rhode Island; Albert B. Cummins, Iowa; Charles Curtis, Kansas; William P. Dillingham, Vermont; Walter E. Edge, New Jersey; Davis Elkins, West Virginia; Joseph S. Frelinghuysen, New Jersey; Frederick Hale, Maine; Warren G. Harding, Ohio; Wesley L. Jones, Washington; Frank B. Kellogg, Minnesota; William S. Kenyon, Iowa; Henry W. Keyes, New Hampshire; Irvine L. Lenroot, Wisconsin; Henry Cabot Lodge, Massachusetts; Porter J. McCumber, North Dakota; George P. McLean, Connecticut; Charles L. McNary, Oregon; Knute Nelson, Minnesota; Harry S. New, Indiana; Truman H. Newberry, Michigan; Carroll S. Page, Vermont; Boies Penrose, Pennsylvania; Lawrence C. Phipps, Colorado; Reed Smoot, Utah; Selden P. Spencer, Missouri; Thomas Sterling, South Dakota; Howard Sutherland, West Virginia; Charles E. Townsend, Michigan; James W. Wadsworth, Jr., New York; Francis E. Warren, Wyoming; James E. Watson, Indiana.

AGAINST RATIFICATION

Democrats, 42: Henry F. Ashurst, Arizona; John H. Bankhead, Alabama; J. C. W. Beckham, Kentucky; George E. Chamberlain, Oregon; Charles A. Culberson, Texas; Nathaniel B. Dial, South Carolina; Duncan U. Fletcher, Florida; Edward J. Gay, Louisiana; Peter G. Gerry, Rhode Island; William J. Harris, Georgia; Pat Harrison, Mississippi; Charles B. Henderson, Nevada; Gilbert M. Hitchcock, Nebraska; Edwin S. Johnson, South Dakota; Andrieus A. Jones, New Mexico; John B. Kendrick, Wyoming; William H. King, Utah; William F. Kirby, Arkansas; Kenneth McKellar, Tennessee; Henry L. Myers, Montana; John F. Nugent, Idaho; Lee S. Overman, North Carolina; Robert L. Owen, Oklahoma; James D. Phelan, California; Key Pittman, Nevada; Atlee Pomerene, Ohio; Joseph E. Ransdell, Louisiana; James A. Reed, Missouri; Joseph T. Robinson, Arkansas; Morris Sheppard, Texas; Furnifold M. Simmons, North Carolina; Ellison D. Smith, South Carolina; John Walter Smith, Maryland; Marcus A. Smith, Arizona; A. Owsley Stanley, Kentucky; Claude A. Swanson, Virginia; Charles S. Thomas, Colorado; Park Trammell, Florida; Oscar W. Underwood, Alabama; Thomas J. Walsh, Montana; John Sharp Williams, Mississippi; Josiah O. Wolcott, Delaware.

Republicans, 13: William E. Borah, Idaho; Frank B. Brandegee, Connecticut; Bert M. Fernald, Maine; Joseph I. France, Maryland; Asle J. Gronna, North Dakota; Philander C. Knox, Pennsylvania; Robert M. LaFollette, Wisconsin; Medill McCormick, Illinois; George H. Moses, New Hampshire; George W. Norris, Nebraska; Miles Poindexter, Washington; Lawrence Y. Sherman, Illinois; Hiram W. Johnson, California (Republican and Progressive).

NOT VOTING

Democrats, none.
Republicans, 1: Albert B. Fall, New Mexico.
Vacancies, 1.

November 19, 1919: Vote on the treaty without reservations:

FOR RATIFICATION

Democrats, 37: Henry F. Ashurst, Arizona; John H. Bankhead, Alabama; J. C. W. Beckham, Kentucky; George E. Chamberlain, Oregon; Nathaniel B. Dial, South Carolina; Duncan U. Fletcher, Florida; Edward J. Gay, Louisiana; Peter G. Gerry, Rhode Island; William J. Harris, Georgia; Pat Harrison, Mississippi; Charles B. Henderson, Nevada; Gilbert M. Hitchcock, Nebraska; Edwin S. Johnson, South Dakota; Andrieus A. Jones, New Mexico; William H. King, Utah; William F. Kirby, Arkansas; Kenneth McKellar, Tennessee; Henry L. Myers, Montana; John F. Nugent, Idaho; Lee S. Overman, North

Carolina; Robert L. Owen, Oklahoma; James D. Phelan, California; Key Pittman, Nevada; Atlee Pomerene, Ohio; Joseph E. Ransdell, Louisiana; Joseph T. Robinson, Arkansas; Morris Sheppard, Texas; Furnifold M. Simmons, North Carolina; Ellison D. Smith, South Carolina; John Walter Smith, Maryland; Marcus A. Smith, Arizona; A. Owsley Stanley, Kentucky; Claude A. Swanson, Virginia; Oscar W. Underwood, Alabama; Thomas J. Walsh, Montana; John Sharp Williams, Mississippi; Josiah O. Wolcott, Delaware.

Republican, 1: Porter J. McCumber, North Dakota.

AGAINST RATIFICATION

Democrats, 7: Thomas P. Gore, Oklahoma; James A. Reed, Missouri; John K. Shields, Tennessee; Hoke Smith, Georgia; Charles S. Thomas, Colorado; Park Trammell, Florida; David I. Walsh, Massachusetts.

Republicans, 46: L. Heisler Ball, Delaware; William E. Borah, Idaho; Frank B. Brandegee, Connecticut; William M. Calder, New York; Arthur Capper, Kansas; LeBaron B. Colt, Rhode Island; Albert B. Cummins, Iowa; Charles Curtis, Kansas; William P. Dillingham, Vermont; Walter E. Edge, New Jersey; Davis Elkins, West Virginia; Bert M. Fernald, Maine; Joseph I. France, Maryland; Joseph S. Frelinghuysen, New Jersey; Asle J. Gronna, North Dakota; Frederick Hale, Maine; Warren G. Harding, Ohio; Wesley L. Jones, Washington; Frank B. Kellogg, Minnesota; William S. Kenyon, Iowa; Henry W. Keyes, New Hampshire; Philander C. Knox, Pennsylvania; Robert M. La-Follette, Wisconsin; Irvine L. Lenroot, Wisconsin; Henry Cabot Lodge, Massachusetts; Medill McCormick, Illinois; George P. McLean, Connecticut; Charles L. McNary, Oregon; George H. Moses, New Hampshire; Harry S. New, Indiana; Truman H. Newberry, Michigan; George W. Norris, Nebraska; Carroll S. Page, Vermont; Boies Penrose, Pennsylvania; Lawrence C. Phipps, Colorado; Miles Poindexter, Washington; Lawrence Y. Sherman, Illinois; Reed Smoot, Utah; Selden P. Spencer, Missouri; Thomas Sterling, South Dakota; Howard Sutherland, West Virginia; Charles E. Townsend, Michigan; James W. Wadsworth, Jr., New York; Francis E. Warren, Wyoming; James E. Watson, Indiana; Hiram W. Johnson, California (Republican and Progressive).

NOT VOTING

Democrats, 2: Charles A. Culberson, Texas; John B. Kendrick, Wyoming.

Republicans, 2: Albert B. Fall, New Mexico; Knute Nelson, Minnesota.

Vacancy, 1.

March 19, 1920:
Final vote on the treaty with 15 reservations:

FOR RATIFICATION

Democrats, 21: Henry F. Ashurst, Arizona; J. C. W. Beckham, Kentucky; George E. Chamberlain, Oregon; Duncan U. Fletcher, Florida; Thomas P. Gore, Oklahoma; Charles B. Henderson, Nevada; John B. Kendrick, Wyoming; William H. King, Utah; Henry L. Myers, Montana; John F. Nugent, Idaho; Robert L. Owen, Oklahoma; James D. Phelan, California; Key Pittman, Nevada; Atlee Pomerene, Ohio; Joseph E. Ransdell, Louisiana; Hoke Smith, Georgia; John Walter Smith, Maryland; Park Trammell, Florida; David I. Walsh, Massachusetts; Thomas J. Walsh, Montana; Josiah O. Wolcott, Delaware.

Republicans, 28: L. Hoisler Ball, Delaware; William M. Calder, New York; Arthur Capper, Kansas; LeBaron B. Colt, Rhode Island; Charles Curtis, Kansas; William P. Dillingham, Vermont; Walter E. Edge, New Jersey; Davis Elkins, West Virginia; Joseph S. Frelinghuysen, New Jersey; Frederick Hale, Maine; Wesley L. Jones, Washington; Frank B. Kellogg, Minnesota; William S. Kenyon, Iowa; Henry W. Keyes, New Hampshire; Irvine L. Lenroot, Wisconsin; Henry Cabot Lodge, Massachusetts; George P. McLean, Connecticut; Charles L. McNary, Oregon; Harry S. New, Indiana; Carroll S. Page, Vermont; Lawrence C. Phipps, Colorado; Reed Smoot, Utah; Selden P. Spencer, Missouri; Thomas Sterling, South Dakota; Howard Sutherland, West Virginia; James W. Wadsworth, Jr., New York; Francis E. Warren, Wyoming; James E. Watson, Indiana.

AGAINST RATIFICATION

Democrats, 23: Braxton B. Comer, Alabama; Charles A. Culberson, Texas; Nathaniel B. Dial, South Carolina; Edward J. Gay, Louisiana; Carter Glass, Virginia; William J. Harris, Georgia; Pat Harrison, Mississippi; Gilbert M. Hitchcock, Nebraska; Edwin S. Johnson, South Dakota; William F. Kirby, Arkansas; Kenneth McKellar, Tennessee; Lee S. Overman, North Carolina; James A. Reed, Missouri; Joseph T. Robinson, Arkansas; Morris Sheppard, Texas; John K. Shields, Tennessee; Furnifold M. Simmons, North Carolina; Ellison D. Smith, South Carolina; A. Owsley Stanley, Kentucky; Claude A. Swanson, Virginia; Charles S. Thomas, Colorado; Oscar W. Underwood, Alabama; John Sharp Williams, Mississippi.

Republicans, 12: William E. Borah, Idaho; Frank B. Brandegee,

Connecticut; Bert M. Fernald, Maine; Joseph I. France, Maryland; Asle J. Gronna, North Dakota; Philander C. Knox, Pennsylvania; Robert M. LaFollette, Wisconsin; Medill McCormick, Illinois; George H. Moses, New Hampshire; George W. Norris, Nebraska; Lawrence Y. Sherman, Illinois; Hiram W. Johnson, California (Republican and Progressive).

NOT VOTING

Democrats, 3: Peter G. Gerry, Rhode Island; Andrieus A. Jones, New Mexico; Marcus A. Smith, Arizona.

Republicans, 9: Albert B. Cummins, Iowa; Albert B. Fall, New Mexico; Warren G. Harding, Ohio; Porter J. McCumber, North Dakota; Knute Nelson, Minnesota; Truman H. Newberry, Michigan; Boies Penrose, Pennsylvania; Miles Poindexter, Washington; Charles E. Townsend, Michigan.

Vacancies, none.

BIBLIOGRAPHY

Bailey, Thomas A., *A Diplomatic History of the American People,* F. S. Crofts & Co., 1942.

Bailey, Thomas A., *Woodrow Wilson and the Lost Peace,* The Macmillan Co., 1944.

Baker, Ray Stannard, *Woodrow Wilson and World Settlement,* Doubleday, Doran & Co., 1923.

Baker, Ray Stannard, and Dodd, William E., Editors, *The Public Papers of Woodrow Wilson, War and Peace,* Harper & Bros., 1925–27.

Bartlett, Ruhl J., *The League to Enforce Peace,* The University of North Carolina Press, 1944.

Berdahl, Clarence A., *The Policy of the United States with Respect to the League of Nations,* Graduate Institute of International Studies; Publications, No. 6, 1932.

Bonsal, Stephen, *Unfinished Business,* Doubleday, Doran & Co., 1944.

Bowers, Claude G., *Beveridge and the Progressive Era,* Houghton Mifflin Co., 1932.

Burlingame, Roger, and Stevens, Alden, *Victory Without Peace,* Harcourt, Brace & Co., 1944.

Carlson, Oliver, and Sutherland, Ernest, *Hearst, Lord of San Simeon,* The Viking Press, 1936.

Chicago Tribune.

Churchill, Winston, *The Aftermath,* Charles Scribner's Sons, 1921.

Colegrove, Kenneth, *The American Senate and World Peace,* Vanguard Press, 1944.

Congressional Record, 1917–21.

Creel, George, *How We Advertised America,* Harper & Bros., 1920.

Creel, George, *The War, the World and Wilson,* Harper & Bros., 1920.

Current Biography, The H. W. Wilson Co.

Darling, H. Maurice, "Who Kept the United States Out of the League of Nations?", *Canadian Historical Review,* September, 1929.

Democratic National Convention, 1920, Official Report of the Proceedings of, Compiled by Edward G. Hoffman, Sec.

Dodd, William E., *Woodrow Wilson and His Work*, P. Smith, 1932.
Fleming, Denna Frank, *The United States and the League of Nations, 1918–1920*, G. P. Putnam's Sons, 1932.
Gilbert, Clinton W., *You Takes Your Choice*, G. P. Putnam's Sons, 1924.
Grand Rapids Herald.
Hansen, Harry, *The Adventures of the Fourteen Points*, The Century Co., 1919.
Harvey, George B., *Henry Clay Frick the Man*, Charles Scribner's Sons, 1928.
Harvey's Weekly, 1917–20.
Hitchcock, Gilbert, *An Address Before the Nebraska State Historical Society*, Lincoln, January 13, 1925.
Hitler, Adolf, *Mein Kampf*, Reynal & Hitchcock, 1939.
Holt, William S., *Treaties Defeated by the Senate*, The Johns Hopkins Press, 1933.
Howland, Charles P., *Survey of American Foreign Relations*, Yale University Press, 1928.
Jessup, Philip C., *Elihu Root*, Dodd Mead & Co., 1938.
Johnson, Gerald W., *Woodrow Wilson*, Harper & Bros., 1944.
Johnson, Willis Fletcher, *George Harvey, A Passionate Patriot*, Houghton Mifflin Co., 1929.
Keynes, John Maynard, *The Economic Consequences of the Peace*, Harcourt, Brace & Co., 1920.
Lansing, Robert, *The Big Four and Others of the Peace Conference*, Houghton Mifflin Co., 1921.
Lansing, Robert, *The Peace Negotiations, A Personal Narrative*, Houghton Mifflin Co., 1921.
Lasswell, Harold D., *Propaganda Technique in the World War*, P. Smith, 1938.
Lawrence, David, *The True Story of Woodrow Wilson*, George H. Doran Co., 1924.
Lippmann, Walter, *Public Opinion*, The Macmillan Co., 1927.
Literary Digest, 1916–20.
Lloyd George, David, *War Memoirs*, Ivor, Nicholson & Watson, 1933.
Lodge, Henry Cabot, *The Senate and the League of Nations*, Charles Scribner's Sons, 1925.
Lowry, Edward G., *Washington Close-Ups, 1921*, Houghton Mifflin Co., 1921.
MacKaye, Milton, "Governor Roosevelt," *The New Yorker*, August 15, 1931.

Marshall, Thomas R., *Recollections of Thomas R. Marshall,* Bobbs-Merrill Co., 1925.
Miller, David Hunter, *The Drafting of the Covenant,* G. P. Putnam's Sons, 1928.
Moley, Raymond, *After Seven Years,* Harper & Bros., 1939.
Myers, Denys P., *Manuscript.*
Nevins, Allan, *Henry White, Thirty Years of American Diplomacy,* Harper & Bros., 1930.
New York American.
New York Evening Journal.
New York Evening Post.
New York Sun.
New York Times.
New York Tribune.
O'Connor, Harvey, *Mellon's Millions,* The John Day Co., 1933.
Pershing, John J., *My Experiences in the World War, Vol. I,* Frederick A. Stokes Co., 1931.
Pringle, Henry F., *The Life and Letters of William Howard Taft,* Farrar and Rinehart, 1939.
Pringle, Henry F., *Theodore Roosevelt; A Biography,* Harcourt, Brace & Co., 1931.
Republican National Convention, 1920, Official Report of the Seventeenth, Copyright 1920 by Lafayette B. Gleason.
Robinson, Corrine, *My Brother Theodore Roosevelt,* Charles Scribner's Sons, 1921.
Roosevelt, Theodore, *America and the World War,* Charles Scribner's Sons, 1919.
Rowell, Chester, "The Foreign Policy of the United States Since the War" in *The Problems of the Peace,* Oxford University Press, 1937.
Schriftgiesser, Karl, *The Gentleman from Massachusetts,* Little, Brown & Co., 1944.
Seymour, Charles, *The Intimate Papers of Colonel House,* Houghton Mifflin Co., 1926–28.
Smith, Arthur D. H., *Mr. House of Texas,* Funk & Wagnalls Co., 1940.
Sullivan, Mark, *Over Here* (Vol. V of *Our Times*), Charles Scribner's Sons, 1933.
Sullivan, Mark, *The Twenties* (Vol. VI of *Our Times*), Charles Scribner's Sons, 1935.
Sullivan, Mark, "America and the League of Nations Six Years After," *World's Work,* January, 1926.
Tumulty, Joseph, *Woodrow Wilson as I Know Him,* Doubleday, 1921.
Villard, Oswald Garrison, *Fighting Years,* Harcourt, Brace & Co., 1939.

Washington Evening Star.
Washington Herald.
Washington Post.
Washington Times.
Watson, James E., *As I Knew Them,* Bobbs-Merrill Co., 1936.
White, William Allen, *Woodrow Wilson,* Houghton Mifflin Co., 1925.
Wilson, Edith Bolling, *My Memoir,* Bobbs-Merrill Co., 1939.
Wilson, Woodrow, *Constitutional Government in the United States,* Columbia University Press, 1908.
Wister, Owen, *Roosevelt: The Story of a Friendship,* The Macmillan Co., 1930.
Young, Roland, *This Is Congress,* Alfred A. Knopf, 1943.

INDEX

Albany Chamber of Commerce, 115-16
Alliances, entangling, 2, 14, 52, 121
Allies, vii, viii, 26, 29, 46, 164 (*See also* France, England, Italy)
America and the World War, by Theodore Roosevelt, 15
American Agricultural Association, 103
American Bankers Association, 197
American Bar Association, 197
American Federation of Labor, 197, 241, 242
American Legion, 155
American Manufacturers' Export Association, 103
American Rights League, 242
American Women Suffrage Association, 103
Armenia, 13
Armies, 9, 13, 32, 43, 71
Armistice (Nov. 11, 1918), 38-39, 50, 100
Ashurst, Henry F., 175, 202
Associated Advertising Clubs, 197, 242
Association of Collegiate Alumnae, 242
Australia, 92, 201
Austria-Hungary, 24

Baker, Newton D., 22
Baker, Ray Stannard, 93
Balfour, Arthur, 34, 99
Balkan nations, 19, 73
Ball, L. Heisler, 78
Baltimore Sun, 261
Bartlett, Ruhl H., 138
Baruch, Barney, 197
Beckham, J. C. W., 135-38
Belgium, 19, 50, 93, 255
Bell, Alexander Graham, 197
Beveridge, Albert, 16, 21, 23, 27, 42, 62, 94, 238
Bi-Partisan Conference, 243-49, 255, 256
Bliss, Tasker H., 40, 178, 237
Bolshevism, 64, 152
Bonsal, Stephen, 105, 205-206, 218, 219
Borah, William E., 55, 61-66, 77, 100-102, 103, 116-18, 120, 126, 129, 141-142, 159, 162, 174-75, 223, 243, 256, 257
Brandegee, Frank B., 68, 69, 73-74, 75, 78, 87, 109, 111-12, 117, 121, 126, 127, 129, 156, 158, 160, 221-22, 238, 243, 246, 254-55, 259
Brockdorff-Rantzau, Count, 106
Brotherhood of Locomotive Firemen and Enginemen, 242
Bryan, William Jennings, 4, 8, 261-62, 267
Buchanan, James, 46
Bulgaria, 24
Bullitt, William C., 107, 178-80
Burbank, Luther, 197
Burns, Allen T., 134
Butler, Nicholas Murray, 275

Cabot, George, 4
Calder, William M., 78
Capper, Arthur, 252
Caroline Islands, 167
Caruso, Enrico, 82
Catholicism, 63, 118-19
Central European nations, 19
Chamberlain-Bayard Treaty, 232
Chamberlain, Thomas G., 148
Chicago Tribune, 36, 45, 56, 103, 110, 116, 117, 161, 175, 196
China, 95, 104, 157, 158, 163, 165-66 (*See also* Shantung)
Church of St. John (Washington, D.C.), 7
Church Peace Union, 104, 241

Churchill, Winston, 38
Clemenceau, Georges, 33-35, 38, 41, 42, 56, 58, 61, 82, 92-93, 106, 180
Cleveland, Grover, 11, 46
Colombia, 14-15
Colt, Le Baron, 130, 133, 242, 243, 244
Congress of the United States, 16, 31, 78, 107, 108, 128
Constitution of the United States, 136-38
Coolidge, Calvin, 66, 141, 266, 273, 275
Council of Jewish Women, 242
Council of League of Nations, convenes, 245
Council of Ten, 56
"Covenanter, The," 109
Cox, James M., 267, 268, 271, 273, 275
Creel, George, 162
Cummins, Albert B., 75, 77, 81, 133, 183
Curtis, Charles, 78, 101, 103, 264
Czechoslovaks, 19, 93

Dairymen's League, 242
Dalmatia, 96
Daughters of the American Revolution, 103
Democratic National Committee, 79
Democratic National Convention (1920), 266-67, 268
Democratic Party, 29, 30, 32, 36, 40, 115-16, 129, 224, 240, 241, 249
Des Moines Register, 74
Dillingham, William P., 78
Disarmament plans, 216
Dodd, William E., 23
Domestic affairs, 90, 91, 215

Edge, Walter E., 77
Edison, Thomas A., 197
Elections: of 1912, 5, 6, 37; of 1916, 3, 5; of 1918, 23, 29, 31, 33, 36, 37; of 1920, 275
Elkins, Davis, 83
England, 11, 35, 50, 52, 53, 63, 64, 86, 96, 97, 105, 125, 135, 159, 201
Erzberger, Mathias, 216
Evangelical Lutheran Church in America, 104

Fall, Albert B., 65, 83, 126, 129, 165, 167, 191, 192, 195, 220, 236
Farmers' Educational and Cooperative Union of America, 103
Farmers' Reconstruction Conference, 103
Fascism, 178, 192, 193, 281
Federal Council of Churches, 104, 241
Fernald, Bert M., 77
Filene, Edward A., 8
Filibuster in the Senate, 78-83
Fiske, John, 14
Fiume, 92, 96, 98, 100, 162, 178, 192
Fletcher, Duncan U., 228, 232
Foch, Marshal Ferdinand, 19, 35-36, 122
Ford, Henry, 37, 197, 235
Foreign Relations Committee of the United States Senate, 11, 28, 29, 37, 65, 66, 108, 126, 127, 128, 129, 156, 158, 161, 162, 163, 165, 176, 207, 232 (*See also* Lodge, Henry Cabot)
Fourteen Points, The, analysis of, 18-19; Col. Harvey's comments on, 21; German acceptance of, 25-26; T.R. demands repudiation of, 26, 27, 28, 33, 37; Clemenceau, Lloyd George, and Orlando comment on, 33-36; Point 1, 54-55; Point 2, 34; Point 9, 34; interpretation by Walter Lippmann, 34; Wilson unwilling to give up, 35; Allied acceptance of, 36; Lodge sets out to demolish, 40, 47; and Senator Borah, 55; and the Peace Conference, 54-56
Fourteen Reservations of Henry Cabot Lodge, 209, 211-12, 214-15
France, Joseph Irwin, 78, 80
France, 19, 24, 35, 38, 50, 52, 53, 58, 59, 60, 64, 86, 96, 105, 159, 191, 201
Franklin, Benjamin, 55, 136
Frelinghuysen, J. S., 77, 246, 254, 255
Frick, Henry Clay, 110-12, 162

Gary, Judge, 197
General Federation of Women's Clubs, 104, 242
Germany; a corridor to the Persian Gulf, 13; destruction and aggression by, 10; peace terms to Russia, new offensive on the West Front, 18, 19; strikes in, 19; flight from Greece and France, 24; German General Staff, 19, 21, 25; ready for peace, 25-26; the Kaiser, 26; negotiations with, 27, 31; notes to and from, 32; defeated by blockade, 34; reparations, 35-36; terms for a military armistice, 36; signing of Armistice

(Nov. 11, 1918), 38; peace treaty with, 48; League of Nations to curb, 92; aggression, 96; Versailles Treaty, 106, 107, 108, 109, 117; capitulation, 122; trade with, 160; hope revived, 181; Junkers, 193; separate peace with, vii, 160, 232, 241, 253, 262, 279; Nazi Party, 252; agreement with Belgium, 255; government, 282; 46, 50, 58, 99-100, 105
Gerry, Peter, 256
Glass, Carter, 267
Goering, Hermann, 282
Goltz, General von der, 193
Gore, Thomas P., 210
Grand Rapids Herald, 131, 184, 274
Grant, U.S., 46
Grayson, Admiral, 168, 169, 187, 188, 190, 194, 195, 236
Grey, Viscount, 250-51, 258
Greece, 24
Greek-Americans, 162
Gronna, Asle J., 78

Hale, Frederick C., 65, 77, 195
Hamilton, Alexander, 55
Harding, Warren G., 63, 77, 127, 129, 147, 157, 227, 265, 266, 269, 270, 271, 273, 274, 275-77
Hardwick, Thomas W., 72
Harvey, George, 20-21, 23, 33, 39, 42, 49-50, 58, 98, 109-13, 196, 263-65, 266, 270, 274, 278
Harvey's Weekly, 110
Hawes, Harry B., 155
Hays, Will, 23, 122, 138, 139, 141
Hearst, William Randolph, 170-71, 234-235
Hearst papers, 56, 110, 134, 170-71, 234-235
Henry, Patrick, 136-37
Hindenburg, Paul von, 27
Hitchcock, Gilbert, 60, 68, 86, 95, 101, 113-17, 129, 168, 198-99, 210-11, 215, 216, 219, 222-23, 225, 226-28, 236, 244, 245, 247, 249, 255, 257, 260, 262
Hitler, Adolf, viii, 37-38, 252-53, 282
Hoover, Herbert, 218, 275
House, Edward M., 33-36, 38, 40, 86, 93, 96, 105, 178, 180, 193-94, 206, 218
House of Representatives, 29, 66, 69
Houston, Herbert S., 171
Hughes, Charles Evans, 3, 5, 6, 95, 101, 122, 275
Hungarian-Americans, 162
Hungary, rebellion in, 19
Hunt, Frazier, 117

Immigration, 16, 68, 72, 93, 115, 130
India, 201
Influenza epidemic, 30
International Federation of Rotary Clubs, 241
International obligations of the U.S.A., 8, 10, 167-68
International understandings, private, 54-56
Internationalism, 27, 36, 152, 153
Ireland, 125
Irish-Americans, 63, 64
Irish reservation, 257
Isolationism, vii, viii, 50
Italian-Americans, 100, 162
Italy, 19, 34, 35, 53, 63, 64, 86, 92, 98-100, 104, 159, 192, 281

Jackson, Andrew, 46
Japan, 63, 64, 86, 92, 96, 104, 158, 159, 163, 165, 166, 167 (*See also* Shantung)
Jefferson, Thomas, 61, 136
Joffre, Marshal, 22
Johnson, Hiram, 5, 6, 27, 55, 78, 109, 116, 124-25, 129, 157, 162, 174, 175, 183, 185, 188, 200-202, 243, 246, 247, 264, 274
Judge, 127

Kaiser Wilhelm II, abdication, 37
Karger, Gus, 139
Kellogg, Frank, 129, 130, 142, 199, 244
Kendrick, John B., 244
Kenyon, William S., 175, 244
Keyes, Henry W., 78
Kirby, William F., 255
Knox, Philander C., 31, 60, 61, 65, 68, 69, 72-73, 74, 75, 77, 87, 109, 110, 111, 112, 121, 129, 158, 162, 164, 179, 254, 265
Koo, Wellington, 95

LaFollette, Robert M., 79-80, 81, 230
Lansing, Robert, 40, 158, 178-80
League for Peace, 8-9, 11, 16

League for the Preservation of American Independence, 124, 174, 196
League of Free Nations Association, 134
League of Nations, vii; not a perfect instrument, viii, 18, 50-51; T.R. detests idea of, 22, 23, 27, 43-45; Col. Harvey's about-face, 23, 27, 28; American people support idea of, 31, 43; Clemenceau, Lloyd George, Orlando, opinions of, 34-35; and Henry Ford, 37; Wilson's power and prestige would insure creation of, 39; and Lodge, 40, 41 (*See also* Lodge, Henry Cabot); first and greatest task before the Peace Conference, 42; Senate support, 43; Lodge outlines strategy to defeat, 45-48; dangers and difficulties, 47-48; and James Watson, 48-49; opposition of Col. Harvey, 49, 50, 58, 98, 109-13; Porter McCumber supports, 52-53, 68-69, 75, 126, 129, 165, 177, 201, 226; made the basis of the peace, 56-57; power of, 58; and Taft, 60, 62, 64-65, 82, 83, 111; triumph for British diplomacy, 62-63; attacked, 61-65; and Coolidge, 66; Wilson's Boston speech for, 66-67; provision for peaceful withdrawal from, 72, 121; Lodge speech on, suggestions for amendments, 70-72; and Senator Hardwick, 72; and Senator Knox, 72-73; press opinion on, 74; resolution of Lodge that the League of Nations be not accepted by the United States, 77-78; round robin, 74-78; filibuster and desire to kill, 78-83; Taft urges nation to support, 82, 83, 115-16; fear abroad that the U.S. will abandon, 83-84; and Henry White (*See also* White, Henry); withdrawal from, 90, 91; special concessions demanded by foreign powers, 92-93, 104-106; press, civilians, soldiers support, 94, 127; endorsement of, 103; actual creation, 107; public endorsement of, 109-10; funds raised to oppose, 110-13; "A Coloured League of Nations," 113; Catholicism and, 118-19; prejudice and passion used against, 120; Foreign Relations Committee plan to fight, 127; Senator Beckham defends, 135-138; Taft flounders on reservations, 138-44; Senator Williams defends, 143-45, 199, 200; Senator Nelson defends, 146; Senator Randsdall defends, 147-49; Lodge reservation needed for ratification, 150; and Senator Reed, 155; Frederick Palmer's opinions of, 155; benefits of, 159; China's guarantee of justice, 165-66; and Taft, 167; and Senator Martin, 168; and William Randolph Hearst, 170-71; war veterans support, 184; group support, 196-197; Lodge's strategy summarized, 198-99; assignment of voting power, 201; religious feeling stirred against, 63, 118-19, 202-203; and Senator Sherman, 202-203; Hiram Johnson amendment, 202; the Preamble, 209-211, 215, 216; Shantung, 215; American delegates to, 216; reservations, 216, 242; and Hitchcock, 95, 113, 222-23, 257, 260; Wilson requests referendum, 240-41; debate, 251-52, 253; final vote on, 257-60; Democratic National Convention supports (1920), 267; Lodge's attack on, 269-70; and James Cox, 268, 271, 273; and F. D. Roosevelt, 271, 273; and Coolidge, 273, 276; and Harding, 274, 276, 277; fight on the referendum, 275-76; and George Harvey, 278-79
League Commission, 5, 7, 90, 93
League Council, 245
League Covenant, 44, 57-61, 65, 79, 82-83, 106, 119, 219, 255; Article No. 1, 1, 211; Article No. 10, 59, 71, 121, 125, 131, 139, 156-57, 166, 172-73, 176, 214-15, 245, 248, 253-55, 258; Article No. 13, 71; criticism and attack on, 60-65; Wilson confers with Senate and House Foreign Relations Committee on, 68-69; Covenant vs. Constitution, 70; Lodge speech on, and suggestions, 70-72; open to amendment, 86; Taft proposes specific amendments, 86, 88; Wilson seeks four amendments, 90, 95; amended and accepted by Peace Conference, 100; amended, 100-102; public sentiment for, 109-10; Taft supports, 115-116; drive to revise, 120-21; in hands of men committed to destroy it, 130; grammar of, 205-206; copy with

Lodge's notations, 206; new reservations (Lodge), 207; Reservation No. 1, 211-12; Reservation No. 2, 214-15; other reservations, 215-16

League to Enforce Peace, dinner, 1; Taft heads, 2; political partisanship thrust aside, 3; developed into strong nation-wide organization, 8, 109-10; speaking tour of Taft, 62, 89, 91, 101, 103; ratifying conventions, 109, 116, 120; survey of the press, 127; and LeBaron Colt, 130; Taft decides in favor of reservations, 138-44; no longer a powerful force, 140, 146, 168; survey, 197, 218; works for Lodge, 238; with American Federation of Labor sponsors conference, 241-42, 275 (*See also* Taft, William Howard; Lowell, A. Lawrence)

Lenin, 64

Lenroot, I. L., 78, 228, 241, 242, 244-255, 259

Lewis, James Hamilton, 36

Liberty Loan drives, 24-25, 30

Lincoln, Abraham, 29, 46, 61, 70

Lippmann, Walter, 34, 276

Literary Digest, 74, 94, 103

Lloyd George, David, 33-35, 38, 41, 82, 92-93

Lodge, Henry Cabot: proposes international league for peace, vii, 1-2, 16, 25; in accord with Wilson and Taft, 3; effort to wreck Wilson's strategy in 1916 presidential campaign, 3-5, 6, 7; character and physique, 5, 7, 76; on the functions and powers of the Senate, 10, 11; address to Senate: opposes international league for peace (Feb. 1, 1917), 12-14, 16; and Frank Brandegee, 73-75, 78, 87, 121, 126, 129, 222, 254-55; and T.R., 15, 16, 27, 43-45, 89; and Beveridge, 16, 42, 62, 94, 238; and Wilson, 28, 29, 30, 33, 40, 41, 54, 66, 68, 69, 100, 150, 170, 191, 208-10, 236, 253, 256; influence in election of 1918, 30, 37; and McKinley, 11, 30, 40, 46; Chairman of Senate Foreign Relations Committee, 37, 107; and Henry White, 40, 41, 84-85, 87, 94-95, 122, 179, 253; League of Nations and the Fourteen Points, 40, 41, 54-56; secret memorandum, 41; and Col. Harvey, 42, 50, 263-65, 266; on world peace, 42-43; opposes any method for actually establishing a League of Nations, 42-43; conferences with T.R. to defeat League of Nations, 43-45; *The Treaty Making Powers of the Senate,* 45; outlines strategy to defeat League of Nations, 45-48; and James Watson, 48-49, 52, 77, 142-143; and Porter McCumber, 52-53, 68-69, 75, 129, 226; attitude toward the Covenant of the League of Nations, 60-61; and Senator Knox, 60, 61, 68, 69, 74, 75, 77, 87, 121, 129, 164, 179, 265; and William Howard Taft, 65, 138-39; speech on the Covenant of the League of Nations, 70-72; engineers signing round robin by 31 Senators to aid defeat of League, 75-78; offers resolution that "Constitution of the League of Nations should not be accepted by the United States," 77-78; and A. Lawrence Lowell, 89, 120; admits people favor a League, 94; and Monroe Doctrine, 97 (*See that heading*); and John Sharp Williams, 97, 152-55, 257; opinion on Italian claim for Fiume, 100; and Borah, 77, 101-102, 103, 120, 126, 129, 141-42, 257; and William C. Bullitt, 108, 178-80; majority leader of the Senate, 108; fear success of League would win a third term for Wilson, 115; drive to revise the Covenant, 120-22; plans to kill Versailles Treaty, 128-29; interview with Allen T. Burns and James G. McDonald, 134-35; Wilson's hatred for, 143, 150; completes formal reading of Versailles Treaty, 145-46; and Knute Nelson, 142, 146, 242; reservations, 150, 161, 165, 207-208, 218, 242, 252; no need for a League, 151-152; presidential inquiry concerning League of Nations, 156-60; on Shantung amendment, 163-67, 195; strategy during Wilson's illness, 191-92, 198; refuses to compromise, 198; on religious sentiment, 204; and Col. Bonsal, 205-206, 218, 219; notations on copy of Covenant, 206; "Fourteen Reservations," 209, 211-12, 214-15; invokes cloture, 215-16; and Senator

Hitchcock, 129, 168, 198-99, 219, 222-223, 225, 236, 244, 249; presents preamble and fourteen reservations to Senate, 220-32; goes down on record as voting for League of Nations and Versailles Treaty, 224; and Senator Fletcher, 232; and Senator Underwood, 239; blocks conciliation, 239-240, 260; Democratic senators attempt reconciliation, 241; conference resolution taken, 242; and Bi-Partisan conference, 243-49; and Viscount Grey's letter, 250-51; separate peace with Germany, 232, 253, 262, 279; proposes change in the preamble to the reservations, 258; and Republican National Convention, 263-66; gives Harding's notification speech, 269; attack on the League of Nations, 269-70; delegate to Conference of Pacific powers, 280-81
Los Angeles Times, 6, 196
Louisiana Territory, 13
Louisville Times, 261
Lowell, A. Lawrence, 89, 91, 120, 140, 275
Ludendorff, General von, 282
Lusitania, 4, 6, 106

Madison, James, 46, 55
Makimo, Baron, 96
Mandate, 90, 91, 150, 215
Marianna Islands, 167
Marshall, Thomas R., 152, 153, 220, 230, 231
Marshall Islands, 167
Martin, Thomas S., 168, 213, 267
Massachusetts Republican State Convention, 197
McAdoo, William G., 267
McClean, George P., 78
McCormick, Medill, 36, 78, 112, 126, 127, 172, 174, 193, 229, 246
McCormick, Robert R., 36
McCumber, Porter, 52-53, 68-69, 75, 126, 129, 165, 177, 201, 226, 228
McDonald, James G., 134
McKellar, Kenneth D., 215, 243, 244, 254, 260, 267
McKinley, William, 11, 30, 40, 46
McNary, Charles, 103, 133, 242
Mein Kampf, 38, 252-53
Mellon, Andrew, 110, 112, 113, 162
Metropolitan Magazine, 16
Mexico, 72
Meyers, Henry, 81
Military training, compulsory, 252
Monroe Doctrine, 9, 13, 14, 16, 43, 48, 53, 70, 72, 88, 89, 90, 91, 95, 96-97, 132, 134, 172, 181, 215
Moot, Adelbert, 127
Moses, George H., 77, 129, 130, 194, 195
Murlin, Lemuel H., 261
Mussolini, Benito, 100, 281

Nation, The, 183-84
National Association of Merchant Tailors of America, 103
National Board of Farm Organizations, 103
National Conference of Social Work, 134, 242
National Council of Women, 242
National Education Association, 242
National Grange, The, 103, 242
National Retail Dry Goods Association, 103
National Society of Christian Endeavor, 104
Nationalism, 27, 153
Navies, 9, 13, 32, 43, 71, 92
Negroes, 113-15
Nelson, Knute, 118, 142, 146, 242
Nevins, Allen, 237
New, Harry S., 77, 129, 189, 244, 246
New York Journal, 134, 262
New York Post, 159, 262
New York State Ratifying Convention, 116
New York Sun, 60, 68-69, 83, 234
New York Times, 4, 6, 32, 61, 108, 123, 148, 164-65, 173-74, 244, 250, 261
New York Tribune, 125, 127, 133, 145, 240, 248
New York World, 233, 261, 276
New Zealand, 201
Newberry, Truman H., 37, 78, 127, 184, 235, 262
"No League of Nations to Enforce War," by Col. Harvey, 49
Norris, George, 163-64
North American Review, 21
Northern Baptist Convention, 104

Order of Railway Conductors, 242
Orlando, 34, 35, 93, 99
Overman, Senator, 180-81
Owen, Robert L., 212-13, 223, 228

Page, Carroll S., 78
Palmer, A. Mitchell, 267
Palmer, Frederick, 155
Panama, seizure of, 15
Paris, 19, 33, 38, 39, 42, 43
Parker, Alton B., 218
Peace: need of world organization for, 1, 3, 7, 15, 18, 42, 56, 57, 154; support in the United States, 1916–17, 7; concert of nations proposed by E. A. Filene, 8; idea opposed by William Jennings Bryan, 8; growing support for idea abroad, 8; League for Peace, 8-9, 11, 16 (*See also* League to Enforce Peace; Taft, William Howard; Wilson, Woodrow; League of Nations)
Peace Conference: Wilson to attend, 39; delegates to, 40; creation of a League of Nations, 42; opens, 54-55; closed to the press, 54; basis of peace, 56-57; Wilson's role, 57; Wilson returns from, 82; Orlando bolts, 99; negotiations, 133; decision about Shantung, 157-58 (*See also* Clemenceau, Lloyd George, Orlando)
Penrose, Boies, 61, 78, 112, 213
People of America, 3, 4, 8, 27, 28, 31, 39, 43, 49, 94, 142, 161
Pershing, John J., 22
Phelan, James D., 118, 257
Philadelphia Inquirer, 234
Phillips, William E., 107
Phipps, Lawrence C., 78
Pittman, Key, 129, 141, 161, 228, 231
Pittsburgh Gazette Times, 261
Poindexter, Miles, 27, 61, 65, 66, 78, 79, 162, 226
Poland, 19, 93
Polk, James K., 46
Pomerene, Attlee, 129, 134, 158, 229, 230, 267
Pope, The, 63, 119
Portugal, 201
Power politics, European, 51
Presbyterian Church, 104
Press, The, vii, 7, 54, 58, 74, 94, 101, 103, 127, 142, 158 (*See headings of individual publications*)
Prettyman, Rev. Forrest J., 220
Princeton University, 20
Pringle, Henry, 15, 22
Progressive Party, 5, 21, 23, 37, 128

Randsdall, Joseph, 147-49
Ratifying Conventions, 109, 116, 120
Redmond, Charles F., 145-46
Reed, Senator James, 64, 65, 66, 113-15, 119, 120, 155, 162, 164, 196, 210
Referendum, 240-41, 258, 273, 275
Reparations, 35, 36
Reparations Committee, 165
Republican National Committee, 122
Republican National Convention (1930), 263-66
Republican Party, 5, 21, 22, 23, 27, 28, 29, 30, 32, 36, 37, 40, 41, 108, 115-116, 120, 128, 192, 224, 240, 249, 264, 274
Reservations, indirect method of, 49 (*See also* League of Nations; Wilson, Woodrow; and Lodge, Henry Cabot)
Review of Reviews, 39
Rhineland, 96, 105
Richardson, Wyman, 148-49
Robinson, Corinne Roosevelt, 44
Robinson, Joe T., 129, 205, 227, 260
Rochester Times-Union, 233
Rogers, John Jacob, 69, 83, 180
Roosevelt, Eleanor, 66
Roosevelt, Franklin Delano, 66, 268, 271-73, 275
Roosevelt, Theodore: election of 1912, Progressive Party, 5, 6; sent arbitration treaties to Senate, 11; ill will for Wilson, 14-15, 22; favored ideas of world organization for peace, 15; and Lodge, 15, 16, 27; article in *Metropolitan Magazine,* 16; and Col. Harvey, 21; plans to oppose Wilson's peace plans, 21-22, 27, 39; desire to command a division in France, 22, 23; and Beveridge, 23, 27; Bull Moose Campaign, 23; demands repudiation of the Fourteen Points, 26, 33, 37; and Wilson, 26, 31-33, 37, 39; his influence, 31-33; and Truman Newberry, 37; election of 1912, 37; entered Roosevelt Hospital (N.Y.C.), 39; and Henry White, 40; conferences with Lodge to

defeat League of Nations, 43-45, 89; death (Jan. 6, 1919), 52; *quoted*, 63, 84, 89
Root, Elihu, 40, 87, 93, 95, 98, 120, 121, 127, 139, 208, 275
Round robin, 74-78, 83
Rowell, Chester, 274
Russia, 19, 62, 64

Saar Basin, 96, 105
St. Louis Globe Democrat, 60, 233
San Francisco Chronicle, 39
Scheller-Steinwartz, von, 181-82
Seas, freedom of the, 18, 34, 35 (*See also* Monroe Doctrine)
Secret Postscript story (of Henry Cabot Lodge), 3-5, 6, 7
Serbia, 50
Shantung, 92, 96, 104, 133, 157-59, 163, 164, 165, 166, 195, 215
Sherman, Lawrence Y., 77, 78, 79, 80, 81, 118-19, 120, 142, 172, 202-203, 221, 243
Shields, John, 129, 177
Short, William Harrison, 238
Simonds, Frank, 192-93, 244
Smith, Alfred E., 267
Smith, Hoke, 195, 245
Smith, John W., 199
Smith, Marcus A., 141
Smith, Roland Cotton, 7
Smoot, Reed, 61, 78, 81, 103, 195
South Africa, 201
Spain, 46, 201
Spanish-American War, 30, 40
Spencer, Selden P., 61, 78, 131, 175
Springfield Republican, 134
Stars and Stripes, 59
Sterling, Thomas, 77, 195
Stimson, Henry L., 275
Sullivan, Mark, 9-10, 104
Sutherland, Howard, 78, 79, 246
Swanson, Claude, 77, 117, 129, 231
Switzerland, 13

Taft, William Howard: President of League to Enforce Peace, 2; in accord with Wilson and Lodge, 3, 6; lectures on peace, 8; proposed arbitration treaties, 11, 134; support of world organization for peace, 27, 62; protests Wilson's election plea, 33; and Philander Knox, 31, 65; election of 1912, 37; not made delegate to Peace Conference, 40; praise of the League of Nations, 60, 62, 64-65; evaluation of certain obstructionists, 65; with Wilson speaks for League of Nations, 82, 83, 111; urges Wilson to amend Covenant, 86; proposes specific amendments to Covenant, 88, 91, 95, 100; and the Monroe Doctrine (*See heading*); and A. Lawrence Lowell, 91, 120, 140; support of the Covenant, 115-16; and Elihu Root, 122; and Senate Foreign Relations Committee, 129; and Arthur H. Vandenburg, 130-32; decides in favor of reservations, 138-140, 142, 146; reports every Senator wants his own reservations, 199; and Kellogg, 142, 199; and Harding, 275
Territorial integrity, 19
Texas, 72
Thomas, Charles, 80, 81, 117, 182-83, 203, 257
Topeka Capital, 174
Townsend, Charles E., 78, 169
Treaties, 11, 45-46, 76-78, 92, 104, 105, 106, 107, 108, 109, 118, 134, 159 (*See also* Versailles Treaty)
Treaty Making Powers of the Senate, The, 45
Treaty of London, 92
Trotsky, 64
Tumulty, Joe, 66, 88, 122, 149, 169, 188, 190, 277, 282
Turkey, 13, 19

Underwood, Oscar W., 219, 227, 230, 231, 239, 245, 262
United Society of Christian Endeavor, 242
United States Chamber of Commerce, 7
United States Peace Delegation, 107
United States Senate: vii; powers of to confirm treaties with foreign powers, 10, 11, 40, 41, 75-78; Foreign Relations Committee (*See heading*); and T.R., 11, 27; Republican control, 28, 36; and McKinley, 40; peace commissions, 40; support of League of Nations, 43, 76; powers and prerogatives, 45; right to revise and reject treaties, 45; on foreign policy, 46; filibuster,

78-83; Wilson's criticism of, 81-82, 83; treaties must be kept secret until Senate votes otherwise, 118; party membership of committees, 128-29; Committee on Immigration, 130; canvas of, 162; approve separate peace with Germany, 229 (*See headings for individual senators*)

Van Buren, Martin, 46
Vandenberg, Arthur H., 130-32, 138, 184, 274
Vatican, 119
Venizelos, Mr., 180-81
Versailles Treaty: Wilson's demand that treaty be kept secret, 116-18; Hiram Johnson's demands, 116; unauthorized copy, 117; signed, 123; laid before Senate, 126; plans to kill, 128-29; Lodge on, 133 (*See also* Lodge, Henry Cabot); approval in British House of Commons, 135; and John Sharp Williams, 143; Lodge completes reading of, 145-46; Harding recommends reservations, 147; Japan and, 158; Senate Foreign Relations Committee starts amending, 163, 166; and Senator Fall, 165; reported to Senate, 176-77; second reading before Senate, 181; ratification by England, France, and Japan, 191-92; Lodge amendment to Shantung provision, 195; vote on, 217; reservations, 218-32; defeated, 224; confusion after defeat, 233-34; 106-109, 151
Victor Emmanuel III, King of Italy, 281
Victory Committee for Women, 104
Villard, Oswald Garrison, 183-84

Wadsworth, J. W., Jr., 77
Walsh, David I., 205, 210, 230, 267
Walsh, Thomas J., 166, 183, 204, 244, 260, 267
War veterans, vii, 184
War Weekly, 21, 23, 49, 98
Warren, F. E., 77
Washington, George, 1, 14, 55, 61, 70, 121
Washington Post, 241
Watson, James E., 48-49, 52, 77, 142-143, 149-50
Weapons of War, 147
White, Henry, 40, 41, 69, 83-85, 87, 94, 95, 107, 122, 178, 179, 237, 253
White House windows, bars on, 194
White, William Allen, 275
Why We Fought, 148
Wickersham, George W., 218
Willard Hotel, Washington, D.C., 1
Williams, John Sharp, 97, 129, 143-45, 152-55, 194, 199-200, 257
Wilson, Edith, 66
Wilson, Woodrow, 1; proposes a commonwealth of nations for peace, 2-3; in accord with Taft and Lodge, 3; story of secret postscript, 3-7; election of 1916, 5; character, 7, 22, 208-209; proposed League for Peace, 8, 9, 11, 16; delineation of powers of the President and the Senate, 10; arbitration with all nations, 11; request for declaration of war (April 2, 1917), 16-17; views on democracy, 17; the Fourteen Points and the League of Nations, 18, 21; speech at Mount Vernon (July 4, 1918), 20, 21; views on peace, 20, 24-25, 36; and Col. George Harvey, 20-21, 23, 39, 196; and T.R., 15, 22, 28, 33, 39, 52; Liberty Loan address (New York City), 24-25; receives German peace offer negotiations, 25-26, 27; and Lodge, 28, 29, 30, 33, 40, 41, 54, 66, 68, 69, 76, 87, 100, 150, 156, 170, 191, 208-210, 232, 236, 253, 256; appeal to the voters for election of Democrats, 29, 33; and Colonel House, 33, 35, 38, 40, 86, 96, 105, 218; and Allied acceptance of the Fourteen Points, 36; plans for peace, 36; and Henry Ford, 37; in election of 1912, 5, 6, 37; to attend Peace Conference, 39; appoints delegates to Peace Conference, 40-41; welcomed in Paris, 42, 43; creation of the League of Nations, 42; warns the League of Nations that the peace will not be perfect, 50-51; interpretation of Fourteen Points, 55; chairman of the League of Nations' Commission, 57; role played in Peace Conference, 57; fears of the Senate, 58; presents Covenant of the League of Nations, 58-60, 65; and Tumulty, 66, 88, 122, 149, 169, 188, 190, 277, 282; speech in Boston, 66-

67; confers with members of Senate and House Foreign Relations Committees, 68-69; criticisms of the Senate, 81-82; returns to Peace Conference, 82; and Taft, 82, 86, 88-89, 111, 168; power and prestige, 83; willing to make constructive changes in the Covenant, 87; and Henry White, 87, 107; and Senator Hitchcock, 87, 116, 168, 199, 210-11, 216, 219, 236, 255; seeks four amendments to Covenant, 90, 91, 95; and Clemenceau, 92-93, 105-106; and Lloyd George, 92-93, 106; and the smaller nations, 93; attack of influenza, 93, 96; importance of the Monroe Doctrine to (*See heading*); adoption of Monroe Doctrine amendment, 96-97; opposes Italian claim for Fiume, 98-99; and compromises, 104-106; called Congress to convene May 19, 1919, 107; remains in Europe to sign Versailles Treaty, 107; desires that Versailles Treaty be kept secret, 116-18; on the reservations, 122-23, 126, 133; on laws of freedom, 124; reception on return to United States, 125; and Porter McCumber, 68-69, 75, 126; lays Versailles Treaty before the Senate, 126; makes effort to persuade Republican Senators not to demand reservations, 133, 135; Taft decides in favor of reservations, 138-40, 142; hatred for Lodge, 143; and James Watson, 149-150; appeal to the country, 151, 161; requests speedy approval of Versailles Treaty, 156; his interpretation of the League to the Senate Foreign Relations Committee, 156-60; tour to West to support League, 161, 162, 168, 171-174, 177-78, 181-82, 185-91; and Senate Foreign Relations Committee, 167; decides to accept some reservations to Versailles Treaty, 169-70; and William Randolph Hearst, 170-71; and Borah, 116-18, 175; and Charles Thomas, 182-83; suffers a stroke, exhaustion and confinement, 190-91, 194-95, 211, 213; and John Sharp Williams, 194, 199-200, 277; Lodge notations to Covenant, sent to, 206-207; on reservations, 133-35, 210, 216, 219-20; informed of the defeat of League of Nations, 233; opposes separate peace with Germany, 240, 262; requests referendum, 240-41, 258, 273; and Carter Glass, 267; gaunt, cadaverous, broken, 268; and James Cox, 268; and Root, 40, 208, 275; and Armistice Day, Nov. 11, 1923, 282

Wilson, Mrs. Woodrow, 21, 86, 169, 218, 236

Winning of the West, The, 6

Women's Christian Temperance Union, 242

Wood, Leonard, 110

World partnership, 60

World Peace Foundation, 242

World War I, vii; declaration of war, 17; German peace offers, 25-26; armistice terms, 26; revolt against the peace program, 28; Japan, 92; cost in lives and money, 147; state of war with Germany (1920), 262 (*See also* Versailles Treaty and the League of Nations)

World War II, viii, 147

Yugoslavs, 93